ETHICS

& Expediency

in Personnel Management

A Critical History of Personnel Philosophy

CHARLES R. MILTON

UNIVERSITY OF SOUTH CAROLINA PRESS
COLUMBIA, SOUTH CAROLINA

CONTENTS

ETHICS
& Expediency
in Personnel Management

I

AN OVERVIEW OF PERSONNEL PHILOSOPHY

To management falls the responsibility of putting together and maintaining the effective organization which can achieve the goals and objectives of the enterprise. This task has both a technical and a human aspect. The human aspect consists of "building a cooperative organization, an organization of people with drive and enthusiasm, who work together, and who are responsive to management's leadership in the common effort to achieve the economic aims of the enterprise." [1] Production, the technical aspect, is no longer the only ultimate objective of an enterprise. While executives have not fully renounced their production-oriented economics, increasingly the goal has expanded to include the general well-being of everyone in society—public, community, and employees. Many employers give as much consideration to sound human relations as to the traditional problems of production, sales, and finance. A humane and satisfying organization, as well as profitable operations, has become a criterion of successful executive performance. The more modern viewpoint does not establish a dichotomy between human relations and technical efficiency; rather, efficiency is recognized as dependent upon industry's human assets.

Today most executives are aware that the wants and needs of workers extend far beyond wages, and they have accepted the responsibility of helping workers fulfill the psychological needs required to make employment a more rewarding and satisfying ex-

[1] James C. Worthy, "Changing Concepts of the Personnel Function," *Personnel* 25 (1948) 3:166–67.

perience. Businessmen have achieved high-level mastery over physical production and many are now endeavoring to meet the challenge of promoting satisfying personal and interpersonal relationships within industry. Sound personnel relations are highly desirable, not merely as a requisite to an efficient and profitable business operation, but as a contribution to society in general, as a fulfillment of moral and ethical demands.

However, an awareness of the human side of business has not always been prevalent. In fact, such a realization is a matter of degree even today. As late as 1925, Hoopingarner observed that "The most practical thing that industry needs today is an industrial philosophy that is human. . . ." [2] Lippman, thinking somewhat along the same lines, concluded, "The social history of the past seventy-five years has been in large measure concerned with the birth pains of an industrial philosophy that will really suit the machine technology and the nature of man." [3] Today the search continues, and is even being accelerated, for a philosophy that will serve to guide thoughts and actions as management deals with the human side of business. Such a philosophy should shape the top executive's concepts and approach to personnel administration.

THE PROBLEM AND OBJECTIVES

Although the quest for an adequate philosophy persists, little understanding exists of how we have reached the present mode of employee-employer relations or the factors that significantly contribute to its form, content, and implementation. The American experience of trying to reconcile the human and technical components of production as it relates to personnel philosophy has not been documented. It is time we did so.

Therefore, the purpose of this study is to determine how employers have tended to view labor during the course of American history,

[2] Dwight Lowell Hoopingarner, *Labor Relations in Industry* (New York: McGraw-Hill Company, 1926), p. vi.
[3] Walter Lippman, *A Preface to Morals* (New York: Macmillan Company, 1931), p. 243.

to discern the prevailing views or assumptions of labor that have guided the treatment of human resources, provided the foundation of employer-employee relations, and influenced labor's utilization of these resources in conjunction with industrial technology. A proper perspective of the historical background of human relationships in business and industry is necessary to convey the basic developmental characteristics of personnel philosophy and to clarify one's understanding of the present state of personnel relations. Provided with insights into the human side of production, one can more intelligently formulate a meaningful philosophy to guide management.

In looking for a philosophy of personnel administration in industry, the study will be devoted to an analysis of the basic management ideas that affect the entire organization and the manner in which its personnel relations are conducted. Such a philosophy has been described as "discoverable in the animating idea of any enterprise, the idea in terms of which all functions are performed, all details organized; the idea that sets the pace and direction for the enterprise." [4] More specifically, a personnel philosophy "represents the fundamental beliefs, ideals, principles and views held by management with respect to organizing and treating individuals at work. . . ." [5]

To facilitate the search for personnel philosophies that have influenced the integration of human and technical factors of production, the following objectives will be pursued:

1. To determine what personnel philosophies are characteristic of American industry—past and present.
2. To structure descriptive models of such personnel philosophies and to evaluate their potential for gratifying basic human needs.
3. To explore the evidence for progressive improvement and the extent to which basic rationales have been dynamic or responsive to forces on the American scene.

In order to achieve the above objectives, one must concentrate on

[4] H. A. Overstreet, "The Meaning of Philosophic Foundations," in *Scientific Foundations of Business Administration,* ed. Henry C. Metcalf (Baltimore: Williams & Wilkins Co., 1926), p. 30.

[5] Lewis K. Johnson, "Personnel Philosophy," *Personnel Journal* 25 (June, 1946), 2:42.

the primary determinants of employment relationships and personnel philosophy. Furthermore, one must discern how such variables have changed over time and evaluate the sensitivity of personnel philosophy to such influences operating in the American environment. Although not exhaustive, the determinants examined in the present survey are as follows:

1. Values and sentiments of the public, community, and employees.
2. Political pressures—federal and state labor laws.
3. Reaction to organized labor.
4. Economic and technological factors.
5. Scientific disciplines—scientific and personnel management, industrial and social psychology, and human relations.
6. Industrial leadership.
7. Concepts of labor.
8. Incentives utilized by management.
9. Emphasis placed on the personnel management function.

The above determinants of personnel philosophy will comprise the framework of analysis used in this study and will be expanded later in the chapter.

REFINEMENT OF THE PROBLEM

It is important to note that personnel philosophy, as examined throughout the following discussion, is not that of the recently specialized personnel or industrial relations departments, although they have stimulated its formation, but rather is structured by the highest level of administration responsible for policy or the formulation of organization goals. Although the personnel department, as well as other levels of the organization, may assist and advise in the formulation of personnel philosophy, the responsibility and authority for structuring this philosophy and implementing it into organization policy and practice should lie with the top management in the firm.

The attainment of personnel objectives depends upon policies that convey to those engaged in the management function the tone of employer-employee relationships intended by the top levels of administration. Policies then become guides to action. Personnel policy may be considered as the "body of principles and rules of conduct that governs the business enterprise in its relationship with its employees." [6] Therefore a close relationship exists between policy and philosophy. Policy naturally stems from the basic philosophy of the enterprise and is in effect "the application of philosophy in the day-to-day operation of the enterprise." [7]

Many useful techniques have been developed to increase productive efficiency and to implement the personnel function. Time and motion analysis, incentive systems, job evaluation, interviewing, and psychological testing have been developed and refined in order to improve industrial relations. Techniques, however, are the tools of personnel management; as such, they are neutral and impersonal. It is the manner in which these techniques are utilized that is important, since they may be used to implement either an autocratic or democratic philosophy of management. How personnel techniques are used and the objectives sought depend upon the philosophy and policy of the individual firm.

Industry frequently has tended to give its entire attention to development, adoption, and utilization of personnel techniques and has failed to develop or explore the underlying philosophy. Furthermore, management has been remiss in explaining to employees the rationale inherent in its utilization of such tools even when consciously formulated. This has often led to the failure of techniques or only a partial realization of their potential capabilities because they have been perceived by employees as a means of exploitation or as a means to achieve goals opposed to their best interests.

METHOD OF ANALYSIS

The problem of examining the evolution of philosophies of personnel administration is similar to the one confronted by Werner

[6] William R. Spriegel, *Industrial Management* (New York: John Wiley & Sons Inc., 1947), p. 535.
[7] William H. Knowles, *Personnel Management* (New York: American Book Company, 1955), pp. 145–46.

Sombart in his *Quintessence of Capitalism* in which he sought to trace the development of the capitalistic spirit.[8] A similar approach to source material will be employed in the present investigation. As Sombart indicates, direct information can be obtained from the personal comments or writings of men actively engaged in industrial activity. Although other sources have been utilized, journals, published by the American Management Association have been selected primarily as the most representative reflection of managerial personnel philosophy since the turn of the twentieth century.

Indirect information has also been used to ascertain the evolution of industrial personnel philosophy. This source, perhaps the most trustworthy one, is derived from the actual achievements of industry in implementing expressed philosophy. In the present study, the development of personnel administration as a function, a staff department of general management, and as an emerging scientific discipline will provide important evidence of the extent to which the expressed philosophy has been followed by concrete action.

FRAMEWORK OF ANALYSIS

In a chronological examination of an idea or movement over a long time span, a framework of analysis is necessary for interpreting causal factors of developments and trends and for explaining the contents found therein—especially when much of the philosophy is implicit in the statements and activities of industrial administrators. A brief outline will be presented below of the investigatory framework, or the factors influencing the development and content of personnel philosophy.

Public Values and Political Pressure. As the philosophies of personnel administration are examined, they will be evaluated in light of their harmony with employee, community, and public values. Should the philosophies prove inconsistent with such values, pres-

---

[8] Werner Sombart, *The Quintessence of Capitalism* (New York: E. P. Dutton & Company, 1915), pp. 363–64.

sures will be exerted to compel industry to modify its materially oriented values in favor of more human ones. Failure to acknowledge human values has led to governmental legislation sanctioned by public sentiment, and has forced industry to conduct its personnel relations on a higher plane. Consequently, attention must be focused upon the extent to which personnel philosophies have been in harmony with those of society in general and the extent to which industry has accepted its social responsibilities.

Reaction to Organized Labor. Organized labor has represented a threat to the unilateral direction and control traditionally exercised by management and as such has been met by the overt hostility of many employers. As the trend toward union affiliation of employees increased and was eventually given legal status by federal law, employers were compelled to examine and formulate new personnel and labor policies. Management had to decide what kind of relationship—conflict, armed-truce, cooperation—should prevail in working with employee representatives and then whether, and to what extent, the personnel function was to be integrated with labor relations. An employer's personnel philosophy determines whether hostility or cooperation will prevail and whether the organization's personnel function will be utilized to combat the union or to complement its labor relations practices.

Economic and Technological Factors. As America moved from a handicraft economy to a more interdependent, factory form of production, pressures were brought to bear upon prevailing personnel relations. New concepts of labor evolved as the close personal relationships and mutual interests among master, journeyman, and apprentice were disrupted by expanding markets and more mechanized production methods. In the nineteenth century, a wealth of natural resources facilitated a highly individualistic, competitive economy that was reflected in repressive working practices. Workers, dissatisfied with economic and working conditions, crystallized their grievances into specific demands and sought relief by means of strikes, public legislation, and trade unions. Subsequently, as the nation's resources became less abundant and labor more restive, management's attention turned to internal organizational problems and labor efficiency. The receptivity of management to personnel practices and philosophy has been strongly influenced by periods of economic upheaval and depression.

Contributions from the Social Sciences. The various concepts of labor have been structured and modified by economic, political, and social pressures but perhaps more so by the contribution of social sciences during the twentieth century. Insights into the human element made possible by these disciplines have gradually been assimilated by many executives and found expression in their personnel rationale and practices. The extent and manner in which accumulated scientific knowledge has been used reflects the personnel rationale of executives since scientific principles may be used to implement either an authoritarian or democratic philosophy. Therefore, the contributions made by scientific management, psychology, personnel management, sociology, and "human relations" will be examined in order to fully ascertain their influence on the content of personnel philosophies.

Industrial Leadership. The framework of analysis must include the kind of leadership displayed by executives, since they are the ultimate determiners of personnel philosophy and of the emphasis placed upon the human factor. Autocratic leadership, in varying degrees, insists upon complete obedience to managerial authority and minimizes individual self-development and freedom. Such leadership has been reluctant to express its intended standard of treatment toward employees because unilateral control is facilitated if there has been no prior commitment to a course of action. As industrial leadership increasingly became divested of ownership, personnel rationales and practices were modified. Implications of leadership will be noted to provide a better perspective of the development of personnel rationales.

Concepts of Labor. An employer's governing philosophy will be largely determined by his concept of labor, and this basic management attitude will in turn affect the consideration and treatment accorded employees. If labor is deemed merely another commodity, no consideration will be given employees as individuals with psychological needs that may be gratified within the industrial structure. Work, therefore, will tend to be boring and monotonous. In such cases the employment relationship can definitely be better structured to permit a more wholesome and satisfying experience, with the value placed upon the human factor determining the extent to which intelligent, planned personnel relations are cultivated.

A variety of labor concepts have been reflected in personnel administration as practiced in America.[9] Some of these concepts emerged, were modified, and often disappeared as a result of contributions made by scientific disciplines and economic, political, and social forces. A few of the more important concepts follow.

1. Master-servant concept of labor. Finding expression in indentured servitude, slavery, and often apprenticeship, the individual is relegated to a servile or at best semi-servile position. The relationship is characterized by complete dependence upon the owner, lack of personal freedom, and the rendering of unquestioning obedience.

2. Commodity concept of labor. This view of labor considers the employee like any other physical resource necessary to produce a product. When the supply is scarce, the price becomes high; when plentiful, the price is low. The commodity concept of labor is founded in the discipline of economics and often confirmed in the market place. This economic law of supply and demand was once considered immutable and impersonal. Significantly, no recognition was taken of the psychological needs of an employee nor was any responsibility acknowledged for his physical or economic welfare.

3. Machine concept of labor. Since the employer buys and sells the products produced by the worker, employees are regarded as

[9] Walter Dill Scott and Robert C. Clothier, *Personnel Management* (New York: McGraw-Hill Book Co., 1954), pp. 2–8. Several concepts of labor used in this study will not be found in this reference, and others have been modified.

machines, or as extensions of the machinery, and capable of a specific output. Like the machine, the employee is discarded when his productive efforts, whether caused by an injury or increasing age, are no longer sufficient to maintain the specified output; therefore the employment relationship is based upon the cash nexus and is continued only if the worker attains his production quota. The machine concept of labor does not view the employee as endowed with human attributes or a multiplicity of human needs.

While the machine concept of labor was generally prevalent from the very beginning of America's industrial revolution, it also became the engineers' viewpoint of economy and output after 1880, at which time the management movement was initiated. Assuming that employees were primarily economically motivated, management devised numerous wage incentive plans to insure that the maximum potential productivity of employees would be realized.

4. Good-will or paternalistic concept of labor. This view of labor recognizes that the welfare of employees has a direct effect on their productivity and job satisfaction. Accordingly employers decide to "do good" and provide adequate work conditions, restrooms, cafeterias, fringe benefits, etc., for their personnel. In turn, it is expected that workers will be grateful, loyal, and productive. Management decides what is best for its employees and becomes very paternalistic as welfare programs are implemented. This attitude fails to recognize that employees are capable of determining their own needs and often prefer to earn things for themselves rather than have everything handed to them by management. It does not acknowledge their need for independence and self-respect.

5. Natural-resource concept of labor. Like the nation's physical resources, labor requires careful utilization and protection from excessive practices of exploitation. This viewpoint was first advocated by statesmen and by some farsighted employers after the turn of the twentieth century. Restrictions placed upon immigration reduced the supply of labor and, coupled with the increased demand resulting from World War I, compelled employers to ultilize labor with more care and consideration. Out of this concept, accompanied by

a wave of humanitarianism, came health and accident legislation, workmen's compensation laws, child-labor laws, and a curtailment of working hours.

6. Uniqueness or individual differences concept of labor. This concept of labor evolved from psychology and the applications of industrial psychology to manufacturing. Men are characterized by individual differences in their basic capacities, abilities, and personality. Some employees can perform certain tasks better than others and, therefore, cannot be indiscriminately placed on the job, transferred, or promoted. Job satisfaction and productivity are promoted if industry utilizes these differences wisely—if the man is matched with the job.

7. Humanistic concept of labor. This basic attitude toward labor approaches the problems of work from the human as well as the production point of view; it is founded upon a concern for both the economic and psychological aspects of work. Management endeavors to enlist the worker's interest, goodwill, and cooperation by treating him as a human being with definite needs, desires, and aspirations. Psychological needs for self-esteem, achievement, security, belonging and self-actualization are viewed as attainable within the industrial organization. Emphasis is placed upon enhancing the employee's personal development, integrity, and dignity. This concept of labor emerged after 1910 and was given content and meaning by industrial psychology and personnel management.

8. Citizenship concept of labor. This concept holds that employees are entitled to have a voice in determining the rules and regulations affecting their welfare in the work environment. An employee's investment of his labor in industry conveys rights similar to those of community citizenship—each individual has inherent rights and is entitled to a voice and vote in determining civil matters. The citizenship concept of labor has been prevalent in the personnel rationale of employers who have sincerely endorsed shop committees, employee-representation, union-management cooperation, and participation of employees in the decision-making process.

9. Consumer-public concept of labor. In the 1930's the viewpoint

emerged that the employee is a customer of the business as well as a producer. Consumers and employees are one and the same. Since the employee is also a consumer, he is entitled to solicitude and concern similar to that given the consumer. The good will of the employee must be obtained as well as that of the consumer, because both are capable of retaliatory or defensive measures if exploited or abused. This concept of labor became prevalent as employers realized that the employee was a consumer and also a member of the public to whom industry was acknowledging responsibilities.

10. Partnership concept of labor. The attitude of partnership is based upon the belief that there is a mutuality of interests between management and employees. Although their interests are divergent in the short-run, in the long-run the needs and interests of both parties coincide and each can attain its objectives. Mutual confidence and respect are implied in this concept of labor and have been manifested in stock-ownership and profit-sharing plans as managements have sought to secure cooperation, productivity, and an identification with company objectives.

11. Social concept of labor. This concept of labor recognizes that work has a social function, that the worker has social as well as egoistic needs. The work environment consists of informal work groups with definite values and attitudes; the employee, while exerting an influence upon the group, is also regulated and controlled by group sentiments. Furthermore each position is characterized by social values and a rank in the social scale; the worker tends to adopt the behavior pattern consistent with the job's social position. Although an appreciation of the social facets of work and social needs of employees had been in evidence prior to the Hawthorne investigations in the late 1920's, it remained at an academic level to most management people. Elton Mayo and his associates succeeded in demonstrating the operation of social forces in basic industrial operations.

Incentives Utilized by Management. The kind of motivation emphasized by an employer to achieve productivity and profits is contingent upon his concept of labor which, in the twentieth century, may have been formulated or strongly influenced by some of the scientific disciplines. Motivation, in many ways indicative of the essence of a personnel philosophy, has ranged from the use of fear and threats to an appeal to the mainsprings of human behavior through persuasion and often participation in the decision-making process. Managements seek the cooperation of employees but do so by extremely different applications of incentives, some appealing only to economic motives while others emphasize in varying degrees both financial and psychological rewards. The kind of motivation utilized by management will largely determine the amount and kinds of satisfaction employees realize from their daily work activities.

Emphasis Placed on the Personnel Management Function. The role played by the personnel function or department will provide the primary criterion of whether pronounced ideals and beliefs by top executives have been implemented into concrete action. Also indicative of serious intent is the status accorded the chief personnel official, who should be placed on policy-making committees to interject the human factor implications before, rather than after, action is taken. Likewise, if the personnel function is taken seriously, it should be placed on a comparable status with line functions.

Several comments pertaining to the conceptual framework outlined above are pertinent. Not all of the factors comprising the framework of analysis are independent; some are interrelated and have been considered separately only for the purpose of clarity. For example, the human values of the public and community are not unrelated to political pressure because when the values of management and the public become too divergent, public dissatisfaction frequently finds expression in legislative enactments. Furthermore, the factors are not all pertinent at a given period of time since their importance and especially their order of appearance vary with the time period under consideration.

MODELS OF PERSONNEL PHILOSOPHY

One of the objectives of the present investigation is to formulate descriptive models of personnel philosophy. Like many models, the personnel philosophies presented will be generally descriptive and not an exact replica of any top executive's philosophy. However, the models endeavor to convey the most objective, tangible, and pertinent aspects of the data disclosed in this survey—although the rationales and their tenets may at times be implicit rather than explicit.

For formulating models of personnel philosophy, a definite structure is required for their presentation. Five factors from the framework of analysis will be utilized: (1) executive leadership, (2) personnel management, (3) concepts of labor, (4) incentives utilized, and (5) reaction to organized labor. These variables were selected because they comprise the most significant ones for conveying the tone of employer-employee relations, or personnel philosophy, as would be found in a given industrial organization. (See Figure 1 for the factors contributing to such a rationale.)

In a chronological survey such as the one being initiated, the question arises: at what point have certain thoughts and ideals become sufficiently prevalent to say that they characterize a given personnel philosophy. As basic principles pertaining to the intended standard of treatment of human resources are crystallized, there tends to emerge an explicit philosophy. "The philosophy of any subject is desirably articulated as soon as its content of principles, ideas, and practices [has] been given some identifiable separateness and unity of its own, some momentum of self-realized existence." [10] To establish these principles of necessity will involve some reiteration of similar expressions or ideas and perhaps cause the reader to feel he has definitely encountered this material before. It is hoped, however, the reader will understand and tolerate some degree of repetition in the interests of a more objective study.

[10] See Ordway Tead's introduction to Marshall E. Dimock's *A Philosophy of Administration* (New York: Harper & Brothers Pub., 1958), p. vii.

FIGURE 1

*Factors Influencing the Development
of Personnel Philosophy*

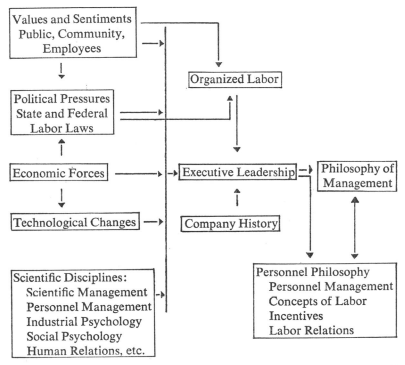

Finally, the descriptive models present a problem of timing their inclusion into the survey of personnel philosophy. Rather than grouping them into a final chapter, the models have been placed after a reasonable amount of concrete expression. Most of the models' components will have been articulated quite extensively and will resemble a summary of preceding material. A few statements of philosophy, however, may not have taken specific or final form in the evolution of ideas as surveyed and consequently become the source of some concern, since they contain concepts not apprecia-

tively developed. While there is no ideal solution to this timing problem, the personnel models have been placed where, it is hoped, they
will facilitate an understanding of the philosophy.

PREVIEW OF PERSONNEL PHILOSOPHIES

The foregoing concepts of labor cover the basic attitudes that
have been held by industrial executives as revealed in their writings,
speeches, and practices. One should not conclude, however, that a
personnel philosophy usually can be summarized or crystallized into
a concept of labor; this a seldom true. Conversely, such a philosophy
most often embraces two or more attitudes toward employees, especially those formulated during the twentieth century. The following descriptions of clearly discernible personnel rationales are presented to orient the reader toward the material that will follow. Only
the most important aspects have been abstracted, but at the same
time an attempt has been made to reveal a brief glimpse of pertinent
accompanying circumstances in order to make each philosophy
more meaningful. They are presented chronologically, in the order
of their emergence, to convey the continuity and dynamic quality of
their evolution.

Pre-Industrial Concepts of Labor. During the Colonial Period in
America, and for some time afterwards, labor was accorded little, if
any, recognition or status. Slaves and indentured servants were part
of an employer's property for a varying number of years, had few
rights, and received little respect or consideration. Slavery implied a
master-servant concept of labor and was complemented by a commodity viewpoint. If the going price of slaves was high, they were
accorded more considerate physical treatment, but, if they became
inexpensive, the physical plane of their existence tended to deterio-
rate. The indentured servant, while occupying a slightly more favorable position in colonial society, was in a semi-servile position until
his obligated term was completed.

The semi-servile, dependent work relationship of the indentured servant was reflected to some extent in the apprenticeship system. However, the apprentice arrangement was definitely paternalistic. Since the apprentice was most often a boy, he was frequently afforded the care and control found in a father-son relationship. The relationship was a close, personal one, providing a period of growth and development, the acquisition of a trade, and a general education as well.

Laissez-Faire Philosophy. During the nineteenth century the nation became more industrialized, and the laissez-faire rationale of personnel became dominant. This philosophy was based upon an extreme individualism which received sanction from economics, political science and biology. Employers, by virtue of their position, which indicated that they were superior and destined to lead according to the Spencerian philosophy popular in the latter half of the nineteenth century, considered themselves entitled to demand complete obedience from employees and utilized their superior bargaining position to compel subjection to administrative authority. It was a materialistic philosophy complemented by autocratic principles of management and void of any consideration for the human factor. Labor was deemed a commodity to be bought at the market price like any other factor of production with only monetary considerations. Employers did not even accept responsibility for providing a decent, safe, or sanitary workplace.

In the last two decades of the nineteenth century, employers turned their attention from an exclusive emphasis on expanding plant facilities and markets to internal problems of production and labor efficiency. Engineers, as technicians and administrators, were primarily responsible for the management movement which marked the first serious attempt to analyze internal managerial problems. With the application of an engineering approach to labor-management problems, there emerged a machine concept of labor; each employee was a machine whose value was determined by the quantity of his output. The employee was regarded merely as a mechanism capable of a certain amount of production, and incentive systems were installed to guarantee the available potential output. Neither the commodity nor machine concepts of labor recognized the employee's right to dignity, respect, and treatment as an equal human individual; the employment relationship was an economic one to be terminated at the employer's discretion. Both concepts were consistent with the laissez-faire philosophy of personnel administration which ignored human values and exploited the human factor in the same manner as physical resources. This personnel rationale was not conducive to cooperation but rather precipitated conflict, inefficiency, and restriction of production.

Paternalistic Philosophy. As industry sought to develop a new pattern of personnel relations to replace the laissez-faire rationale which had become inadequate as industrial technology and organizational structure changed, some executives turned to paternalism, the only other model of personnel administration available at that time. For a majority of the employers having a paternalistic philosophy, it was designed to promote productivity and/or to maintain an unchallenged position of unilateral control. Paternalism found its most organized form of expression in welfare management or industrial betterment that emerged at the close of the nineteenth century. Welfare programs, often poorly organized and administered, were implemented by paternalistic executives who implicitly assumed the employee was similar to a child whose work required close supervision and control. Often employer direction was extended to the worker's home life and home management. Improved work conditions and economic rewards were provided with the expectations that employees would accept the direction of their activities with gratitude and appreciation and, consequently, become more loyal, cooperative, and productive. While there was an awareness of the human factor, although misdirected, the paternalistic philosophy failed to appreciate the employee's drive for integrity, self-respect, self-direction, and dignity.

Technique Philosophy. For many industrial leaders, the laissez-faire rationale of personnel was gradually discarded in favor of an emerging technique philosophy in the years between 1900 and 1920. The technique rationale, as it originally emerged, was primarily different from the laissez-faire administration of personnel problems in that the human factor was given more consideration (since exploitation was no longer deemed an appropriate managerial practice). Labor was perceived as a natural resource that should be protected from excessively long working hours, low wages, and inadequate work conditions. Basically motivated by the high cost of turnover and the problem of labor shortages, employers gave an unprecedented amount of attention to the human factor, thereby serving to ameliorate some of the harsh practices carried over from the nineteenth century. Additionally, adopting the principle of individual differences from industrial psychology, many employers were inclined to consider each employee as unique. Efficiency demanded proper utilization of each individual's differential abilities and capacities. The natural resource and uniqueness concepts of labor were consistent with the machine concept of labor as modified by scientific management that specialized the worker's task, divided it into basic elements of motion and time, and separated planning from performance of the job. All three concepts—natural resource, uniqueness, and machine—fail to recognize basic human needs, desires, and aspirations, or to assist the individual in fulfilling these needs within the organizational structure.

After the turn of the twentieth century, industrial leaders ceased to be autocrats with unrestricted power since their free hand in labor practices was increasingly limited by state and federal statutes. Every means possible was used to maintain their position of undisputed authority or to at least prevent its further erosion. This approach initially led to a strong defense of the status quo and was particularly noticeable for its divergence of managerial values from those of the public, community, and employees. However, as the technique philosophy of personnel developed, especially after the onslaught of federal labor laws in the 1930's, many chief executives became more sensitive to the public's human values and the importance of their influence upon the legislative bodies of the nation.

Consequently the technique rationale in its modern form is characterized by flexibility rather than a rigid defense of the status quo and many executives willingly accept their social responsibilities and perceive themselves as trustees of the interest of the stockholders, public, and employees.

Although employee relations are recognized as an important social responsibility, the prevalent concept of personnel relations is extremely narrow and is primarily implemented by personnel techniques and programs centered around economic motives. The techniques developed by the social sciences are used extensively for designing a program of personnel relations, but the behavioral concepts from these sources are ignored. Scientific disciplines have been used primarily for promoting efficiency, manipulation, and control rather than for planning a work environment conducive to meeting the employee's needs.

Do-Nothing Philosophy. The do-nothing rationale of personnel administration, like the technique philosophy, emerged during the period between 1900 and 1920. Founded upon an unswerving dedication to preservation of the existing order, the numerous potential contributions from the various sources dealing with personnel relations were ignored. Whereas the technique philosophy demonstrated considerable flexibility, after an initial period of rigidity, with respect to the alignment of company and public values as well as to the acceptance of social responsibility for employee welfare, the do-nothing rationale has never done so; it has remained dedicated to preserving the status quo. In functioning so, the do-nothing rationale has responded only to legal pressures. Employers basing their personnel practices on this philosophy have never made a sincere effort to align their policies and practices to reflect the values and sentiments of employees or public. Based upon the commodity and machine attitudes toward labor, motivation is accomplished through the use of fear or penalties. No attention is given to inspiring employees with a sense of the significance of their work or to fulfilling their psychological needs within the employment environment.

Humanistic Philosophy. Having its inception in the industrial psychology and methods of personnel management which emerged after 1910, this rationale has as its objective the intelligent promotion of the psychological welfare of employees as well as their economic well-being. Basic psychological needs of self-esteem, achievement, security, sense of belonging, and self-actualization are considered attainable within the business organization. Since technical efficiency is seen as contingent upon sound personnel relations, management strives to secure the worker's interest, goodwill, and cooperation by treating him as an individual with definite needs, desires, and aspirations.

The humanistic philosophy is primarily a composite of the uniqueness and humanistic concepts of labor and implicitly the social concept for some executives. Although there are an awareness and an appreciation of the social implications of work which aid in understanding employee behavior, the humanistic rationale places primary emphasis on the individual. Behavioral contributions by the social sciences have been assimilated, in varying degrees depending upon the science in question, into this rationale and scientific knowledge and techniques used to achieve a more gratifying work environment rather than for the purposes of employee manipulation and control.

Executives having a humanistic philosophy of personnel administration strive to harmonize company personnel relations with the values and sentiments of employers, the community, and the public, Legal requirements affecting employment relations, as expressed in governmental labor policies, are regarded as a minimum standard rather than an optimum one, and additional efforts are made to enhance employee programs.

As reflected in the preceding preview of personnel philosophy, personnel administration is by no means restricted to the twentieth century although its acceptance as a top administrative function has been fairly recent. Throughout American history there have been activities in which individuals and groups cooperated to attain specific objectives. Inevitably someone directed the endeavor, whereas others were active in following such directives. In the process, coordination of materials, tools, techniques, and human effort was required. Force and persuasion were utilized in varying proportions to achieve this coordination and attainment of objectives as work relationships changed from slavery, serfdom, and indentured servitude to economic, social, and political freedom. Whatever the nature of employment relationships throughout time, human effort was organized and integrated with material and technical resources to achieve designated goals, usually the production of goods and services.

By the turn of the twentieth century, America was predominantly an industrial nation with a very complex factory system and a body of industrial workers completely dependent upon the factory system for a means of livelihood. It was in this period and context that modern problems of personnel administration became acute, and management became sufficiently aware of the personnel problem to begin taking concrete action toward the formulation of techniques, policies, and expressions of personnel philosophy, Analysis of the developing philosophies of industrial personnel administration will cover the period 1900 to 1960. However, to provide continuity and an understanding of factors relevant to the time span under consideration, the following chapter will trace the emergence of personnel rationale during the colonial era and its nineteenth-century development, when America experienced its industrial revolution.

II

PERSONNEL ADMINISTRATION IN AN ERA OF
DEVELOPING INDUSTRIALIZATION

While the primary focus of this chronological study is concerned with America's industrial society after 1900, a brief survey of colonial labor systems will be made to discover precedents in employment relationships for a slowly industrializing economy. Then the rapidly changing status of labor and implicit personnel philosophies of small-scale enterprise from 1790 to 1860 will be evaluated. Employer-employee relations were modified even more with the growth of large-scale manufacturing firms and the concomitant concept of laissez-faire from 1860 to 1900. The resulting laissez-faire personnel philosophy of this period will be outlined in a descriptive model and an appraisal made of its influence on employee relations.

When the settlers came to America they brought with them traditional views of labor that had a profound influence upon the colonial labor system. These views, however, were soon modified by a new environment. The immediate needs of frontier life dictated self-sufficiency. It was necessary to resort to agriculture for a subsistence and, in addition, to supply one's own home, furniture, clothing, tools, and equipment. Manufactured articles were primarily the products of household and farm, and every family became a self-reliant unit. This household stage of production was characteristic of England from which many of the settlers had migrated. Most homes had spinning wheels and a large number possessed looms; women did the spinning, whereas, both men and women performed the chore of weaving. Such production often was given legislative encouragement, for in "1656 every family in Massachusetts was re-

23

quired by law to make at least three pounds of cotton or woolen yarn for thirty weeks in the year." [1]

In the seventeenth century, and until after the Revolutionary War, there was little capital in the colonies and few manufacturing enterprises of any size. Foreign markets were few and the domestic purchasing power of self-independent colonial families was small. During the Colonial Period the methods of production were simple; the factory system had not emerged. Labor systems consisting of slavery, indentured servitude, and apprenticeship tended to accord labor a very low status. In some colonies, the distinction between classes of labor was blurred, and statutes often failed to make clear the distinction between slaves, indentures, and apprentices. Some statutes were applied equally to these groups and each had a semi-servile status in the society.

MASTER-SERVANT CONCEPTS OF LABOR

The demand of sparsely settled colonies for labor led to indentured servitude. England had an excessive supply of workers but their relocation was a problem of meeting transportation costs; indentured servitude provided the simplest solution. However, indentured servitude consisted of two categories—voluntary and involuntary. Voluntary servitude included men and women who sold themselves to the shipmaster or other persons for a period of years in return for paying the expense of their passage. Some individuals, "free-willers," sought to sell themselves under more favorable conditions on their arrival in America and were bound to the captain only if they failed to do so within a specified period of time (usually thirty days). On the other hand, the involuntary servitude group included children bound out as apprentices by English local authorities and disposed of in America, adults and children forcibly

[1] Louis Ray Wells, *Industrial History of The United States* (New York: Macmillan Company, 1922), p. 76.

seized and brought over against their will, debtors, and political and civil criminals.[2]

The length of servitude varied from five to ten years, but the period could be legally prolonged for running away and other offenses. Since the administration of the law was by magistrates who were frequently holders of servants themselves, the abuse of power was considerable. Furthermore, as a semi-servile class indentured servants were unlikely to make complaints since their appeal would be to those whose interest were inimical to their own. The interests of those who had invested money in servants were carefully protected.

Colonial governments foresaw that employers would endeavor to protect their capital by making supervision of their workers severe and harsh. Legal safeguards, therefore, were provided for the physical protection of laborers brought from overseas. The indentured servant had certain rights that were recognized in varying degrees; such legal requirements sought to provide a minimum of protection to those in an extremely dependent position. No servant could be sold out of the province in which he agreed to serve without his consent. The servant was also protected against excessive cruelty and bodily injury, but this was a period in which corporal punishment was used for children and servants. At the end of his service, the indentured servant was granted some land to cultivate for himself or given clothing, tools, and a store of food. The long-range point of view dictated that the system not be permitted to degenerate to an extent that it would discourage immigration of labor, an extremely limited factor of production in the colonies.

From an economic standpoint the indenture system had great advantages. Employers were provided a source of labor that could be organized under specific direction and for a definite purpose. The duration of service supplied the master a source of labor that could be utilized in undertakings for which the economic return was uncertain or distant. Although many of these laborers were from the

[2] Ernest Ludlow Bogart, *Economic History of the American People* (2nd ed.; New York: Logmans, Green & Co., 1935), pp. 97–100.

lowest economic and social groups, some were skilled artisans. For those without training the system provided a trade or agricultural apprenticeship. It supplied a force of skilled labor that became free laborers, independent proprietors, or master craftsmen.[3]

As more of the indentured laborers attained freedom and economic independence, their status in colonial society increased. This demanded of employers a different kind of personnel administration than that used when a majority of laborers occupied a semi-servile position. The attraction of free land and a strong demand for skilled craftsmen provided an economic stimulus that compelled employers to treat employees more favorably and to provide better work conditions.

In addition to indentured servitude, another solution to the problem of colonial labor shortage was the institution of human slavery. Although slavery existed in all the colonies, it did so to a very different degree in the different sections. In New England, slavery was practically nonexistent because it was economically unprofitable in an area best suited to industrial and commercial activities. In the Middle Atlantic section, slavery was more prevalent than in New England but slaves were treated with considerable leniency. In the South, devoted primarily to large-scale agricultural activity, slavery provided an answer to the scarce labor problem. Slavery was preferred because the term of service was for life whereas hired labor and indentured servants could be relied on only for shorter durations. There was no interruption of work because of departure of the worker, and the landlord was assured of a permanent and controllable labor supply. Maintenance costs of slaves were less than for white servants, there were no free-dues of land, clothing, etc., and the children of slaves became the property of the land holders. Finally, the physical strength and endurance of generally docile slaves were better suited to the simple southern agriculture.

Slavery as a system of labor accorded the slaves no rights or privileges—only obligations. Except for a minimum of basic physical protection required by colonial statutes, a slave was given little per-

[3] *Ibid.,* pp. 100–102.

sonal consideration. Economic conditions frequently made it mandatory, however, that the physical necessities provided be increased and work conditions improved. If the price of slaves was high, he was given more careful maintenance; if the price was low, he was more expendable. Treatment tended to vary with the law of supply and demand.

Management problems were relatively simple under the system of slavery. Being a part of the slaveowner's property, the slave was treated like any other form of property; he was bought, sold, or abused, as the owner desired. The slave required close supervision, and corporal punishment was frequently relied upon to promote efficiency. Under such conditions, the slave had no interest in his work; he had no incentive because there was no opportunity for advancement or freedom.

A PATERNALISTIC CONCEPT OF LABOR

Another system of manufacture had grown up along with the household method, however, and was especially prevalent in the making of textiles. This was the handicraft system, based on the local market rather than the household. Frequently a weaver would set up a loom in a community and take in wool to be woven, or, an itinerant weaver would go from one house to another seeking employment in some phase of the weaving process. In this development, one observes the breaking-up of household activity and the beginning of specialized work. In the shoe industry, for example, the work was done for a definite customer on specific demand; frequently this was designated as "bespoke" work. Later there evolved extra sales work which involved making boots and shoes for stock. In the shoe trade this was the characteristic type of production until the Revolution.[4] No large group of consumers, however, was dependent upon others for a living. Lack of a sufficient labor supply, capital, and a market caused the continued existence of household and handicraft manu-

[4] Paul H. Douglas, Curtice N. Hitchcock, and Willard E. Atkins, *The Workers in Modern Economic Society* (2nd ed.; Chicago: University of Chicago Press, 1925), p. 168

facturing in many communities until long after the factory had super-seded the household and domestic system in England.[5]

Toward the end of the Colonial Period there were evidences of a sharper division of labor. With the passage of time, "increasing wealth had created greater purchasing ability, the households had trained skilled workmen, and small capitals were being accumulated." [6] As a result of these conditions, men went into the business of weaving, making shoes, etc., for an emerging domestic market which rarely extended beyond the community. Master craftsmen purchased materials and sold the finished product or contracted to complete a product for others who supplied their own materials. In the larger towns, especially in the northern colonies, masters employed journeymen and apprentices; this was the domestic phase of production technology.

The system of apprenticeship was somewhat related to inden-tured servitude and even slavery although different in many respects. A large proportion of the craftsmen came directly from England and brought with them work traditions and apprenticeship regula-tions that had evolved long before America was settled. Colonial apprenticeship was like the English system in two respects: it was a system of poor relief and a penalty for idleness in some instances. It differed from the English system in that "(a) the seven-year term was not as universal, (b) apprenticeship became a means of acquir-ing a liberal education, (c) practically all apprenticeship regulations were administered, not by guilds, but by town and country offi-cials." [7] Apprenticeship in the colonies had four functions.[8] It was a punishment for debt. Both Pennsylvania and Massachusetts stipu-lated that debtors who were unable to meet their obligations could be sold into service. Because of the frequently undifferentiated states of apprenticeship and indentured servitude and ambiguity of the law, many of these indentures were made out for apprenticeship

[5] Wells, *op. cit.*, p. 75.
[6] *Ibid.*
[7] Paul Howard Douglas, *American Apprenticeship and Industrial Educa-tion* (New York: Longmans, Green & Co., 1921), pp. 49–50.
[8] *Ibid.*, pp. 41–42.

rather than true servitude. Apprenticeship was a penalty for idleness and also served as a system of poor relief. Finally, apprenticeship was the earliest state-directed educational system. In general, masters were "required by statute law, to impart not only trade training, but to give instruction in the liberal arts, and to inculcate sound morality as well." [9] If the masters failed to give such training, both trade and intellectual, the apprenticed children could be taken away and indentured to other masters who would fulfill their obligations.

In the few southern colonies, notably Virginia and South Carolina, apprenticeship provisions resembled some of the aspects of slavery and "the same laws were made applicable to Negro slaves and to white apprentices." [10] In some of the more northern colonies apprenticeship was frequently a transition stage between servitude and freedom. In Pennsylvania the Negro passed through the stage of apprenticeship as he attained his freedom under the Abolition Act of 1780. At a later date, New Jersey and Illinois followed similar plans. Under these conditions, apprenticeship resulted in a semi-servile status.

As with slavery, there were some aspects of apprenticeship that closely paralleled indentured servitude. "Both [apprentice and servant] were under contract to serve for a period of years, both were subject to the same regulations as regarding running away and breaking the contract, and the same statutes were often applied to both classes." [11] Differences are to be noted, however; the apprentice, by law, was to receive instruction in a trade and the elements of an education whereas the indentured servant was not. In addition, the apprentice was usually a minor born in the colonies whose indenture was under the supervision of the colonial government, while the indentured servant was most frequently an adult from abroad whose work relationships and conditions were harder to control.

An appraisal of apprenticeship as one of the earliest forms of em-

[9] *Ibid.*, p. 43.
[10] *Ibid.*, pp. 20–21.
[11] *Ibid.*, pp. 28–29.

ployment relationships in America is extremely difficult. There were, without doubt, many occasions of cruelty and injustice. The system created a semi-servile status since the apprentice was dependent upon the master for food, clothing, and shelter. Many apprentices were compelled to perform unrelated household and farm duties in the process of learning the mysteries of the trades. Also, the system permitted exploitation since many of the trades could be mastered in considerably less time than required by the term of apprenticeship, especially if the apprentice possessed superior ability.

There were additional features of apprenticeship, however. The master in most cases was required to teach the apprentice his trade, which also worked to the master's advantage, and to impart sound morals as well as elements of an education. In many respects, it resembled a dependent, father-son relationship. Failure to meet these terms of apprenticeship could result in either a fine or the loss of the apprentice, who represented an investment on the part of the master. As industrialization under the economic doctrine of laissez-faire later advanced, responsibility of any form toward the worker was to be disclaimed by the owner or entrepreneur.

In many instances the personal relationship was congenial and friendly; the master and the apprentice worked side by side and often performed the same tasks. No strong divergence of interest existed and there was little difference in the status between the master, the journeyman, and the apprentice. The laborer in this context was not deemed a commodity or machine, as he was later in the nineteenth century, but as an individual with specific rights and, equally important, specific responsibilities to the master. Cooperation was elicited, not primarily because of the dependent relationship, but because apprenticeship was an avenue to economic independence. Motivation was inherent in a task that provided status and an outlet for creativity and advancement.

In summation, the economic interests of those administering basic employment relationships were paramount in the coordination of labor with land and capital; treatment accorded colonial laborers was dictated primarily by economic conditions. Indentured servants and apprentices were economically dependent upon the employing group—labor had not achieved political or social equality; consequently, the working class had few privileges or rights. Apprenticeship was generally a more favorable employment relationship but it was also founded on a dependent, paternalistic basis. The prevalent rationale of personnel administration consisted of a master-servant concept of labor which relegated employees to a semi-servile position.

Employers had not expressed an intended standard of treatment toward those employed such as is found currently. Legal documents which stipulated the conditions of employment between employers and indentured servant or apprentice often were couched in terms of a master-servant relationship. There was no humanitarian point of view nor were there any principles of social science, characteristic of the twentieth century, to focus attention upon the employee's need for dignity and self-respect.

PERSONNEL ADMINISTRATION IN EMERGING SMALL-SCALE ENTERPRISE, 1790–1860

Between the American Revolution and the commencement of the Civil War, there was a period of industrial transition; household and domestic production gave way slowly to the machine and factory system. Progress was uneven, and diverse forms of production and personnel administration were coexistent. The conceptions of personal relationship between employer and employee stemmed from current thinking and practices. As industry emerged, traditional ideas and customs of servile labor systems still prevailed. "Labor" still implied somewhat of the servile status characteristic of the master-servant relationship. James O'Neal concluded, "It is no exaggeration to say that the society of colonial time, and long after the revolution regarded labor as a badge of shame." [12] This situation tended to be reinforced by the political situation. The Revolution had failed to establish political equality; the right to vote and hold

[12] James O'Neal, *The Workers in American History* (4th ed.; New York: Leopard Press, 1921), p. 89.

office was coupled with property ownership qualifications. Laborers who did not own property were more or less second-class citizens. The property class utilized their political power to promote manufacturing and other interests of property-holding groups.

For twenty years after the Revolution, manufacturing by machinery made slow progress in America. After 1807, however, an industrial revolution similar to that in England took place rapidly in America.[13] This year provides a convenient line of demarcation between United States dependence upon European countries and the development of numerous internal, diversified industries. Prior to this transition, colonial production procedures and basic labor systems had changed little since the Revolution; agrarian and commercial activities still predominated. Ernest Bogart records that "with the passage of the Embargo Act, the Non-Intercourse Act, and finally the outbreak of the War of 1812, foreign trade was greatly hindered if not destroyed and the country thrown back upon its own resources." [14] Domestic production of commodities previously imported sprang up immediately.

There were numerous and rapid changes in employee-employer relationships accompanying this outburst of industrial activity. One of the most important developments was the gradually growing distinction between employer and employee. In the handicraft stage of production, there was no separation of the productive process into managerial functions. The handicraftsman had his own shop and worked with his own materials for customers who were usually his neighbors; functions of merchant, master, and journeyman were performed by the same person. As the population grew and demand increased, the master workman began to employ journeymen and apprentices and goods were made in advance of orders. The journeyman did not own either raw materials or shop but both he and the apprentice had an opportunity of becoming a master craftsman and of owning their own business. Personal relations between the master and the journeyman tended to be harmonious. They worked side by

13 Wells, *op. cit.*, p. 151.
14 Bogart, *op. cit.*, p. 383.

side; they were not greatly differentiated by earnings or social position and conflicts over wages or hours were infrequent.

However, pressures were brought to bear upon this mutuality of interests as improvements in transportation began to expand markets. Some merchants and enterprising masters sought orders for goods to be produced and delivered later. Competition from others also seeking orders compelled the merchant to sell as cheaply as possible, and employers were therefore forced to reduce wages so they could meet competitive prices. Under these conditions there developed, in a nation still predominantly agricultural, capitalists or merchant-manufacturers who operated wholesale businesses created by market expansion. The master became a business contractor who employed more journeymen and sold the product to a merchant wholesaler rather than directly to customers. Production was based on an order from the wholesaler, price was determined by competition rather than custom, and wages became competitive. The journeyman became a wage earner who did not own his own tools and saw less opportunity for advancement.[15]

As independent workers, journeymen sought to protect themselves from rapidly changing technical and economic conditions, and also from concomitant administrative practices that tended to undermine their economic welfare, status, and values. Their perception of community of interests between journeymen and employer, pride in craftsmanship and its accompanying status, and psychological rewards of self-respect, dignity, and independence were being destroyed. Protection was sought by forming unions whose objectives consisted of securing higher wages and maintaining the status of journeymen by insisting upon a term of apprenticeship before becoming a qualified worker. Likewise, master workers or employers who had formed local associations to control prices and selling practices now extended their objectives to presenting united resistance to the increasing demands of workers. Employers sought, and obtained, the support of the courts. The Journeymen Cordwainers (shoemakers) of Philadelphia were successfully prosecuted for com-

[15] *Ibid.*, pp. 421–23.

mon law conspiracy in restraint of trade in 1806. However, the courts were not utilized as the primary deterrent to labor's action since employers usually found it quicker and cheaper to meet strikes and lockouts either by employing strikebreakers or by direct negotiation.

The first complete factory was established in the textile industry in 1814; all manufacturing processes such as spinning and weaving, complemented by the power loom, were performed in one factory.[16] After introduction of the power loom, manufacture of cotton and woolen goods passed rapidly from the household to the factory. Concentrated factory systems did not immediately dominate the systems of production; there came, rather, a period of transition which spread gradually into other industrial fields. Even in textiles, where the first integrated factory was established, domestic production continued to predominate until 1830. In the shoe industry, domestic manufacturing prevailed until almost 1855, at which time invention of shoemaking machinery drove out this system.[17] Transition from domestic to factory machine production had a devastating effect upon the journeyman and apprentice. Mechanization tended to split established trades into different jobs and to increase the possible division of labor; all-round skilled craftsmen were not required. In colonial days, the craftsman had been protected by apprenticeship regulations which prohibited a master from engaging more than three apprentices without employing a journeyman for each additional apprentice. With a growing demand for cheaper goods, many employers and manufacturers began recruiting employees from other than legally trained journeymen to obtain a cheaper labor supply. Employers took a large number of boys and taught them only one or two processes instead of the whole trade. As their wages were low, it was much cheaper to hire boys to perform simplified tasks than regular journeymen. Full-fledged journeymen were displaced by such corruptions of the apprentice system and the substitution of power-driven machinery for hand tools. Effects upon the appren-

[16] *Ibid.*, pp. 384.
[17] Douglas, et al., *op. cit.*, p. 168.

tice were equally great, for the industrial revolution divested apprenticeship of its trade and civic educational features.[18]

Parallel to disruption of the apprenticeship system, industry began employing women and children as factory operatives. Alexander Hamilton, one of the earliest advocates of industry, saw industrialization as a means of creating prosperity and power for the new nation. He visualized the utilization of women and children to supplement family income as one of the advantages of industrialization and also as a solution to the labor shortage. Mechanical power was to lighten factory labor so that women and children could easily cope with their jobs. Farming was considered to be the primary occupation; manufacturing was deemed a secondary vocation.

It would be incorrect, however, to conclude that industry compelled women and children to work; their employment had been a necessity from the time the colonies were founded. "That their toil was limited to the home and to agriculture and to domestic industry was merely due to the fact that there were no other opportunities for employment." [19] Industrialization merely changed the kind of work and its location.

Being the primary form of economic activity, the agricultural system of labor influenced factory hours of labor. On the farms, hours were from sunrise to sunset and it seemed entirely natural to establish the summer routine of the farms in the cotton mills. Lowell, a model American industrial factory, worked children from fourteen to fifteen hours daily in the early period of its existence; factory operatives from nearby surrounding farms returned ordinarily to their country homes where similar hours prevailed.[20]

Administrative practices of industrial organizations were partially derived from the family system rather than from governmental forms. Early "factories" or production systems were family affairs. A master workman assisted by his family and possibly a few outsiders comprised the requisite personnel. The father or husband had

[18] Douglas, *op. cit.*, pp. 54–60.
[19] William L. Chenery, *Industry and Human Welfare* (New York: Macmillan Co., 1922), p. 23.
[20] *Ibid.*, pp. 38–39.

absolute power in such an organization; this became the model upon which much of early American industry was unconsciously organized.

Another precedent for personnel administration of the period stemmed from feudal, militaristic types of management practices.[21] Entrepreneurs assumed the spirit of autocracy that had previously been held by feudal masters. Thus the business class, on the basis of being better informed and having greater ability to lead, regulated the conditions of work, compensation, and production. Consistent with military traditions, a master expected unquestioning obedience and absolute self-denial from his employees. This concept of management ignored completely the human element.

The period was marked by a transition from hand to machine production, from a close personal relationship with the employee to an impersonal one as manufacturing establishments grew in size, and from feelings of personal concern and responsibility for the employee to a condition where all responsibility was denied. In the spirit of laissez-faire, everyone looked to his own interests. However mixed personnel administrative practices might be, development of a definite trend toward a laissez-faire philosophy was evident. The first entrepreneurs were individuals embarking upon an undertaking with money generally saved by their own thrift and hard work. Everything the entrepreneur generally possessed was tied up in such a venture and the vividness of personal interest tended to make his practices narrow and selfish. Immediate self-interest was his sole guide and personal supervision was frequently severe, backed by threat of force or discharge. Expanding markets and growing competition further increased the pressures applied by early entrepreneurs. The close, personal relationship and mutuality of interests characteristic of master craftsman, journeyman, and apprentice—fairly typical of the domestic system—gave way first in the factory which at first mostly employed women and children. "The factory operators had no strong traditions of this nature to overcome. They

[21] Eugene Wera, *Human Engineering* (New York: D. Appleton and Co., 1921), pp. 27–96.

did not so much assert the opposite principle as simply ignore the tradition itself, partly because it had never been theirs and partly because the reality was more evident in the factory than elsewhere." [22]

It was not until the emergence of such mill towns as Pawtucket, Rhode Island, and Lowell and Lawrence, Massachusetts, in the 1820's that America witnessed the establishment of the real factory system. Out of these early developments emerged two forms of personnel administration which would become prototypes of later employment relationships. The Lowell system of factory organization and administration was initiated by Boston capitalists of Puritan tradition who had a strong desire to avoid well-known degraded conditions of English operatives. To overcome aversions of women and girls to factory discipline and the publicized notorious conditions in England, factories were designed to attract women into the mills and guard them from immoral influences. The production system established at Lowell was considered by many to be a model of factory organization and the perfect industrial community.

Utilized generally throughout Massachusetts and New Hampshire, the Lowell system of factory organization depended more on automatic machinery and less on operative skill and strength; this facilitated employment of women and young girls. Corporate ownership and organization were typical of these factories in which paternalism was the basic form of personnel administration. There were company boardinghouses for female operatives who were under the supervision of a boardinghouse keeper. The girls were required to be in at 10:00 P.M. and were discharged for immoral conduct. Church attendance was compulsory. Wages and hours were established by an understanding among corporations, and a blacklist was used to bar from employment anyone suspected of advocating the union cause. [23]

One finds here that the paternalistic features of the fading apprentice system carried over into the factory system. The latter embraced

---

[22] Norman Ware, *The Industrial Worker* (Boston and New York: Houghton Mifflin Co., 1924), p. xix.
[23] *Ibid.*, p. 74.

the same objectives which were inherent in the practice of welfare management at the turn of the twentieth century. Both on-the-job and off-the-job activities were given close supervision and arrangement. Additionally, administration was dedicated to maintaining unilateral control and direction. Any diminution of managerial authority or prerogatives by the encroachment of unions was deemed intolerable. Achievement of this objective was facilitated in New England cotton textile concerns by standardized wage rates and working hours. Workers were left comparatively helpless in bargaining to improve their condition.

In sharp contrast to the puritanical paternalism found at Lowell, there was the Rhode Island system which was popular in the Middle States but was also found at Fall River, Massachusetts. This was the English system of laissez-faire. Rather than the corporate ownership found at Lowell, individual or joint stock ownership was prevalent in this section. It was the original method of cotton manufacture established in 1794 at Pawtucket by Samuel Slater, a textile worker who had immigrated from England. The manufacturing process was an adaptation of the English system and utilized existing technology and procedures.[24] Personnel administration was based upon the English philosophy of laissez-faire, which sanctioned no interference with the personal freedom or self-interest of others. In contrast to Lowell where adults were employed almost exclusively, whole families were employed and child labor was more prevalent. No attempt was made to guard the morals of employees or to do anything for them within or outside the mills. Instead of the cash wages paid at Lowell, factory stores were established and store orders issued—a further means of employee exploitation.

A brief consideration of the paternal system at Lowell and the laissez-faire system found in Rhode Island might lead one to conclude that Lowell was infinitely superior. However, the first attack by intellectuals on the factory system was centered against Lowell; furthermore, the operatives' revolt against industrial conditions began there. Norman Ware concluded that the facts would suggest

[24] *Ibid.*, p. 72.

"that there were elements in the Lowell situation that were regarded as even more harmful than bad conditions, and that the Fall River system left the operatives greater initiative." [25] The crucial difference between these two systems of personnel administration, paternalism and laissez-faire, was psychological, i.e., the constraints placed on individual freedom of choice and action.

In the last half of the nineteenth century, the laissez-faire system became the more prevalent form of employment relationship although paternalism continued to some extent and emerged later in a different form and in a modified economic and social context. As the Lowell corporation passed from its original founders and largely into the control of stockholders, whatever appeared commendable in the system faded. The typical attitude of employers toward their employees was disclosed by a Lowell official who recorded the following conversation with a Fall River plant manager in 1855:

I inquired of the agent of a principal factory whether it was the custom of the manufacturers to do anything for the physical, intellectual, and moral welfare of their people. . . . We never do, he said. As for myself, I regard my work-people just as I regard my machinery. So long as they can do my work for what I choose to pay them, I keep them, getting out of them all I can. What they do or how they are outside my walls I don't know, nor do I consider it my business to know. They must look out for themselves as I do for myself. When my machines get old and useless, I replace them and get new ones, and these people are part of my machinery.[26]

In factories and small businesses of this era, the philosophy of personnel administration moved away from concepts of master-apprentice paternalism and the puritanical paternalism characteristic of Lowell to a laissez-faire rationale which was divested of all personal interest and responsibility toward employees. Paternalistic features persisted, especially in small establishments, although they were not as extensive as the laissez-faire philosophy.

A majority of companies, unlike Lowell, were small and in the

[25] *Ibid.*, p. 77.
[26] Quoted in Ware, *op. cit.*, p. 77; cited in Mass. Senate Doc., No. 21, 1868, p. 23.

hands of individual owners. An establishment with a hundred workers was considered large, whereas those with only two or three employees were common.[27] The 1840 Census showed probably the greatest development of small manufacturing firms which this country has ever seen. Manufacturing tended to become diffused as the population increased and moved into new territory but this was not counteracted by a trend toward concentration which followed improvement of transportation facilities.[28] Greatest expansion of the factory system in the United States came after 1850. The Twelfth Census report of 1900 stated: "Until about 1850, the bulk of general manufacturing done in the United States was carried on in the shops and the household, by the labor of the family or individual proprietors, with apprentice assistants, as, contrasted with the present system of factory labor, compensated by wages, and assisted by power." [29]

Owners of small establishments were scarcely conscious of management as a separate function. Although growth of larger mills necessitated a more complex managerial structure, this rarely extended beyond a distinction between laborers, clerks, foremen, and minor officials. A good administrator could keep informed of all business operations and know lesser managers as well as older workmen. As a result, there were few difficulties in coordinating various managerial functions. This situation was fortunate since management problems were solved by rule of thumb or experience. There were no published books or professional societies to analyze administrative functions or personnel management.

Most entrepreneurs regarded wages and hour standards as fixed by the demands of competition. If an employer paid the traditional or prevailing wage rate and required the customary hours of labor, he was dealing justly with his employees. Despite this viewpoint, a majority of operatives were underpaid and overworked; further-

---

[27] Chenery, *op. cit.*, p. 154.
[28] Bogart, *op. cit.*, p. 157.
[29] Twelfth Census (1900), Vol. VII, p. liii.

more, they were left to shift for themselves in case of sickness or injury.[30] Personnel administration was premised upon the commodity concept of labor—economic determinism—which was incompatible with workers' aspirations of economic betterment and security.

Work relationships during the colonial era provide an interesting contrasts to the system of laissez-faire developing in the first half of the nineteenth century. Regulation of labor relationships by colonial statutes, although of dubious effectiveness, was prevalent. These statutes were provided to ensure the laborer, whether slave, indentured servant, or apprentice, a minimum of protection against wanton abuse. The legal requirements stipulated that the employer had specific responsibilities, depending upon the labor system, for the laborer's welfare. Under the laissez-faire philosophy of personnel administration, legal provisions protecting the worker were to disappear and emerge again in the twentieth century on an unprecedented scale after the demise of the laissez-faire rationale.

During the period of transition from handicraft to factory production, the paternalism characteristic of the apprenticeship system became an established philosophy in a few larger factories as well as in many of the smaller establishments. A laissez-faire approach to personnel problems, however, increasingly became more prevalent. The master-servant and paternalistic philosophies were giving way to the commodity and machine concepts of labor. Minimal protection of work conditions and environment stipulated in colonial statutes was swept away by an economic climate that neither provided nor acknowledged protections of any kind. Concomitantly, acceptance of some degree of responsibility for a worker's welfare was repudiated and neglect or unconcern became the dictum. Ties of mutual personal interest often found in domestic production were replaced by tenuous economic conditions which precipitated a sharp diversion between worker and employer. As the factory system expanded into all spheres of production, the independent artisan became a depen-

[30] Harold F. Williamson, *The Growth of the American Economy* (Englewood Cliffs, N. J.: Prentice-Hall, Inc., 1946), pp. 310–14.

dent wage earner; the skilled craftsman was compelled to perform a highly specialized task. Transition of the worker's share in the production process can be generalized from Figure 2.[31]

FIGURE 2

Role of the Worker in Early Production Systems

Role	System		
	Handicraft	Domestic	Factory
Supplied own raw materials	X		
Distributed own product	X		
Provided own work place	X	X	
Furnished own tools	X	X	
Devised own methods	X	X	X
Set own work pace	X	X	X
Used his skill	X	X	X
Gave his time	X	X	X

A worker in the handicraft system participated in every phase of the production process—from securing his own materials to distributing the product he had created. Subsequent forms of production, however, removed many of the functions that previously had been an integral part of his job. As the factory became the predominant

[31] Eugene J. Benge, *Standard Practice in Personnel Work* (New York: W. H. Wilson Co., 1920), p. 6.

form of production, work became an increasingly unrewarding experience—dull and monotonous. A sense of achievement and pride in workmanship was diminishing; self-esteem and self-respect were no longer engendered by a task that had become exceedingly restricted as the trend toward job specialization increased.

Furthermore, the transition from handicraft output to the factory system was unmitigated by more personal and humane treatment on the job. Top executives or owners in rapidly expanding industries were no longer able to keep in touch with local conditions. Imperceptibly the dictatorship of the foreman began to assert itself; motivation was by sheer force or authority of position and backed by a willingness and delegated authority to fire anyone who manifested a tendency toward disobedience of orders. It was a form of supervision founded upon autocratic practices and backed by the institution of private ownership. Administration of the developing factories was not sensitive to the need for loyalty, good will, and cooperation of employees.

PERSONNEL ADMINISTRATION IN AN ERA OF LAISSEZ-FAIRE, 1860–1900

The decade prior to the Civil War had witnessed the golden age of the small manufacturing business.[32] Most manufacturing concerns were owned by a single entrepreneur, a small number of stockholders, or by a family. The subdivision of managerial functions found today in modern industry was unknown. An entrepreneur handled purchasing, sales, finance, and all other administrative tasks if they were required. After the Civil War, industrial manufacturing expanded geographically and in size, but there was also a corresponding concentration into fewer large establishments. Industrial establishments had emerged from the Civil War with expanded plant capacities and greater demands for raw materials. Improved transportation facilities opened still larger markets and provided access

---

[32] Harold Underwood Faulkner, *American Economic History* (3rd ed.; New York: Harper & Brothers Publishers, 1935), p. 519.

to physical resources which were being developed at an unprecedented rate. Many small producers with limited capital, unable to survive this transition, were slowly supplanted by larger and more complex industrial establishments that enjoyed the economics of large-scale production. The period of predominantly small-scale industrial and managerial operations was over. The post-Civil War era was one of "rapid settlement of the public domain, eager appropriation and exploitation of natural resources, extension of railroad facilities across the continent, and expansion of industries on a national scale. It was a period of unbridled laissez-faire operating in a territory whose expanse seemed limitless and whose wealth seemed boundless." [33]

Employers' Philosophy of Progress. Reinhard Bendix, a sociologist, has observed that "wherever modern industry is first introduced, entrepreneurial activity is accorded little social prestige." [34] The American experience has tended to corroborate this statement. Industrialists before the Civil War were a minority or subordinate group in a growing nation dominated by commercial and agricultural groups. By the end of the Civil War, however, the industrialists emerged as one of the most powerful and influential groups on the American scene. Of more significance, however, were the basic beliefs and values of those engaged in business. They assimilated and advocated a credo that permeated much of the American society; furthermore, it became the foundation upon which personnel administration was based.

The businessman's philosophy of progress was crystallized in the concepts of individualism and laissez-faire that flourished unabated for most of the last half of the nineteenth century. Economics, political doctrine, and biology combined in the advocation of individualism. The economics of Adam Smith were well known in America and his conceptions of the supreme value of individual liberty and

[33] Bogart, *op. cit.*, p. 526.
[34] Reinhard Bendix, *Work and Authority in Industry* (New York: John Wiley & Sons, Inc., 1956), p. 199.

the pursuit of one's own interests were consistent with the American viewpoint. Self-interest was God's providence which, if pursued without state intervention or other artificial barriers, would promote the welfare of all. "America had already adopted a philosophy of laissez-faire before the influence of the English idea manifested itself, and, indeed, the reason for the popularity of English theories in America was that they represented a more completely worked out formulation of the prevailing ideas." [35]

The philosophy of individualism also had found expression in the American Constitution. Both federal and state constitutions reflected the individualistic spirit of the time. Constitutional sanction was given to the doctrine of non-interference with the individual's freedom which could not be abridged by governmental interference.

Finally, the philosophy of individualism was reinforced by the biology of Charles Darwin and Herbert Spencer which gave the force of natural law to competitive economic struggle. This philosophy was most thoroughly formulated by Spencer, an Englishman, and seemed not only to have captivated businessmen but most of America. Spencer applied the biologic scheme of evolution to society as a whole. Survival of the fittest found its counterpart in his theory of social selection, published even before Darwin stated his theory. According to Spencer, pressure of subsistence upon the population had been the cause of progress, stimulated human advancement, and selected the best for survival. Adaptation of human character to natural conditions of life was fundamental to all ethical progress because in the process evil tended to vanish. The progress of such natural events should not be impeded by state intervention even though the intervention consisted only of aid or relief to the poor, since such individuals were unfit and the best interests of society could be fulfilled by their elimination. Artificial preservation was a violation of the selection principle.[36] The struggle for existence in

[35] Willard E. Atkins and Harold D. Lasswell, *Labor Attitudes and Problems* (New York: Prentice-Hall, Inc., 1924), p. 196.
[36] Richard Hofstadter, *Social Darwinism in American Thought* (rev. ed.; Boston: Beacon Press, 1955), pp. 38–44.

the realm of nature resulting in the emergence of the superior species found its counterpart in those competitors who had been most effective and successful in the arena of economic conflict. Those individuals who emerged victorious comprised the elite; wisdom dictated that no restrictions should be placed upon their leadership if society were to achieve perfection.

Spencer's philosophy was consistent with the aspirations, conduct, and social viewpoint of American businessmen and provided them a "guide to faith and thought perfectly in keeping with the pattern of their workaday lives." [37] The extent to which this philosophy prevailed can be noted in comments by two prominent industrial leaders of that era. John D. Rockefeller declared: "The growth of a large business is merely a survival of the fittest. . . . The American Beauty rose can be produced in the splendor and fragrance which brings cheer to its beholder only by sacrificing the early buds which grow up around it. This is not an evil tendency in business. It is merely the working out of a law of nature and a law of God." [38] Andrew Carnegie, one of the most devoted followers of Spencer, placed great emphasis on the biological foundations of economic competition. He wrote, "It is here; we cannot evade it; no substitutes for it have been found; and while the law may sometimes be hard for the individual, it is best for the race because it insures the survival of the fittest in every department." [39]

These streams of thought were inevitably used to explain the position and behavior of the employing class. Men were divided into two groups; the few who had excelled, and were thereby entitled to lead in positions of authority, and those who had failed to demonstrate leadership or other requisite qualities for success. Workers were commanded to obey those whose success entitled them to direct business enterprises. It was evident that workers would live in dire poverty if it were not for their entrepreneurial guidance. The em-

[37] Thomas C. Cochran and William Miller, *The Age of Enterprise* (New York: Macmillan Co., 1942), p. 119.
[38] John D. Rockefeller, quoted in Richard Hofstadter, *op. cit.*, p. 45.
[39] Andrew Carnegie, quoted in Richard Hofstadter, *op. cit.*, p. 46.

ployer had demonstrated his right to a position of authority because of his success; success, in turn, was indicative of superior abilities and virtue. Therefore, the authority relationship in industry was justified. Employers interpreted their own success in the competitive struggle as sufficient justification for their absolute authority in an enterprise; anyone who had not been successful had to submit to their authority without qualifications or reservations.

Conflicts between workers and employers were attributed to the employees' unwillingness to exert themselves and not to their rightful engagement in the economic warfare. Employers failed to concede that employees were justified in their protective measures against harsh industrial practices and in participating fully in the economic struggle. Employer response to employee countermeasures was exemplified by the former's reaction to the union movement. The Knights of Labor, organized in 1869, had grown sufficiently strong by the mid-eighties to challenge employer's unilateral authority. After a couple of successful strikes, a strong reaction to the challenge of managerial authority began; labor's demands were deemed unlawful and unjust. Employers organized strong associations to combat this threat and sought to eradicate any form of organization among wage earners.[40]

Despite the limited success of such strikes, they did succeed in directing attention to employee problems which had been neglected in the haste to expand product markets and adopt new technologies into continually expanding industrial organizations. The labor ferment periodically compelled employers to focus attention upon their human resources and take stock of managerial practices. However, the problem was not considered of sufficient importance to warrant instituting personnel practices or policies designed to promote long-range peaceful employer-employee relations.

Employers held a laissez-faire philosophy of personnel administration which was based upon absolute authority. Each employer had the right of absolute proprietorship and arbitrary decision. Con-

[40] John R. Commons and Associates, *History of Labor in the United States, Vol. II.* (New York: Macmillan Company, 1918), p. 414.

trolling the means of production, entrepreneurs were in a position to see that the worker could not engage in making his livelihood except by their permission; the employee was compelled to work at terms, including wages, hours, and work conditions, designed to maximize profits for the employer. Emphasis was upon materials, markets, and production; the human element was neglected. It was a materialistic philosophy complemented by autocratic principles of management.

Autocratic management embraced and applied basic principles that are analogous to those observed in an autocratic form of government. In general, the autocratic manager believes that the worker exists for the sake of industry. Furthermore, the worker's abilities and capacities are hopelessly inferior. And, finally, the worker must be governed by authority; it is for his own good and welfare.[41] It has been noted how such a philosophy was embellished and given scientific substantiation by Spencer. The industrialist personified the survival of the fittest—which justified his position of authority and his right to demand unqualified submission to such authority.

Employers based their personnel practices upon a commodity concept of labor; an employee's services were bought like other factors of production. Wages were high when labor was scarce in relation to its demand and low when the labor supply was in excess of demand. Classical economics taught, and experience confirmed, that the price for labor was determined by supply and demand like any other commodity. Considered only another factor of production, employees received scant attention as individuals with needs, desires, and aspirations that could be satisfied within the framework of the industrial organization. Employers felt little or no responsibility for the working conditions, health, safety, or job security of their operatives, but rather viewed employee relations solely as an economic association to be severed at their discretion. Satisfying personnel relationships were not deemed a managerial objective or a fruitful approach in assisting the company to attain or achieve its objectives.

[41] Wera, *op. cit.*, p. 116.

The Management Movement. Intense competition prevailed throughout most of the period from 1860 to 1900. Natural resources were exploited and markets expanded; business methods were individually profitable but technically wasteful. It did not matter to most industrialists whether business practices were economical or uneconomical, just or unjust, legal or illegal. However, as geographical frontiers were reached and exploitation of natural resources made increasingly difficult, these industrial methods were no longer appropriate to meet new conditions.

The individualistic spirit and unrestrained competition endorsed by American businessmen produced some unanticipated results. Large-scale production had facilitated certain economies due to minute divisions of labor, constant utilization of expensive and complicated machinery, employment of more skilled managements, and the mass purchase and marketing of goods; however, there remained unavoidable losses unless prices could be maintained at profitable levels and output stabilized. The purported benevolences of competition were marred by the emergence of monopoly and unfair competition. Industrial combinations were deemed one of the best means to alleviate these problems, and during the last quarter of the nineteenth century a tremendous number of combinations, mergers, or trusts of competing plants into larger enterprises occurred. This was an attempt to escape or mitigate the competition engendered by the employers' philosophy of laissez-faire.

In response to the decline of easily exploited resources and terrific competition which forced profits to very narrow margins, employers also turned their attention to internal conditions of production and labor efficiency. The management function became increasingly important. Concern for internal management did not mushroom overnight; it was an evolutionary process. Some evidence to this effect is demonstrated by the scarcity of publications on management problems. Prior to 1881 there were no such publications; from 1881 to 1900 there were 27; 240 from 1900 to 1910, and a rapid increase thereafter.

The typical self-made entrepreneur had scarcely taken any interest in a serious examination of the management problem; his attention was focused on prices and markets; his mental attitude and methods were still more like those of the pioneer.[42] Rather, awareness of the management problem came first from engineers, who were the initiators of the management movement.

Engineers were the first academically trained group to enter industry where they sought to utilize an objective approach in the analysis of industrial managerial problems. Prior to their entrance into industry and for some time afterwards, management was not systematized; the benefits of plant layout, new ways of handling materials, and scientific research were not greatly appreciated. Founded in 1880, the American Society of Mechanical Engineers originally confined itself to engineering problems and accepted the existing type of general management. "Gradually they realized that something more than machinery and physical equipment [was] needed to bring about desired production. . . . The first need they saw was that of an incentive method of wage payment as a substitute for the direct supervision which was depended upon in the earlier small shops to make laborers work industriously." [43]

Whereas an individual entrepreneur previously had performed practically all managerial functions of the smaller business unit, it became necessary to subdivide duties and delegate authority in order to cope with organizations functioning on an unprecedented scale. Supervisors, having supreme authority over all processes and men under their jurisdiction, and yet often untrained for their task, were small tyrants. Relying on motivation by fear, foremen demanded that workers follow orders or else. It was a mailed-fist approach implying that employees should be "treated rough" and made to like

[42] Harlow S. Person, "Basic Principles of Administration and Management: The Management Movement," in H. C. Metcalf, ed., *Scientific Foundations of Business Administration* (Baltimore: Williams & Wilkins Co., 1926), Human Relations Series IV, p. 201.

[43] Don D. Lescohier and Elizabeth Brandeis, *History of Labor in the United States, 1896–1932, Working Conditions* (New York: Macmillan Co., 1935), III, p. 304.

it; the methods were dictatorial, militaristic, and void of any consideration for the human factor. Employees generally found their highly simplified tasks unmotivating, and their personal treatment failed to offset the lack of achievement and satisfaction in the job itself.

As managements began to focus attention on internal problems, they found poor work attitudes were prevalent. "Experience with unemployment during the 'seventies' had convinced workers that there was not enough work to go around, experience with the cutting of piece rates had caused distrust of management, and generally, morale and voluntary effort were low. Throughout American industry management's concept of a proper day's work was what the foreman could *drive* workers to do and the workers' conception was how little they could do and hold their jobs." [44] Efficiency aspects of the labor problem, therefore, first engaged the attention of management; wage systems were thought to provide a solution. As plants had increased in size, the span of supervisory control had been overextended, and it was hoped workers under less direct supervision could be motivated by financial incentives. Previously, time payment and piece rates had been the standard methods of wage payments; both, however, were found to have severe disadvantages. Utilizing a wage incentive approach to labor-management problems, H. R. Towne in 1886 submitted a premium system of payment to industry, while Frederick W. Taylor devised a differential piecework plan. F. A. Halsey, influenced by his study of the epidemic of strikes during the 1880's, formally presented his premium plan of wage payment in 1891.[45]

Under the influence of science and engineering, the machine concept of labor became more widespread. The value of labor was determined by the quantity of its product. With this mechanistic viewpoint in a technologically oriented era, employers tended to regard their employees as machines, or an extension of such, capable of a

44 The Taylor Society, *Scientific Management in American Industry,* ed., H. S. Person (New York: Harper & Brothers Publisher, 1929), p. 2.

45 L. P. Alford, "The Status of Industrial Relations," *Mechanical Engineering* 41 (May, 1919), 6:614.

certain output. Wage plans, advocated by engineers, sought to guarantee that this potential output would be assured. This approach
was noteworthy because it reflected a lack of human values and an
understanding of employee motivation; it was based on the implicit,
but erroneous, assumption that employees were primarily economically motivated. The machine concept of labor failed to consider
factory operatives as individuals who possessed rights, desires, or
human aspirations. Industry was not aware of the necessity for such
human understanding.

After wage incentives, cost systems were the next problem to engage managerial attention. This approach was an improvement and
advance over efforts to increase labor efficiency by piece rates, premium systems, tasks, and bonuses. Managements' ". . . attempt to
solve their problem through wage devices was really putting the
solution up to the workers; their attempt to solve it by better cost
systems was placing the responsibility where it belonged—on management. Also it was the beginning of a new method—an analytic
attack on the problem." [46]

An additional wage approach was utilized to solve labor difficulties
after the 1880's—profit sharing; by 1893 over a hundred concerns
were using various forms of profit sharing. Some of the profit-sharing
schemes were inspired by industrial unrest while others were deemed
necessary to combat socialism and producers' cooperatives. For
other industrial managers it was an attempt "to restore the feeling
of association in a common cause which had characterized the relations of master and men in simple industrial times." [47] Because of
the growing impersonality and specialization of labor, some managers thought of profit sharing as necessary to motivate the employee
to give an honest day's work and to visualize himself as a part
of industry and, therefore, vitally concerned with its technical
efficiency.

Other sporadic and isolated efforts were made to promote indus-

[46] Person, *op. cit.,* p. 202.
[47] Ida M. Tarbell, *The Nationalization of Business, 1878–1898* (New
York: Macmillan Co., 1936), pp. 172–73.

trial peace; these were along welfare and paternalistic lines, but they indicated a growing awareness of the labor problem. The Pullman Car Company in 1880 founded a model town in Pullman, Illinois, which, in addition to homes and community facilities, even supplied a physician and medicine. The N. O. Nelson Manufacturing Company also established a similar town in Leclaire, Illinois, in 1890. Although these towns were ideal in many respects, residents had little or nothing to say about the administration of community affairs.[48]

A few employers were beginning to explore the possibilities of various welfare projects. Although welfare management dates back to Robert Owen's work in England and the efforts of Lowell, Massachusetts, welfare practices were not general and failed to attract appreciable attention until the last decade of the nineteenth century. The recognition, however, had become sufficiently developed to warrant foundation of the American Institute of Social Service in New York in 1898. Its objective was to promote industrial betterment which was broadly defined as ". . . various phases of improvement in the promotion of better relations between employer and employee; arbitration, trade unions, employers' associations, trusts, wages, hour of labor, housing, education and recreation and other movements." [49] This designation, industrial betterment, was soon changed to welfare work by popular usage.

The first association formed to implement industrial betterment principles was founded by the Cleveland Chamber of Commerce in 1900 in recognition of the growing distance between capital and labor. The organization was dedicated to the belief that "anything which tended toward more intimate relations and a more kindly feeling between these two classes would result in a better understanding and a nearer approach to mutual cooperation." [50]

Another notable effort to achieve harmonious labor-management

48 *Ibid.*, pp. 175–77.
49 William H. Tolman, *Social Engineering* (New York: McGraw-Hill Book Co., 1909), p. 44.
50 *Ibid.*, p. 45.

relations took place in the declining years of the laissez-faire era, but it was conceived in conflict and ultimately degenerated into the same. The Stone Founders' National Defense Association, the first employers' organization operating on a national scale, was organized in 1886 for the protection and defense against the demands of labor. While generally successful against the Iron Molders' Union, the struggle was expensive and demoralizing. Seeking a more harmonious solution to their problems, both groups formulated a method of peaceful settlement. In 1891, it was decided to settle their differences amicably and to abandon strikes and lockouts. The ensuing success of this venture stimulated additional foundries, other than stoves, to organize the National Founders Association in 1898 "with the distinct understanding and the knowledge that a labor organization existed, had a right to exist; that men had a right to join each other for their mutual benefits." [51] Although this search for a different avenue to labor problems ended in conflict in 1904, it was indicative of an awareness for a novel approach, a willingness to experiment with something new, and a recognition of the inadequacy of prevalent labor-management relations.

Despite the promising trend noted above, the prevailing approach to personnel relations came under close scrutiny and attack. Employers had used their superior bargaining position, based on right of ownership, to compel employees to work on their own terms, which were frequently oppressive and inconsiderate. The association of employee and employer was an individual relationship based upon the cash nexus and lasted only so long as the employer had a job to offer. An employee was viewed either as a commodity or machine, not endowed with human attributes. In keeping with the individualistic spirit of exploitation, employers ignored the human nature of employees instead of utilizing such human drives and needs constructively for their mutual advantage. Industry was unaware of the necessity for human understanding or the need for a personnel rationale compatible with employee needs and values. Consequently,

---

[51] Tarbell, *op. cit.*, p. 169.

employer-employee relationships precipitated conflict rather than mutual cooperation and restriction of production rather than efficiency. The laissez-faire philosophy of personnel administration, prevalent throughout the last half of the 19th century, which was instrumental in creating these conditions is summarized below.

LAISSEZ-FAIRE PHILOSOPHY OF PERSONNEL ADMINISTRATION

1. Leadership. Leadership under the laissez-faire philosophy was autocratic and therefore insistent upon complete obedience to managerial authority; autocratic control was freely exercised without respect to moral or human considerations. Exploitation of both physical and human resources was identified with progress; top management leadership was dominated by materialistic and acquisitive values. Employers had the right of absolute proprietorship and administered the enterprise on the behalf of personal ownership and economic interests.

   Executive leaders considered themselves the elite of society, equipped to command because of their superior hereditary endowment; they had demonstrated a right to positions of authority by their success in the competitive economic struggle for survival. Workers who had been unsuccessful in economic affairs were expected to submit to the employer's authority without qualification or reservations, thereby giving managers an unquestionable right to determine work conditions and labor practices.

2. Personnel Management. Personnel management was based upon the concepts of individualism and self-interest which repudiated any responsibility for the employees' physical, economic, or psychological welfare. Since neither personnel management as a scientific approach to employee relations nor the personnel department had come into existence, the personnel function was handled by foremen untrained for their task. Supervisors were small tyrants who had supreme authority over all processes and men under their jurisdiction; personnel methods were dictatorial, militaristic, and lacking in consideration for the human factor.

3. Concepts of Labor.
   Commodity concept. An employee's services were bought like any other factor of production; wages were high when labor was scarce and low when the labor supply was in excess of

demand. Considered only as another factor of production, employees received scant attention as individuals with needs, desires, and aspirations that could be satisfied within the framework of the industrial organization. Employers felt no responsibility for working conditions, health, safety, or job security of their operatives, but viewed employee relations solely as an economic association to be served at their discretion.

Machine concept. The employee was regarded as a machine, or an extension of such, capable of a certain output; wage plans, designed by engineers, sought to guarantee management that this output would be attained. When extended to personnel relations, it reflected a lack of human values and little understanding of employee motivation. Furthermore, it was based upon the erroneous assumption that employees were primarily economically motivated.

4. Incentives. Relying on motivation by *fear* and *drivership*, management demanded that workers follow orders or else. In keeping with the individualistic spirit of exploitation, employees were compelled to work on the manager's terms which were oppressive and inconsiderate. There was no awareness of the necessity for human understanding or personnel relations compatible with employee needs and values.

5. Labor Relations. Conflicts between labor and management were attributed to employees' unwillingness to exert themselves rather than to the workers' right to participate in competitive economic struggle. Employers failed to concede that employees were justified in their protective measures against harsh industrial practices; labor's demands were unlawful and unjust. Consequently, employers organized strong associations to combat the threat to their unilateral control by organized labor and sought to eradicate any form of organization among wage earners. Industrial leaders based their cause, among other things, upon freedom of contract and the industrial liberty of the citizen.

The laissez-faire philosophy of personnel administration created and reinforced workers' dissatisfactions with social and economic conditions which had gradually worsened between 1860 and 1900. Feeling more personal and economic consideration was due them, employees were beginning to crystallize their desires into definite propositions and to seek improvements through public legislation and trade unions. Labor had been increasingly active in directing attention to harsh and oppressive industrial practices and in pressing for social legislation, but had met with little success. Prior to 1900, a few states had laws regulating child labor, employment of women, and health conditions; however, these statutes were extremely limited in scope, lacking in enforcement provisions, and of questionable constitutionality. The courts tended to view such laws as class legislation and also as an interference with the freedom of contract. This legalistic point of view, however, tended to reflect the sentiments of a majority of the community.

While there seems little doubt that the public and community embraced the laissez-faire outlook and the promise of unlimited economic opportunity during most of the late nineteenth century, a wave of national self-criticism was rising. The plight of many citizens and the abuse of consumer and labor interests alike could no longer be ignored. In the eighties the value of manufactured products had surpassed that of agriculture, and by 1900 America was an industrial nation with a permanent body of dependent, industrial workers. As the century drew to a close, the general public could no longer ignore the evils of stemming from economic and social malpractices in industrial operations. A tide of humanitarianism was mounting that would precipitate sweeping changes; the values of the employee, the community, and the public were increasingly out of step with the laissez-faire philosophy.

However, while conflict was widespread, there was developing an awareness that cooperation was necessary since large-scale enterprise prohibited the close, personal relationship and supervision formerly characteristic of small enterprises. Wage incentive plans, profit sharing, and welfare activities were sporadically employed to promote efficiency. These techniques ignored the problems of human relations. Employers failed to realize that problems of improving employee cooperation and efficiency could best be solved by considering the worker as a human being. Although such remedial efforts failed to achieve their objective they reflected a realization that the existing personnel rationale and practices were inadequate; labor-management difficulties could not be resolved by the businessman's philosophy of laissez-faire.

III

PERSONNEL ADMINISTRATION AND ITS
ANTECEDENTS, 1900–1920

The laissez-faire approach to personnel administration had proved inadequate, but an unparalleled number of promising innovations in personnel practice and philosophy made an appearance at the turn of the twentieth century. In this section we will follow the modern personnel function from inception to its application to manpower problems of World War I. The philosophy and techniques of scientific management and industrial psychology will be analyzed for their impact on personnel management. Additionally, the relationship between welfare management and personnel management will be examined for compatibility of purpose and function.

A study of the reaction of top business leaders to these new contributions, of the extent to which such contributions were utilized, and the purpose for their adoption will indicate the significance to employees of changes in personnel philosophy. Finally a descriptive model of the fairly prevalent paternalistic philosophy will be structured and its adequacy for fulfilling human needs evaluated.

ORIGIN OF PERSONNEL ADMINISTRATION
AND ITS RATIONALE

At the beginning of the twentieth century, factories had grown in size but there were no parallel developments in improving human relations. The typical factory was characterized by high accident rates, excessive labor turnover, and extremely inefficient operations. A small number of employers were installing better heating, lighting, sanitary facilities, and first-aid-stations. A few progressive ones were experimenting with welfare projects, health programs, and profit sharing to promote greater efficiency, loyalty, and profits. Problems of personnel relations were ignored; scientific management and personnel administration were as yet in the future.

The years from 1900 to 1920 were notable for the new ideas advanced and for the beginning of concepts leading toward an improved philosophy of personnel administration. In the last decade of this interim, personnel management emerged as a young discipline and was recognized by some of the more progressive employers as a basic function of management. The philosophy of this embryonic managerial function was distilled from Taylor's philosophy of management, the welfare management approach to personnel administration, and the basic principles of industrial psychology.

The newness of employment management, or personnel management as it was later known, was indicated by Meyer Bloomfield, who, writing in 1920, stated: "You may ransack the literature of industrial management written ten years ago and you will not find the phrase 'employment management' used or the work of the personnel or employment supervisor mentioned. No college or university school of business training of that day dealt with the problem. And the reason for this is simple. Neither the work of employment management nor the functions of an employment executive were recognized in the scheme of industrial organization as it was commonly carried out." [1] The personnel movement grew out of efforts of those hiring employees to share common experiences and problems, to establish definite techniques of manpower management, and to formulate standards of good practice. Foundation of the Boston Employment Managers Association in 1913 indicated a growing consciousness of the personnel function and its importance. The association originated with the idea that "building up of a working force and dealing with men in their work relations was a job which had a real professional content." [2] It was an effort to introduce

[1] Meyer Bloomfield's introduction to *Employment Management*, ed. Daniel Bloomfield (New York: H. W. Wilson Co., 1919), p. 1.
[2] Daniel Bloomfield, "Man Management: A New Profession in the Mak-

scientific analysis and a human note into personnel procedures that previously had been conducted on a hit-or-miss basis. Individuals in this novel personnel profession were impressed by the fact that they held one of the most important and difficult of all executive jobs. One finds here the beginning of the modern art of handling men.

Employment and personnel associations spread throughout the country and in 1917 the first national conference on this subject was held. The implications of the new movement were summarized by Eugene Benge, management engineer, as follows:

> It is safe to believe that we are now living in a nascent era of industrial changes whose main characteristic when crystallized will be the attention to the human relations of man to man. A new profession has arisen. Out of the nebula of inefficiency, paternalism, exploitation, . . . there has been formed the new profession of industrial relations, whose aim is to help each other. Beginning, as it did, with a realization of the evils and losses due to bad employment policies, this new profession has gradually broadened until it is now considered by many to be the most important single factor in management.[3]

Although it is questionable whether personnel management met the qualifications of a profession, being more of an art than a science at this stage of development, it did bring a new emphasis on the human factor into industry. The personnel dictum became: "Study the human nature you deal with in order to win leadership by cooperating with it." [4]

The personnel function had been given impetus by the economic argument of high costs of labor turnover. Professor John R. Commons, in 1909, reported a study of a Pittsburgh machine shop which "in a single year of prosperity (1906) hired 21,000 men and women to keep up a force of 10,000." [5] Later, in 1914, Magnus W. Alex-

---

ing," in *Problems in Personnel Management*, ed. Daniel Bloomfield (New York: H. W. Wilson Co., 1923), p. 10.

[3] Eugene J. Benge, *Standard Practice in Personnel Work* (New York: H. W. Wilson Co., 1920), p. 7.

[4] Bloomfield, *Problems in Personnel Management*, p. 9.

[5] Don D. Lescohier and Elizabeth Brandeis, *History of Labor in the*

ander of the General Electric Company again focused attention on this labor problem when in an address he stated that among a group of twelve factories in 1912 "about six and one-third times as many people had to be engaged during the year as constituted the permanent increase of force at the end of the period." [6] Findings such as these had an impact upon employer personnel policies. As industrialists began to realize that labor turnover was indicative of worker discontent, they began to get the economic implications, in dollars and cents, of turnover previously taken for granted.

Personnel activities also were influenced by the passage of workmen's compensation laws. In 1911, the first compensation law passed the Supreme Court's scrutiny; within two years twenty additional states passed similar laws. Responsibility for injuries was placed upon employers, and juries began to award large sums in suits for personal damages. Such pressures made it economically profitable for employers to utilize individuals specialized in accident prevention and safety. Training and education programs were initiated to protect operatives from accidents. Specialization in safety and training was given formal expression through the National Association of Corporation Schools.[7]

In general, employers were not greatly concerned about turnover or procurement problems prior to World War I because labor generally had been plentiful. As a result of the war, however, immigration was severely curtailed, employees went into military service, and expanding wartime production made jobs plentiful. Problems of securing a sufficient labor force and getting maximum production from the existing work force became crucial. To meet these problems, personnel management was introduced to reduce labor turnover, improve labor selection, improve the training of workers, and

---

United States, 1896–1932, Working Conditions (New York: Macmillan Co., 1935), 3:331.

[6] Magnus W. Alexander, "Hiring and Firing: Its Economic Waste and How to Avoid It," *Personnel and Employment Problems in Industrial Management*, The Annals, LXV (May, 1916), 128–44.

[7] Thomas G. Spates, "An Analysis of Industrial Relations Trends," *AMA Personnel Series* (1937), No. 25, 1–24.

increase per capita productivity. This functionalized division of management was not entirely new since a few firms already had established separate departments for hiring, training, and the promotion of welfare activities. Functions of hiring, training, and firing were taken from the foreman and centralized in the employment office where they could be handled more objectively and scientifically. Investigations were made of discharges and quits to deter turnover and to salvage as many employees as possible. Welfare activities, job standardization, motion study, time study, and correction of unfavorable work conditions tended to be brought under the direction of one executive.

A summary of the functions and objectives of employment management as it developed in the more progressive firms discloses that they are very similar to modern personnel administration. The basic rationale expressed in its formative years is summarized as follows:

1. Employment management is human engineering, a continuing and intelligent handling of men.
2. The main purpose of employment management is to increase the efficiency of labor.
3. Employment management is a specialized function and must be scientific in its method.
4. Employment management is a staff function whose executive should have equal rank with other executives.
5. Primary functions of the employment department are selection, training, medical care, and welfare.
6. The functions of employment management are based on careful job analysis as a prerequisite for effective implementation of personnel administration.
7. The employment manager must secure the cooperation of labor if high efficiency is to be obtained.
8. Employment management is dedicated to increasing the social and psychological, as well as the economic, satisfactions of employees.
9. Each worker is developed for a particular task.
10. Fair treatment, good wages, and favorable work conditions are sound production policies.

11. Services and welfare work are indirect methods of promoting employee efficiency.[8]

Although not as elaborate as modern personnel philosophy, basic objectives of the emerging personnel function represented a great advance beyond previous thinking and approaches. It is doubtful if the implications and ramifications of this rationale were understood as they are today but their significance rests in an awareness of basic principles and the first efforts to articulate these into a system of beliefs that serve as a basis for action. It cannot be claimed that this rationale was universally accepted. Rather,

The movement represented more an ideal, a goal, than an accomplishment with definite, codified procedure. There were, consequently, many degrees and variations even among the firms who aspired toward its realization. The type of work varied no more than did the names applied to those in charge of its performance: Employment Manager, Personnel Manager, Industrial Relations Secretary, Employees Service Director, Labor Manager—even the term Welfare Manager was used in spite of its besmirched connotation.[9]

The above principles did not emerge fully developed; they were a synthesis of concepts and philosophies from scientific management, welfare management, and industrial psychology. It is necessary to trace their contributions to a personnel rationale and its subsequent refinement.

Contributions of Taylor's Scientific Management to Personnel Administration. The first explicit philosophy of industrial administration was formulated by Frederick W. Taylor. Taylor deemed high wages and low labor cost the best foundation for management

[8] Edward D. Jones, "Employment Management," pp. 118–28; Ernest M. Hopkins, "A Functionalized Employment Department as a Factor in Industrial Efficiency," pp. 149–58; R. C. Clothier, "Function of the Employment Department," pp. 158–66, and E. C. Gould, "A Modern Industrial Relations Department," pp. 193–96, in Bloomfield, ed., *Employment Management.*
[9] Lescohier and Brandeis, *op. cit.,* p. 326.

and a means or achieving harmony between labor and management. From first-hand experience and research he concluded that this objective had not been achieved because employers lacked specific knowledge of the various kinds of work performed. To remedy this, it was necessary to develop a science for each element of an employee's work. A further cause of failure to reach harmony was the "indifference of the employers and their ignorance as to the proper system of management to adopt and the method of applying it, and further their indifference as to the individual character, worth, and welfare of their men." [10]

Taylor indicted the previous philosophy of management which left problems of initiative and incentive to be solved by the individual workman; in contrast, he felt that the "philosophy of scientific management places their solution in the hands of management." [11] The employer was to assume duties previously left to the workers because a scientific division of work demanded the performance of activities for which each was logically responsible.

Management's new responsibility consisted of collating all traditional work knowledge into basic rules and laws; a science of work would be developed from this body of information and complemented by a science for each element of an employee's work. Furthermore, management was to work closely with employees in order to be assured that all work was consistent with the derived scientific principles. Supplementary managerial duties consisted of scientific selection and training. In addition, Taylor's scientific management required a disciplinarian to handle cases of insubordination, lateness, absences, readjustment of wages, and grievances. The disciplinarian was also the employment supervisor. "The knowledge and character of the qualities needed for various positions acquired in disciplining the men should be useful in selecting them for employment. This man should of course consult constantly with the

10 Frederick Winslow Taylor, *Shop Management* (New York: Harper and Brothers Publishers, 1903), p. 30.
11 Frederick Winslow Taylor, *Principles of Scientific Management* (Harper and Brothers Publishers, 1911), p. 103.

various foremen, both in his function as disciplinarian and in the employment of men." [12]

One finds here the precursor of the personnel manager who appeared during the second decade of the twentieth century. Taylor, having been a foreman himself, realized that dealing with employer-employee relationships required special abilities and was sufficiently important to constitute a separate function of management.

Scientific management was not an efficiency device, cost accounting system, piecework or bonus system, time study, or functional organization. The essence of scientific management was, rather, a complete mental revolution on the part of both the workingmen and the employers.[13] For the employee, now hired for work commensurate with his ability, trained, and paid higher wages than ever before, had a new image of his job duties and a new attitude toward co-workers and employers. A completely new concept was being formulated by management as to their obligations toward the workers and their own daily tasks and problems. The principal objective of management was to secure maximum prosperity for each employee; this required the development of each employee to a state of maximum efficiency and resulted in higher wages. Long-run employer prosperity was contingent upon the prosperity of the employee and both received what each most desired—higher wages for the worker and low labor costs for management.

In addition to this mental revolution which Taylor envisioned as being the essence of scientific management, one other requisite change in viewpoint was considered necessary: "Both sides must recognize as essential the substitution of exact scientific investigation and knowledge for the old individual judgment or opinion, either of the workman or the boss, in all matters relating to the work done in the establishment." [14] Taylor was advocating science rather than rule of thumb, cooperation rather than individualism, harmony

[12] Taylor, *Shop Management*, p. 119.

[13] Frederick Winslow Taylor, "Taylor's Testimony before the Special House Committee," reprinted in *Scientific Management* (New York: Harper and Brothers Publishers, 1947), pp. 29–30.

[14] *Ibid.*, p. 31.

rather than discord, maximum production rather than restriction of production, and the development of each worker to his greatest efficiency and prosperity. For most industrial managers, these ideas were entirely new.

Taylor's approach to the relations between employers and workers involved a complete change in traditional philosophies of personnel administration. Like previous employers, he assumed that employees were motivated primarily by economic interests and that an incentive system would induce better performance. However, Taylor took one step forward by associating the worker's prosperity with that of the employer. An employee under the laissez-faire rationale of personnel administration had been entirely responsible for his failure to achieve success in the industrial world; now the employer had the responsibility of scientifically determining not only the best way to perform a job but also of placing the employee on the job for which he was best suited. This called for duties, techniques, and responsibilities that, by and large, were unrecognized and nonexistent at the start of the twentieth century. During the nineteenth century, if the worker seemed unable to perform the task he was discharged. This approach to employment problems had appeared most feasible because the labor supply, swollen by natural growth and immigration, was abundant.

This new approach to industrial management assumed some responsibility toward the worker and was supplemented by an emphasis upon cooperation. Industrial harmony, now a goal of employers, was to replace the antagonism and conflict too long prevalent in industry. Having assumed that the principal objective of management was to secure maximum prosperity for each employee, Taylor believed the true interests of labor and management were identical. Scientific investigation would establish objectively a fair day's work and a fair day's pay. Since this, according to Taylor, had always been the chief source of misunderstanding, the natural laws of cooperation would operate and industrial harmony would follow. Occupational maladjustment would be reduced because each man was fitted to the job most consistent with his abilities. Training promoted maximum wages since misunderstandings over duties and methods were eliminated. Discipline was to be handled more objectively by a disciplinarian rather than by a foreman, and grievance machinery would be established to hear and scientifically investigate sources of friction. With such treatment, employees would naturally cooperate with management.

Despite the emphasis placed on mutuality of interests, selection, training, a grievance procedure, and consideration of the human factor that was entirely new to the traditional approach of personnel administration, Taylor's concept of labor was essentially mechanistic. His functional management called for removing all mental work from the shop to a planning department; each employee was to do only what he was told and perform his job in the exact manner prescribed by scientific management.

> It is the aim of Scientific Management to induce men to act as nearly like machines as possible, so far as doing the work in the one best way that has been discovered is concerned. . . . Experience has shown that, whether or not the men may be called machines, they fare better and profit more when the management takes the time to have a trained planning department, cooperating with the best workmen, determining every step in the process and every motion in the step, and the effect of every variable in the motion.[15]

It is true that each worker had been selected to perform the task for which he was best suited, but this, in Taylor's scientific management, implied that some workers, like machines, could perform more complex operations. This viewpoint was deemed consistent with modern industrial development.

Scientific management also stipulated a new type of leadership; the old-fashioned, autocratic, and dictatorial methods utilized in the exercise of authority were to be eliminated. Management was to assume its rightful responsibilities, abandon rule-of-thumb approaches to personnel administration, and abide by the findings of science, with the understanding that the workers were also to abide by these

[15] Frank B. Gilbreth, *Primer of Scientific Management* (New York: D. van Nostrand Co., 1912), p. 50.

findings. Under scientific management, arbitrary power and dictation were to be replaced by the scientific investigation of each problem and reduced to scientific laws. Taylor's philosophy, supporting techniques, and scientific procedures eliminated the personal exercise of authority. In essence it substituted the authority of science. He had criticized the previous failure of management to assume its proper responsibilities and the use of rule-of-thumb procedures; Taylor had questioned the judgment and superior ability attributed to employers. Many employers found scientific management an interference with their authority and managerial prerogatives as well as an attempt to substitute techniques for judgment.

Taylor was instrumental in demonstrating the importance of careful, intelligent handling of employees, and his system of scientific management required a disciplinarian or employment supervisor to manage human problems arising from employment relationships. Furthermore, by demonstrating that personnel problems could be attacked by scientific methods, Taylor originated and outlined the first functional scientific personnel organization in American industry. This structure failed to include welfare activities or a rationale of human behavior but it outlined some of the primary functions and approaches that were later incorporated into employment, or personnel, management.

The ultimate purpose of scientific management was to increase the efficiency of labor. This also became the primary goal of personnel management, and the criterion of its success was its demonstrated ability to achieve a more effective application of labor to production. Personnel administration was unique, however, in that increased efficiency was achieved by engaging the workers' interest in their work, by human engineering which required a knowledge of the human element unavailable to Taylor. Scientific management sought to make labor more effective by selection and training, firmly established on job analyses as a basis for job requirements and specifications; eventually personnel management followed suit. Taylor considered employees as motivated only by economic incentives, whereas personnel management recognized a variety of psychological and social motives as important as the economic. Taylor's scientific management, despite its limitations, must be credited with making the first big stride toward recognizing the importance of the human factor.

As it evolved, personnel management came to consider fair treatment, good wages, and adequate work conditions as sound policies to promote production and efficiency. Taylor's approach had not only previously demonstrated the feasibility of such policies, but also provided a means for their realization. Employees were given a specific and acceptable standard task, scientifically determined and within the capacities of properly selected and trained operatives. Workers were induced, rather than forced, to perform the stipulated task by incentives. Initiative, special skill, and creativeness were rewarded, and promotion based upon achievement rather than seniority or other arbitrary methods. Even fatigue was considered, and rest periods were provided. These principles, modified and expanded, became an integral part of personnel administration.

Substitution of cooperation for conflict between management and labor was the heart of Taylor's system, and he was the first to promote such conditions on an organized and objective basis. Personnel administration, even in its formative stages a decade later, adopted cooperation as its means of achieving efficiency. Using human engineering as a basic approach, force, drivership, and exploitation were repudiated as methods for obtaining long-range harmonious relations with employees.

Finally, Taylor's philosophy held that there was a mutuality of interests between management and employees with regard to industrial efficiency. The emerging personnel function accepted this viewpoint. However, personnel management has also been cognizant of the areas of conflict and inevitable disagreement; its approach has been to minimize friction by creating a work environment conducive to harmonious relationships. This objective has been sought by intelligent management of the labor force and efforts to harmonize the objectives and values of the business enterprise with those of employees.

Much of Taylor's philosophy, modified, reinforced, and given greater insight by industrial psychology, was reflected or assimilated into the early rationale of personnel administration as a discipline and much later integrated into the philosophy of industrial executives.

Welfare Management and Personnel Administration. Toward the close of the nineteenth century, welfare work, or industrial betterment as it was first called, began to attract the attention of industrial leaders. The United States Bureau of Labor Statistics defines welfare management as "anything for the comfort and improvement, intellectual or social, of the employees, over and above wages paid, which is not a necessity of the industry nor required by law." [16] Welfare work preceded Taylor's scientific management but was most extensively developed during the period when scientific management was evolving.

Louis A. Boettiger concluded that there are three distinct stages in the development of welfare work. During the first stage welfare activities are spasmodic, paternal, and often inquisitorial in nature; the economic advantages are understood to some degree, but the welfare work is not functionalized on an economic basis, and such activities are crude and frequently badly managed. This was characteristic of welfare management before and during the first decade of the twentieth century. In the second stage, welfare activities are better formulated and delegated to trained specialists, such as social secretaries and welfare agents. These individuals are directly responsible to the top executive but exercise very little authority. Growth along such lines as outlined in the second stage was especially noticeable in the first decade of the twentieth century. Finally, there is a third stage in which welfare activities become major staff functions under the direction of specialists designated as employment managers or personnel administrators; welfare activities and

[16] United States Bureau of Labor Statistics, Bulletin 250 (February, 1919), p. 8.

employment work are integrated into one department. Writing in 1923, Boettiger concluded from statistics compiled by the Department of Labor: ". . . the greater part of welfare work carried on in this country at the present time is in the first stage of development; approximately one-third is in the second stage, while only a relatively small number of establishments have developed the work as far as the third stage." [17]

The immediate ends sought by employers were varied. Welfare management was a trial-and-error attempt to reestablish the close personal relationship between worker and employer that existed when production systems were small. For some it represented a growing awareness that the wage earner must be treated as a human being if cooperation was to be secured. Other employers saw in welfare work a means of stabilizing employment by minimizing the cost of excessive hiring and discharging of employees. For other companies, however, it was an insincere attempt to obtain the workers' loyalty for less than the price of a fair wage, means of mitigating a bad reputation caused by poor business practices, and a method of good advertising or public relations.[18] It also represented a means of discouraging the growing trend of employees to join unions, which were viewed as an unwarranted interference with managerial authority. Numerous companies had found cultivation of the workers' good will by welfare plans such as profit sharing, bonus and premium systems a more useful policy than efforts to suppress unions or intimidate workers who joined. International Harvester Company, Bell Telephone Company, and General Electric were typical firms with extensive welfare programs that assisted in the maintenance of an open shop.[19]

Another force behind welfare management, although it probably served multiple objectives simultaneously, was the "belief that what-

[17] Louis A. Boettiger, *Employee Welfare Work* (New York: Ronald Press Co., 1923), p. 125.
[18] Harold U. Faulkner, *The Economic History of the United States* (New York: Rinehart & Co., Inc., 1951), p. 269.
[19] Lescohier and Brandeis, *op. cit.*, p. 317.

ever promoted the loyalty and interest of the worker was an industrial asset and therefore 'good business.' " [20] It was thought to be a means of achieving greater production at lower costs. National Cash Register Company, the first concern to concentrate its welfare activities in one department, explained the reason for its welfare work as follows: "In 1892 registers worth over $50,000 were returned because of defective workmanship. We decided that more interest would have to be taken in our employees to make them better and we then started welfare work and found that it paid in a better product." [21]

Organized labor, with few exceptions, opposed welfare work of every kind. The unions frequently recognized it as a means of sugarcoating the introduction of scientific management, to which they were generally opposed. Labor considered welfare management as a substitute for fair wages, better working conditions, and, foremost, as a method to counteract unionism; it was a technique that further entrenched autocracy and encouraged paternalism by the employer.

On the other hand, welfare management was never completely accepted by a majority of employers. "Out of 37,194 firms in New York State in 1904, about 110 had one or more welfare features. Of the 18 million wage earners in the United States in 1908 probably one and a half million came within the scope of welfare management." [22]

Many concerns which initiated extensive welfare programs curtailed them because of a lack of employee response. One prominent industrialist stated:

We have considerably curtailed our work along the line of industrial betterment . . . we are not quite so enthusiastic over it now. . . . I feel perfectly convinced that, so far as we are concerned, it was a mistake to have started it, . . . we have satisfied ourselves that we shall never again make the attempt. . . . In other words, we shall buy our labor as we buy our material, and we are thoroughly convinced

[20] *Ibid.*
[21] Quoted *ibid.*, cited in *Welfare Work*, The National Cash Register Company, Dayton, Ohio.
[22] Lescohier and Brandeis, *op. cit.*, p. 326.

that those who sell their labor will give us as little as they possibly can for what they sell us without regard to whether or not we attempt to go more than our half of the way.[23]

Some employers had expected too much from welfare measures and were chagrined when such programs failed to meet expectations; others simply did not realize that workers, in addition to resenting interference in their personal lives, detected the motives behind such programs and reacted negatively.

The rationale of welfare management stemmed from a realization that employee welfare had a direct effect on productivity. Industrial strife, low productivity, and high turnover were evidences of an unsatisfactory relationship between management and employees. Welfare activities were utilized to solve the problem; employers provided better work conditions, restrooms, lunchrooms, recreation programs, safety, first aid, visiting nurses, and a horde of other ameliorating conditions in an effort to improve employment relationships and increase production. The employer, often with the best of motives, assumed an attitude of absolute direction in the personal lives of workers. This approach failed to provide an opportunity for initiative and responsibility; it lacked a basic understanding of employee needs, desires, and aspirations, and how they could best be fulfilled; it generally failed to promote cooperation and mutual understanding. The significance of this good-will or paternalistic concept of labor was that it indicated a growing awareness that labor as a factor of production could no longer be ignored.

Welfare management was a continuation of the paternalistic apprenticeship system and the factory system found at Lowell, Massachusetts, during the first half of the nineteenth century. It was a form of personnel administration that assumed the worker was a child whose work and play must be arranged and supervised by the employer. Employees were dependent upon the employer, who retained undisputed authority and responsibility for their well-being; it was managerial paternalism based on autocratic leadership. Founded on

[23] Quoted in *Social Engineering*, William H. Tolman (New York: McGraw-Hill Book Co., 1909), p. 356.

the premise that there should be no diminution of managerial authority, benevolent programs were conducted to insure that no one would challenge this authority and to eliminate competing loyalties and ideas.

Variations of welfare management continued, and from 1915 to 1920 there was a rapid development of labor policies closely related to welfare work. Labor shortages, high turnover rates, and the assimilation of large numbers of new personnel to meet the war demand gave a great impetus to welfare functions. With all its diversity of employer motives, hostility of unions, and errors of poor administration, ". . . welfare management contained some elements of liberal labor policy and those features which responded to a real need were later reincarnated into another form of managerial policy, the modern policy of functionalized labor management covering the whole range of employer-employee relations." [24] The ultimate sanction of welfare work in personnel management was to rest on its social utility because social well-being demands certain guarantees in respect to hours of work, wages, working and living conditions, and periods of economic uncertainty. Such welfare activities were to be confined largely to those programs having a direct bearing on the security and efficiency of employees and also on the business establishment. Divested of its paternalistic approach, welfare activity became a part of the philosophy of the new profession of personnel administration.

Contributions of Psychology to a Philosophy of Personnel Administration. To an extent not generally realized, the scientific management movement originated by Taylor facilitated the development and utilization of industrial psychology. By proving that it pays to use specialized techniques for selection and training of employees, as well as for studying the most effective methods, Taylor paved the way for industrial psychology. He demonstrated that it was economically profitable to study human behavior with the objective of increasing the effectiveness of the human element. Industrial psy-

[24] *Ibid.*, p. 321.

chology was concerned with similar problems, but developed and applied a knowledge of human behavior not available to Taylor.

The application of psychology to manpower problems was stimulated by a growing awareness of the limitations of past personnel administration and the promise of more effective methods for handling personnel and production problems. Utilization of psychology was also due to the slow realization that the ". . . development and rational utilization of labor saving mechanical devices must be supplemented by a more complete and effective utilization of human energy, human abilities, and of human will-to-work to ensure the success of the individual industrial plant." [25] For some it was one more means of thwarting further extension of the trade union movement. And too, the movement was facilitated by a wave of humanitarianism sweeping America; it was a reaction against the practice of ignoring the human factor. Viteles states that the applications of industrial psychology were made possible to some extent as a result of the "replacement of the let-it-alone by the humanistic concept of work." [26]

The application of psychology to industrial problems was first advocated by Hugo Munsterberg, founder of this area of applied psychology. He outlined three fundamental areas in which psychology might be applied:

We ask how we can find the men whose mental qualities make them best fitted for the work which they have to do; secondly, under what psychological conditions can we secure the greatest and most satisfactory output of work from every man; and finally how we can produce most completely the influences on human minds which are desired in the interests of business. In other words, we ask how to find the best possible man, how to produce the best possible work, and how to secure the best possible effects. [27]

Advancement of human efficiency has been one of the foremost ob-

[25] Morris S. Viteles, *The Science of Work* (New York: N. W. Norton and Co., Inc., 1934), p. 43.

[26] *Ibid.*, p. 41.

[27] Hugo Munsterberg, *Psychology and Industrial Efficiency* (New York: Houghton Mifflin Co., 1913), p. 23.

jectives of industrial psychology. However, it was realized that true efficiency in industry could not be achieved by sacrificing human values to achieve economic goals. A decrease in the physiological and psychological cost of work was found to be the only permanent means of increasing economic efficiency.

In addition to an emphasis on the human factor in studying work problems, industrial psychology popularized an "individual differences" concept of labor which recognized that each person possessed a different mentality and had different physical capacities and personality characteristics. This viewpoint indicated the importance of differential selection and placement; men could not be indiscriminately selected or shifted to other jobs. Taylor had indicated scientific management could effectively utilize such individual differences to the advantage of both employers and employees. Lillian Gilbreth, a psychologist who was also closely associated with the development of scientific management, sought to integrate psychology with Taylor's scientific management.[28] In doing so, she recognized individuality as a fundamental principle of scientific management in the study, selection, and motivation of employees. However, it was left to the discipline of psychology to demonstrate the full significance of individual differences and to develop the tools for their measurement.

Industrial psychology, an applied science based on individual differences, developed testing devices to assist in individual measurement and facilitate the prediction of job success. Psychological testing also was considered a means of reducing turnover, minimizing labor strife, and promoting greater productivity. Both the behavioral and instinctive schools of psychological thought had pointed to the individual as being comprised of a conglomerate of traits, abilities, and aptitudes; although they did not agree as to their origin, these human components were considered essential to job success in varying degrees and measurable by properly devised tests. Psychological testing by the army during World War I indicated the contribution such measurements could make in finding the right man for a job,

---

[28] L. M. Gilbreth, *The Psychology of Management* (New York: Macmillan Co., 1919), pp. 27–37.

and industry was quick to capitalize upon its possibilities. Tests were eagerly welcomed. Managers, and some psychologists, soon realized that their exaggerated expectations of test results would not be realized. Many traits important to job success could not be measured.

An outstanding contribution of psychology to the philosophy of personnel administration was an approach which explained the problem of work from a behavioral point of view. Instinctive behavior as a means of explaining human behavior and adjustment was given wide circulation after 1908 by William McDougall's *An Introduction to Social Psychology*.[29] This approach to understanding the complexity of human behavior soon found its way into business activities, and in 1910 Ordway Tead published a text on *Instincts in Industry*.[30]

As a psychological approach to human behavior and values, the study of instinctive behavior emphasized the importance of the individual personality, innate and acquired traits and habits, and the relationships among these factors and the complex problems of motivation, adjustment, and behavior in the industrial environment. The relationship between job satisfaction and employee output was considered to reside in instincts, rather than primarily in the pay envelope. Satisfaction from work stemmed from the fulfillment of human needs which were innate predispositions toward certain forms of behavior. Such instincts as workmanship, property acquisitiveness, and self-assertion, coupled with intelligence and modified by experience, were the driving or motivating forces underlying human conduct. Factors in the industrial environment such as injustices in hiring and firing, specialized work, and monotonous tasks were forces that thwarted the instinctive expression of innate modes of behavior. Employers by properly structuring the industrial environment could appeal to the basic instincts of workers and thereby promote efficiency, cooperation, and employee satisfaction.

[29] William McDougall, *An Introduction to Social Psychology* (Boston: John W. Luce & Co., 1908).
[30] Ordway Tead, *Instincts in Industry* (New York: Houghton Mifflin Co., 1918).

The study of instincts as a means for understanding, motivating, and forecasting employee behavior had a great influence upon personnel thought and practices until the late 1920's. Previous concepts of labor had visualized the worker as either a commodity, machine, or simply as an economic man. Industrial relations had reflected these concepts and had been found inadequate. Administrators had become very uncertain of the traditional concepts of labor in view of their failure to obtain cooperation and the continuation of restricted production, excessive turnover, violence, and strikes.

A different approach to understanding human behavior, behavioral or objective psychology, rejected the assumption of innate instincts and contended behavior was the result of environmental forces. Regardless of divergent explanations of human behavior, both viewpoints maintained that an environment could be provided which would result in predictable behavior; one could understand, predict, and control human modes of conduct. Thoughts and actions of employees were amenable to control by properly structuring the work environment. Attitudes could be shaped, motivating factors utilized to manipulate workers' behavior, and human drives channeled into the productive efforts of industry. This implied that industrial psychologists and personnel administrators could accomplish with individual workers what engineers had accomplished with machines. In 1917, an article entitled "Human Engineering" stated: "It seems to be largely a question of knowing or judging what given individuals or groups of individuals will do under a given set of conditions, and knowing from experience, which seems to be our only guide as yet, what people have done under such circumstances; provide suitable means so that the circumstances and what follows from them may go along the line which will bring the greatest profit to the company employing the men." [31] This approach offered great hopes for the management of labor, and was consistent with traditional practices of employers in seeking to control the work performance

[31] E. H. Fish, "Human Engineering," *Journal of Applied Psychology* 1, (1917), 174.

of employees. Since industrial relations were largely psychological, the objectives of personnel management were sought through the science of predicting and controlling employee behavior. Personnel administration became synonymous with human engineering.

Industrial psychology, however, never advocated any single, basic philosophy, as did Taylor's scientific management. Rather, industrial psychology in its efforts to become and remain an exact science deliberately sought to avoid consideration of objectives. "Psychology will always be limited by the fact that while it can determine the means to an end, it can have nothing to do with the determination of the end itself. . . . In short, it may determine means, but the determination of ends and their values is beyond its sphere." [32]

Although industrial psychology did not have an explicit philosophy, it did make significant contributions to personnel administration and its rationale; it generated a humanistic philosophy. The most significant contribution of industrial psychology was the orientation of the work problem from the human as well as from the production point of view. In its scientific analysis of work conditions, the primary interest of industrial psychology was to increase human efficiency by decreasing the physiological and psychological costs of work. Considering the novelty of this approach in light of the prevailing concepts of employee work performance, one realizes that such psychology was no small advance toward a better understanding of industrial relations and thus the promotion of more peaceful, cooperative relationships. Employment management as it developed during World War I adopted this point of view; it too was dedicated to promoting labor efficiency, but equally to increasing the psychological and social satisfactions of employees.

Industrial psychology also contributed an individual differences concept of labor. Each employee had unique mental and physical capacities as well as temperamental characteristics. Personnel administration adopted this concept of labor and utilized psychological

[32] H. L. Hollingworth and A. T. Poffenberger, *Applied Psychology* (New York: D. Appleton & Co., 1919), p. 20.

tools and techniques to promote the objectives of employee adjustment, job satisfaction, and efficiency.

In addition to their stress on the individual and individual differences, industrial psychologists were also aware of social implications. In McDougall's *Social Psychology*, this sociality was considered an instinct of gregariousness, a minor or secondarily defined phenomenon of human behavior. The herd instinct, which recognized that the individual's behavior will be determined by the people with whom he associates, was emphasized by Tead. In the first textbook devoted to personnel administration, the desire for association was noted as an important factor in achieving work satisfaction.

It is because the desire to associate is so innate that the demand for the approval of those with whom we associate is also dominant. Indeed, if properly used this desire to be thought well of by our fellows is an immensely constructive force. . . . The problem of rendering the association a voluntary and willing one is urgent because it is in association which is reasonably self-initiated and spontaneous that the most effective work is done and the most pleasurable atmosphere prevails.[33]

Despite these insights into the social implications of work, which anticipated the discoveries of the Hawthorne investigations of Elton Mayo, the psychological orientations to human behavior in industry remained individualistic in both philosophy and practice.

Psychology provided theories of human behavior that gave a clearer comprehension of the human factor in industry; personnel administration immediately assimilated this new viewpoint. Despite the severe scientific limitations of instinctive and behavioral approaches to human behavior, psychology made a significant contribution to a better understanding of the human element. No longer could the worker be viewed as an "economic man" motivated only by financial rewards. Psychologists made management more aware of non-financial incentives and demonstrated the complexity of the human factor. "In every industrial country of the world the accom-

[33] Ordway Tead and Henry C. Metcalf, *Personnel Administration* (New York: McGraw-Hill Book Co., Inc., 1920), p. 17.

plishments of industrial psychology have been effective in promoting output and adjustment—in making work more tolerable and more productive. These results have been made possible by the recognition that the operation of industry is primarily dependent upon the capacities, interests, impulses, sentiments, and passions of human beings." [34]

Finally, psychology, by revealing the complexities of the human element and its diversity of motives, demonstrated the possibilities of a better regulated work environment. By intelligently managing the work situation, basic psychological needs of employees could be satisfied so that efficiency, cooperation, and job satisfaction would result. This was the first realization that basic needs and objectives of employees, other than economic, might be integrated with those of the industrial organization. It became apparent that the psychological atmosphere of the work place could no longer be left to chance but must be the subject of careful attention and study. Early expressions of personnel management as a discipline adopted this objective from human engineering. Industrial psychology had generated a humanistic philosophy, but it remained the task of personnel administration to implement this approach in daily work relationships.

EXECUTIVES' PHILOSOPHY OF PERSONNEL ADMINISTRATION

One should keep in mind that the personnel rationale just examined was that of personnel administration as a new discipline, and such views were held by those engaged in or closely related to the personnel function. There is little evidence to show that these new insights were equally shared by industrial executives who in the final analysis formulated the philosophy of personnel administration. It has been typical to find executives of industrial relations and personnel departments more conscious of human relations problems than the top executives to whom they report. The unending task of

---

[34] Viteles, *op. cit.*, p. 56.

personnel executives has been to educate and shape their superiors' thinking on such problems.

Executive Reaction to Scientific Discipline. Executive reaction to scientific management and principles of industrial psychology was indicative of the prevailing level of management's thinking and of its failure to adopt an enlightened personnel philosophy. Taylor himself anticipated and witnessed one of the least desirable reactions to scientific management. He had admonished: "The mechanism of management must not be mistaken for its essence, or underlying philosophy. . . . The same mechanism which will produce the finest results when made to serve the underlying principles of scientific management, will lead to failure and disaster if accompanied by the wrong spirit in those who are using it." [35] Many industrialists, however, had mistaken the mechanism or techniques for the underlying philosophy they involved. This neglect of the essence or basic philosophy of scientific management was confirmed by Robert Hoxie, who directed the investigation of the United States Commission on Industrial Relations into the practices of scientific management. Hoxie found that no single plant had completely installed scientific management principles. The machines and organization of the production process had been overlooked, motion study had been neglected, and time study was superficial. Businessmen had been unwilling to pay for the necessary research and had made quick adaptations of the various techniques in hope of immediate results. Scientific managers, usually termed efficiency experts, many poorly trained and frauds, were performing their tasks to achieve the results desired by employers. Numerous employers clothed their autocratic decisions with the so-called findings of science, considered to be beyond question by employees, and further fortified the practice of industrial autocracy.[36] In his testimony before the House committee,

[35] Taylor, *Principles of Scientific Management*, pp. 128–29.
[36] Industrial Commission on Industrial Relations, *Final Report* (Washington: U.S. Government Printing Office, 1915), XV, 209–33.

Taylor summarized his experience with the employers as follows: "Nine-tenths of our trouble has been to bring those on the management's side to do their fair share of the work, and only one-tenth of our trouble has come on the workman's side. Invariably we find very great opposition on the part of those on the management's side to do their new duties and comparatively little opposition on the part of the workmen to cooperate in doing their new duties." [37]

The reaction of managers to psychology was similar to that given to scientific management. Some industrial psychologists, as professionals, had demonstrated a willingness to sacrifice economic for human values; but it was questionable if industrial executives were equally willing to do so. Management's basic motive for accepting industrial psychology was summarized by Viteles as follows: "As a matter of fact, industry has largely accepted psychology as an aid because of what it can contribute toward the cheaper production and merchandising of goods." [38] Munsterberg recognized that industrial psychology was primarily an employer psychology, but he was optimistic, and perhaps rightly so to a large degree, that some advantages would accrue to the workers. "We must not forget that the increase of industrial efficiency by future psychological adaptation and by improvement of the psychological conditions is not only in the interests of the employers, but still more of the employees; their working time can be reduced, their wages increased, their level of life raised." [39]

Viewed pragmatically, it did not matter that the principles of industrial psychology or the more liberal practices of personnel administration were motivated by the desire to increase profits; the results tended to benefit labor also. From the standpoint of executive philosophy, however, it is significant that good labor relations were only a means to an end. Industrial thinking and practice had not de-

[37] Taylor, "Taylor's Testimony Before the Special House Committee," p. 43.

[38] Morris S. Viteles, *Industrial Psychology* (New York: W. W. Norton and Company, Inc., 1932), pp. 8–9.

[39] Munsterberg, *op. cit.*, p. 308.

veloped to the extent that sound personnel relations were conceived as an end objective or even a complementary objective to profit maximization.

Executive Concern for Employee Welfare. In general there was little employer concern expressed for the physical, psychological, and social well-being of employees prior to 1915. After taking note of the great concentration of ownership, usually corporations, and the tremendous number of workers employed in this type of industrial structure, the Industrial Commission on Industrial Relations in 1915 made the following statements concerning the conditions of employment:

... These industrial dictators for the most part are totally ignorant of every aspect of the industries which they control, except the finances, and are totally unconcerned with regard to the working and living conditions of employees in those industries. Even if they were deeply concerned, the position of the employees would be merely that of the subjects of benevolent industrial despots. Except, perhaps, for improvements in safety and sanitation, the labor conditions of these corporation-controlled industries are subject to grave criticism, and are a menace to the welfare of the nation.[40]

Failure of such prominent owners of industrial wealth as the Rockefellers, Morgans, and Vanderbilts to shoulder any responsibility for industrial conditions was disclosed by the investigation. The testimony revealed the extent to which effective action and direct responsibility for working conditions had been shifted to executive officials. John D. Rockefeller, Jr., stated: ". . . those of us who are in charge there elect the ablest and most upright and competent men whom we can find, insofar as our interests give us the opportunity to select, to have the responsibility for the conduct of the business in which we are interested as investors. We cannot pretend to follow the business ourselves."[41] The committee chairman then questioned J. Pierpont Morgan: "In your opinion, to what extent

[40] Industrial Commission on Industrial Relations, *op. cit.*, p. 118.
[41] *Ibid.*, p. 31.

are the directors of corporations responsible for the labor conditions existing in the industries in which they are the directing power?" To which Morgan replied: "Not at all, I should say." [42] Industry was found, in general, not only lacking in concern for working conditions, but to be opposing improvements by legislative means. It was noted in committee hearings that legislators had been remiss in pressing for adequate remedial measures, and that judicial interpretations had been unfavorable toward statutes designed to improve the lot of labor.

Still another powerful influence was found at work by the Industrial Commission. The National Association of Manufacturers and allied organizations had been extremely active in applying pressures in both Congress and state legislatures to the end that legislation designed to improve labor conditions should not be enacted. Opposition of the National Association of Manufacturers to laws designed to prevent child labor, to shorten working hours, to eliminate night work for women, and to provide safety measures was disclosed by the investigation. Employers had not acted to improve work conditions and had resisted remedial legislation which would require them to do so.[43]

Under the impact of the war from 1915 to 1920, the poor working conditions found by the Industrial Commission were radically changed. The stimuli of acute labor shortages and need for greater productivity turned executive attention to labor problems as never before. This newly emerging concentration of concern was pointed out in a letter written by Thomas A. Edison: "Problems in human engineering will receive during the coming years the same genius and attention which the nineteenth century gave to the more material forms of engineering." [44]

As World War I produced a shortage of workers, employers began to conceive of labor as a productive resource that should be

[42] *Ibid.*
[43] *Ibid.*, p. 42.
[44] Quoted in Meyer Bloomfield, "Relations of Foremen to the Working Force," *Industrial Management* 53 (June, 1917), 3:341.

protected and carefully utilized in order to secure maximum production. Industry adopted a "natural-resource" concept of labor. As geographical frontiers closed and exploitation of natural resources became less acceptable as a method of business operation, federal statutes were enacted to protect the nation's natural resources. Some Congressional leaders likewise began to conceive of labor as a natural resource which required similar protection from exploitation; health and accident legislation, shorter hours for women and children, and proposals for child labor laws evolved from their thinking. A few visionary employers had been in the vanguard promoting more favorable work conditions, and legislative enactment sought to bring other industries to, or nearer to, such improved industrial conditions.

The natural-resource concept of labor is significant because it marks a change in public thinking that had been previously dominated by the philosophy of laissez-faire and individualism. Aroused public sentiment and labor agitation had prompted some governmental intervention in industrial operations which had previously been exclusively executive functions. An increasing number of industrial leaders realized that if they abused or failed to utilize adequately the human resource, then governmental action, sanctioned by public sentiment, would compel them to change their methods. Others, under the pressure of economic necessity, sought to conserve and effectively utilize the restless and limited labor force during the war years. Taylor had shown the possibilities of selection and training for improving efficiency, and industrial psychology had confirmed and extended such possibilities. Personnel or employment management using these and similar techniques was employed, often in desperation, to conserve labor. Furthermore, many executives found that conservation of labor paid greater dividends than exploitation.

Attention was turned mainly to the physical well-being of employees, with considerably less evidence of an awareness of psychological and social well-being or of the rights of employees as cooperators in industrial production. The concern for even physical well-being was novel: "The comparatively modern policy of providing comfortable working quarters for men and women employees had been accepted as an obligation by many leading industrial corporations of our country. Apparently these immense business enterprises have begun to realize that the maintenance of a steady, permanent working force, capable of giving its best service, depends in a large measure on the physical conditions surrounding employment." [45]

Many employers found it difficult to secure the cooperation of labor even in a concerted effort to win the war. One employer advocated, in addition to efforts of labor maintenance, the establishment of personal contact as a remedy for poor labor-management relations. A personal interest in the home life and families of the workers was considered a means of overcoming the impersonal atmosphere of industry. ". . . Best of all, from the human standpoint learn to know them, if not personally, at least through accredited channels, and make sure that they know you. . . . Personal contact is of inestimable value. No commodity in the world responds so quickly to kind treatment as labor, and no investment yields such great returns." [46] A few of the more progressive employers were becoming aware of the mental or psychological aspects of worker satisfaction.

But the policy which aims at high standards in production does not stop with the working methods of individuals in the organization. The view of the broadminded men of industry extends beyond the immediate influences which adhere only to the working hours and takes in the influences which bear upon the worker's health, well being, and happiness. This means a regard for the cleanliness and purity of the working plant and of the homes, for the peace of mind of the workers which can come only with a fair measure of prosperity, and for contentment which comes only, when to the above is added general confidence in the fairness and good faith of the management.[47]

[45] John Roach, "Hygienic and Sanitary Equipment," *Industrial Management* 54 (October, 1917), 1:20.

[46] J. J. Gillespie, "Indifferentism: The Present Danger in Manufacturing," *Industrial Management* 57 (January, 1919), 1:3–39.

[47] P. F. Walker, "Ethical Tendencies in Modern Industrialism," *Industrial Management* 53 (September, 1917), 6:2.

However, even the thinking of progressive employers was considerably behind that generally characteristic of personnel officials. The lag between the outlook of the evolving personnel discipline and the perceptions of top executives was perhaps never greater than during the period from 1900 to 1920. Considerable time would elapse before these two levels of thinking began to merge significantly.

Reactions to Organized Labor. While employers had previously resisted employees' efforts to form and affiliate with unions, the opposition to trade unions was provided with national organization and leadership by the National Association of Manufacturers in 1903. This group recognized the right of workers to organize, but dedicated itself to the suppression and destruction of independent unionism and its tactics. Theoretically, unions and collective bargaining were sanctioned unless officials outside the local plant area were involved. The Commission on Industrial Relations, which held hearings for two years beginning in 1912, found such a viewpoint common among employers: "out of 230 representatives of the interests of employers, . . . less than half a dozen have denied the propriety of collective action on the part of employees." [48] However, the commission also observed that a majority of employers indicated a refusal to deal with a national labor organization. From the testimony collected, the commission drew the following conclusions:

> The underlying motive of such statements seems to be that as long as organizations are unsupported from the outside they are ineffective and capable of being crushed with ease and impunity by discharging the ringleaders. Similarly, the opposition to the representation of their employees by persons outside their labor force, seems to arise wholly from the knowledge that as long as the workers' representatives are on the payroll they can be controlled, or, if they prove untractable, they can be effectually disposed of by summary dismissal.[49]

Significantly, collective bargaining with company unions or shop

48 U.S. Industrial Commission, *op. cit.*, p. 5.
49 *Ibid.*, p. 6.

committees was not objectionable. Such organizations were not a significant threat to unilateral control; without outside support, they were generally ineffective.

Further evidence of a continuation of this viewpoint was demonstrated at the first National Industrial Conference called by President Wilson to meet at Washington on October 6, 1919. Representatives of employers, labor, and the public were to examine means of promoting close cooperation between labor and capital. Representatives of employers and employees, however, were unable to agree upon a definition of collective bargaining. Both the public and labor delegates supported the principle of the right of employees to bargain collectively through representatives of their own choosing; employer representatives, however, refused to agree to such a definition and the conference group disbanded. Employers still refused to accept independent trade unions as the basis of collective bargaining.[50]

The employers' stand on unionism had a philosophical basis similar to the restraints placed by the Constitution upon the invasion of the rights of life, liberty, and property. The right of free contract, management reasoned, is basic to the enjoyment of property. Since the buying and selling of labor imply a contract, any restrictions of the process is a violation of the liberty to contract; thus, any violation of freedom to contract is a violation of the rights of private property. The wage earner was conceded the right to seek employment and to acquire property in the form of wages, whereas the right to contract for services and freely operate a business was deemed a part of the property rights of the employer.[51] Organized labor, therefore, was considered as a threat to the freedom of contract, and the fight to maintain an open shop was based upon the property right. The philosophy reflected a continuation of the spirit of individualism and the doctrine of natural rights so popular in the

[50] William Jett Lauck, *Political and Industrial Democracy, 1776–1926* (New York: Funk and Wagnalls Co., 1926), p. 77.

[51] Albion Guilford Taylor, *Labor Policies of the National Association of Manufacturers* (University of Illinois Studies in the Social Sciences, Vol. 15, 1927), pp. 162–67.

last half of the nineteenth century. It was a philosophy that nourished continued hostility and opposition to organized labor.

In contrast, one notable form of labor-management joint endeavor was initiated by the federal government during World War I, when the National War Labor Board sought to minimize the effect of industrial conflict upon the war effort. Work councils or shop committees were organized in which employee representatives actively participated in the adjustment of employment problems. Principles and policies employed by the board recognized the right of workers to organize and bargain collectively through their chosen representatives, permitted organized labor to maintain existing union security conditions, and allowed employers to bargain individually and collectively when the firm was divided between union and nonunion groups and to bargain collectively on provisions relating to hours and wages. As a result of such vigorous promotion of employee representation by the government, local shop committees became prevalent throughout industry. At first labor unions gave hesitant endorsement to various forms of employee representation but endorsed the board's policy of compelling employers to bargain with shop committees when they refused or were reluctant to do so. It appeared to organized labor that shop committees would eventually become trade unions. Employers had other ideas, however, and as soon as the government ceased its regulation of industrial relations, they initiated an open shop drive. For some managements, work councils or shop committees were to be substituted for independent unions; shop committees became company unions.[52]

Developments in Personnel Philosophies. In seeking to establish better personnel relations, such major approaches were utilized to alleviate the conditions of industrial unrest as profit sharing, incentive methods of wage payment, safety programs, employment management, and shop committees or joint control. None of the methods, however, was part of an integrated, coherent philosophy of personnel administration; they were sporadic efforts to deal with persistent

[52] *Ibid.*, p. 42.

labor problems. In addition to these approaches to industrial relations, L. P. Alford, an educator and industrial management consultant, detected three tendencies in the development of industrial relations.[53] One was acceptance of the motive of service which recognized the rights and needs of those engaged in or dependent upon industry. However, at least a decade was to pass before one could consider the service motive a significant phenomenon, and even then it had not been extended appreciably to employees. The second tendency was to consider workers in groups rather than as individuals. This was thought by Alford to be the viewpoint of the industrial psychologist. However, this newly observed trend did not become a significant concept until approximately twenty years later, after the Hawthorne investigations and the legal sanctioning of collective bargaining in 1935. Finally, a discernible tendency to practice mutual or joint control through shop committees was thought to exist. This expression of democratic ideals, brought about largely at the insistence of the federal government during World War I, soon degenerated into an open shop movement at the termination of the war, helping to stop the growth of unions. Therefore, while the methods of dealing with personnel problems and the tendencies observed by Alford are noteworthy in the evolution of personnel practices, they were not indicative of a significant change in personnel philosophy.

Although the typical executive was aware of the importance of favorable work conditions in attracting and maintaining labor and of the application of scientific principles as an aid in increasing productivity, few bothered to formulate policies which reflected their philosophy of personnel administration.

The president or the general manager will impress upon the employment manager that "there is no more important job in the organization" than the handling of men. But . . . these are empty words, spoken . . . because it is nowadays considered proper to speak of employment work in this way. Too often the big man's ideas of

[53] L. P. Alford, "The Status of Industrial Relations," *Mechanical Engineering* 41 (May, 1919), 6:513–56.

employment work, beyond the motive of supplying help to the operating divisions, are very hazy.[54]

I have myself been almost dumbfounded to find how few large employers of workers have any definite constructive labor policy. . . . But if pressed by direct questioning, he will . . . finally admit that he has only a negative policy or a policy of expediency.[55]

The above statements reflect a widespread, although implicit, do-nothing rationale of personnel administration held by a majority of executives during the first twenty years of the twentieth century. The do-nothing philosophy was based upon preservation of the existing industrial order and the refusal to seriously consider the numerous potential contributions from the various sources dealing with personnel relations. While many of the economic, individualistic, and political values held by a great proportion of the populace during much of the period of laissez-faire were harmonious with those of industrial leaders, these attitudes shifted to a more humanitarian and protective view toward labor. Many industrial leaders, however, held to a perspective more compatible with the past. Therefore a do-nothing philosophy was now feasible to an extent not previously possible. Now it was possible to do nothing in the face of value systems more divergent than ever before and to do nothing in the face of scientific approaches to personnel problems which were previously nonexistent. Many employers did nothing to bridge their social and economic values with those of the public and likewise no constructive effort was made to examine or utilize newly discovered behavioral concepts.

Industrial executives had not adopted a humanistic philosophy of labor reflected in the contributions of psychology and incorporated in personnel management. No attention was given to planning a work environment which effectively met the diversity of human needs or provided a fuller expression of the human personality. Likewise, there existed little appreciation of the fact that workers

54 J. H. Richardson, "Why Employment Departments Fail," *Industrial Management* 57 (May, 1919), 5:412.

55 Dudley R. Kennedy, "Employment Management and Industrial Relations," *Industrial Management* 58 (November, 1919), 1:355.

have psychological needs that must be satisfied in their daily work activity if management is to secure their interest, loyalty, and full service. Industry was unwilling to accept the moral obligation of aiding the individual in achieving his basic needs, thereby promoting his personal development. To some extent welfare paternalism had recognized the importance of the mental factor in productivity and industrial harmony; but lacking a sound understanding of human behavior, it sought to give benefits rather than permitting employees to secure them on their own initiative and develop as independent personalities. This approach failed to appreciate labor as a human resource with a right to achieve its human aspirations.

As noted in the previous chapter, paternalistic personnel relations were found throughout most of the early history of American work relationships. This was discernible in master-apprentice paternalism, the puritanical paternalism found in the emerging factory system, and paternalistic practices by a few large industrial enterprises during the last twenty years of the nineteenth century. As industry sought to create a pattern of personnel relations to replace the laissez-faire rationale which had been found inadequate, it turned to paternalism, the only other model of personnel administration available at that time. In terms of relatively recent industrial history, paternalism found its most organized form of expression in the welfare management or industrial betterment which appeared at the close of the nineteenth century. The basic philosophy inherent in paternalism, however, was incompatible with that of personnel administration as it emerged as a separate function of management.

PATERNALISTIC MODEL OF PERSONNEL PHILOSOPHY

The following model of a paternalistic personnel philosophy will serve to outline the basic tenets of this expression of personnel administration.

1. Leadership. The executive was a "benevolent autocrat" who sought to maintain unilateral direction and control of his labor force. Employees were made dependent upon the employer who asserted undisputed authority and responsibility for their well-

being. Assuming a fatherly role of superiority and authority, the employer took the position that he knew what was best for his "people," whose activities both on and off the job required close direction and supervision. Pleasant work conditions and various economic rewards were provided with the expectation that employees would accept the direction of their activities out of gratitude and appreciation. Executive leadership remained insulated from the new behavioral concepts emerging from industrial psychology and personnel management that would have provided new insights into the human factor and provided a firmer foundation for personnel relations.

2. Personnel Management. The personnel function was expressed primarily by means of welfare practices. Most welfare activities, however, were not justified on a social utility basis and were crude, poorly managed affairs. This was indicative of a lack of sincere concern for the human factor or a deep desire to promote employees' physical and psychological welfare. At best, this variety of "personnel management" indicated an awareness, relatively new at the time, that labor could no longer be ignored, abused or exploited.

3. Concepts of Labor.
   Good will or paternalistic: Adopting the relationship frequently characteristic of that of father-son—one of over-solicitude—employers gave direct and indirect financial rewards and provided safe, sanitary, and more pleasant work conditions. Employer direction was often extended to the employees' home life and home management. Such provisions were designed to keep workers docile, obedient, and productive.

   Partnership: Occasionally associated with the promotion of more pleasant work conditions was the practice of profit sharing which sought to promote a mutuality of interests between employee and management and also an identification with company objectives.

4. Incentives. The motivation of employees was sought by forcing employees to rely upon management for the satisfaction of their needs. It was expected that employees would accept the close direction of their activities because to do otherwise would represent a serious reduction in need satisfaction.

   Managerial emphasis was upon economic incentives and the anticipated stimulating effect of better physical work conditions and plant services such as cafeterias and first aid stations. This demonstrated concern for employee welfare avoided the difficult task of making personnel relations and the work itself intrinsically more gratifying. Rather, management sought to purchase the employee's loyalty, cooperation, and productivity. Such motivation failed to recognize the employee's needs for independence, self-respect, and dignity.

5. Labor Relations. Since paternalism was founded upon the premise that there should be no diminution of managerial authority, the newly emerging labor unions were strongly opposed. Dedicated to the elimination of competing loyalties and ideas, paternalistic activities were utilized to discourage the growing trend of employees to join unions.

There is little evidence to demonstrate that the paternalistic philosophy was motivated by a sincere desire to promote a working environment conducive to gratifying basic human needs and therefore psychologically sound. Even if the motives for utilizing this rationale were of a higher order, the approach to personnel relations so lacked a sound understanding of the human factor that failure was inevitable. Paternalism was, to some extent, a response to the public's concern over oppressive working conditions, low wages, and the long hours of industrial workers. More directly it was a means of mitigating industrial strife and securing the cooperation and productivity of workers. Additionally, paternalism was utilized to make union affiliation less attractive to employees. Significantly, however, paternalism represented a growing awareness of the labor problem and a departure from the blatant exploitation that prevailed through much of the last half of the nineteenth century.

The laissez-faire rationale of personnel was gradually displaced by technique and paternalistic philosophies early in the twentieth century. Many employers never experimented with paternalism but gradually moved directly to a technique philosophy of personnel administration. As in the practice of paternalism, the human factor was given more consideration since exploitation was no longer deemed an appropriate managerial practice. Better utilization of its human resources became an objective of management. Several concepts of labor were found compatible with the technique philosophy in the early stages of its evolution. The simplest was to view labor as a natural resource that should be protected and utilized with the same discretion as were physical resources. A similar, but broader, concept of labor was to consider each employee as unique, or as having different capacities and abilities. Appropriate consideration of these basic individual differences by judicious selection and training would enhance employee efficiency and effectiveness. The natural resource and uniqueness concepts of labor were still consistent with the machine concept of labor, as embellished by scientific management, which further specialized the worker's task, divided it into basic elements of motion and time, and separated planning from doing the job. All three concepts, natural resource, uniqueness, and machine concepts, have a basic similarity—they all fail to recognize basic human needs, desires, and aspirations and cause the individual to fail in fulfilling these needs within the organizational structure. While some advantages accrued to the workers from these approaches to labor, they were a by-product rather than a program designed specifically to enhance the employee's well-being, an obligation neither recognized nor accepted as a basic tenet of the technique personnel philosophy.

Sometimes found with the natural resource, uniqueness, and machine concepts of labor was the "partnership" attitude toward labor. Recognizing a need for cooperation, this philosophy stressed the mutual interests of employee and management. Stock ownership and/or profit sharing became devices to secure identification with company objectives. This approach was limited in effectiveness, however, because of its singular emphasis on the economic motive, its failure to invite direct participation in its formulation and administration, and its lack of a direct relationship between effort and reward.

Although based upon neglect of the human side of labor, or at best considering it to be a minor matter, the technique approach to personnel administration demanded obedience and strict allegiance to management. Backed by a superior bargaining position, the employer motivated primarily by fear, drivership, or negative incentives rather than by a planned program for the fulfillment of employee drives and desires. As for positive motivation, economic incentives were relied upon almost exclusively; psychological and social incentives were ignored or at best given minor consideration. Seeking to maintain the status quo, the technique rationale during its initial formative period responded only to social, legal, and economic pressures. Statutes to improve the wages, hours, and working conditions generally were resisted and viewed as unwarranted interference by the government.

Industrial leaders, however, were no longer unrestricted autocrats as they had been in the nineteenth century; their free hand in labor practices was being increasingly circumscribed by legislative regulations. Their authority was gradually being limited. Industrial executives sought by every means possible to maintain their position of undisputed authority or to at least prevent its further erosion. This course of action was supplemented by the persistent viewpoint that such men held their position of leadership because of natural superior endowment. Industrial managers were admonished, "Remember, even though you may have the heritage of more brains than your employee, he does not think so." [56] Strongly influenced by the persistent concepts of laissez-faire and survival of the fittest, managers were still inclined to consider themselves as the elite, as unaccountable to anyone—public, community, or employees.

SUMMARY

The years from 1900 to 1920 were notable for contributions made by scientific management, industrial psychology, and personnel management. Generally, however, the philosophical concepts of these disciplines made no significant modifications in the prevailing philosophies of personnel administration held by a majority of executives. Several decades were to pass before such ideas were to be assimilated by those leaders who formulate and implement the philosophy and policy of business enterprise. The scientific method, first advocated by Taylor, was adopted extensively for solution of production problems, but it had not found extensive use in the man-

[56] J. P. Brophy, "Bringing Capital and Labor Together," *Industrial Management* 50 (January, 1918), 1:40–41.

agement of industrial relations or personnel administration. Co-operation had not been substituted for industrial conflict as the basic form of labor-management relationship. There was little recognition of mutuality of interests between labor and management even with regard to industrial efficiency; Taylor's mental revolution had not occurred.

The philosophy of personnel administration, in its modern form, strives to harmonize objectives and values of industry with scientific knowledge and values of the community and employees.[57] However, the prevailing philosophies of this period made little effort to integrate the objectives and values of industry with scientific principles embodied in scientific management and industrial psychology. Philosophical concepts of these approaches to personnel relations were ignored; their techniques, when employed, were primarily used to justify and extend unilateral managerial action. Furthermore, executives' rationales of personnel administration were increasingly out of phase with community values. Employers had exploited labor by requiring excessively long hours, by hiring women and children at extremely low wages, and by failing to provide safe, decent, and sanitary work conditions. This rationale, firmly held by industrialists, had been so lacking in basic human values that public sentiment had eventually compelled enactment of state and federal remedial statutes.

Objectives and values of employees likewise were given scant attention, and corrective measures were suppressed whether initiated from within or without the industry. An inferior bargaining position of employees had given industrialists almost complete control over wages, hours, and work conditions; they were dedicated to maintaining this unilateral position. The leadership philosophy of management required that the absolute prerogatives of management be maintained to insure efficiency and a profitable organization.

Although there existed a growing concern for the physical well-

57 William H. Knowles, *Personnel Management* (New York: American Book Co., 1955), p. 145.

being of employees, stimulated by labor shortages and governmental statutes, employers demonstrated little awareness or concern for psychological and social needs of workers. Concern for the human factor, other than physical well-being, as promoted by personnel management and industrial psychology had not found extensive application by 1920.

IV

DEVELOPMENTAL PERIOD OF PERSONNEL
PHILOSOPHY, 1920–1929

Personnel management as a new managerial function had demonstrated some success in coping with a restive labor force and solving many personnel problems, especially during World War I. Under different economic and social conditions in its period of development, this function encountered refinements and new directions. Imperceptible changes in the top leadership position from ownership to managership became more clearly evident in the post-war years. New economic viewpoints coupled a service motive with the profit objective, while mass production and consumption were related to high wages. This chapter will study the implications of such stimuli for personnel philosophy.

Not all executives were influenced by the new developments, however; many industrial leaders sought to maintain the status quo and continued to base their employee relations on a do-nothing personnel philosophy. This rationale will be outlined and its impact on employees' psychological needs evaluated.

PERSONNEL MANAGEMENT

Personnel Management Reconsidered. After termination of World War I in November, 1918, the war boom continued for a short time, but slowed down in 1919. By the middle of 1920 industrial firms were compelled to curtail production or to shut down entirely. By the spring of 1921, industrial stagnation and extensive unemployment were prevalent. Numerous commercial and industrial enterprises suffered losses or failed, and for nearly two years the nation experienced a depression. Collapse of the post-war boom apparently removed the reason for maintaining the new function of personnel administration in many industries. The war period and subsequent business boom had rapidly accelerated slowly developing trends in personnel administration and numerous executives hastily adopted personnel methods and techniques to meet these abnormal conditions. Personnel methods and techniques that offered possibilities of promoting industrial harmony, cooperation, and efficiency were utilized. Personnel functions were grafted to the industrial structure without proper consideration of their relationship to other departments. Time had not permitted an evaluation of the contributions of personnel management to industrial production or an extensive realization of its emphasis on the human factor. During the depression, when the labor supply was plentiful, many executives felt no need to placate labor; there was a strong movement to minimize financial losses by returning to pre-war labor-management conditions.

In their frantic efforts to reduce production costs, business executives immediately attacked those recent innovations which had a few months before seemed so necessary and worthwhile. In a considerable number of concerns, personnel managers were dismissed, shop committees collapsed, service and attendance bonuses were withdrawn, welfare activities were discontinued. The employer again had the whip-hand of a scarcity of jobs. Penalizing and threat of discharge again took the place of rewards and incentives. *It was evident that the philosophy of personnel management had not been accepted fully nor its real significance understood.*[1]

There are many reasons to be found for the deflation of the personnel movement. During the discipline's rapid expansion during World War I, many individuals who were inadequately trained and lacking in business experience were employed to handle this new function of management. Few colleges were prepared to train in this area. Many personnel executives had failed to perform the most

[1] Don D. Lescohier and Elizabeth Brandeis, *History of Labor in the United States, 1896–1932: Working Conditions* (New York: The Macmillan Co., 1935), III, 326–327. Emphasis added.

basic task of personnel administration; they had concentrated their efforts on employee activities rather than on management of employee relationships. "They had failed to come to grips with the vital matters in the industry's labor problems and the workers' interests." [2] The personnel department had not established a real human touch with the workers but usually entered only when crucial issues arose. Managers in this emerging profession had aroused the resentment and criticism of production and managerial staffs by extending their activities into areas unjustified by objectives of the enterprise and had concentrated functions in the personnel department that should have been worked out cooperatively with the line. One survey of ninety-four companies revealed the lack of standardized practices in hiring, discharging, and transferring. There were sharp disagreements as to the proper role of line and staff in these matters.[3] Indeed there was only a vague conception that personnel was a staff function. One industrialist explained the prevailing situation as follows: "Because of its newness as a distinct activity there has been a certain amount of hesitation and uncertainty as to its definite place in the organization. . . . Management and personnel executives alike have at times failed to see that personnel work is fundamentally a part of production." [4]

Clarification of the Personnel Function. The personnel movement, however, was not finished. Numerous personnel departments were abolished, but many others were started and those that prevailed were given new functions. In addition, there was a decrease in the authority of personnel managers, but this tended to enhance good personnel procedure. The foreman regained the exclusive prerogative of discharge over his crew. Preliminary selection continued in the employment office, but line supervisors and executives made the final decision on acceptance. Personnel executives

[2] *Ibid.*, p. 327.
[3] "Hiring, Discharge and Transfer," *Industrial Management* 58 (September, 1919), 3:242–46.
[4] Charles H. Paull, "What Have We Learned about Industrial Relations?" *Industrial Management* 72 (September, 1926), 3:154.

suggested and formulated labor policy; but the line had actual control over such policies. The personnel staff attempted to promote good management-employee relationships without interfering in the actual control of personnel; activities were conducted as a vital part of line management rather than as a separate function.

Robert Lovett, who analyzed the personnel departments of seventy-four firms in 1923, found there was already evident a trend for responsibility in personnel matters to be placed back in the hands of department heads and foremen. He concluded: "There is a marked tendency to centralize control and decentralize execution of personnel work." [5] Throughout the 1920's there were efforts to properly analyze and categorize this new managerial function. By the end of 1930, however, the National Industrial Conference Board was able to conclude that:

> The administration of industrial relations programs is seen to be approaching the end of a completed cycle. Originally delegated to the line organization with the foreman occupying the key position, this function was gradually withdrawn and turned over to a specialist. This change occurred partly because the foreman was not considered to be equipped to handle the more complex personnel program and partly to concentrate more directly on the technical features of his work. In recent years, however, the pendulum has swung back, and the tendency has been to restore to the foreman and other line officials actual administration of all matters directly affecting their subordinates.[6]

However, from the very inception of the movement, professional people in personnel administration had indicated that this task was a staff function and, as such, advisory in nature. The chief of the personnel activity was to be on the same level as the production manager and would report directly to the top executive official in order to be most effective in representing the interests of employees. Administration of production and personnel were supplementary

[5] Robert F. Lovett, "Present Tendencies in Personnel Practice," *Industrial Management* 65 (June, 1923), 6:327.

[6] National Industrial Conference Board, *Industrial Relations: Administration of Policies and Programs* (New York, 1931), p. 60.

phases of the productive process, and both were to assist in maximization of output.[7] Industry, however, was by trial and error to discover these principles during the 1920's and make readjustments along the lines already advanced.

During the 1920's and especially after 1925, managements began to measure their industrial relations activities by such yardsticks as caliber of applicants, turnover, waste, accidents, absenteeism, labor strife, production, quality of product, and morale. Evaluating the worth of personnel activities by the rate at which they were being added or deleted from company programs between 1925 and 1930, the National Industrial Conference Board surveyed 302 companies to ascertain the value of such activities.[8] It was found that insurance, usually a contributory plan, was the most frequently added activity with medical services and lunch facilities ranking second and third, respectively. In all, twenty-seven various activities had been added to the industrial relations programs of the responding companies. The report concluded that:

> The nature of the activities that are being added in greatest number is illuminating substantiation of the thesis that industrial relations programs are swinging from paternalistic endeavors to "do good" for employees toward those sounder activities that provide employees with definite service and at the same time may reasonably be expected to be of some benefit to the employer. Activities that aid cooperation of management and employees are also gaining favor.[9]

The new philosophy of industrial relations programs held that unless the expenses of welfare activities were justified, they must be terminated. Such activities must contribute to general efficiency, productivity, or smoother management-employee relationships. The desire of public-spirited employers to do as much as possible for their

---

[7] Ordway Tead and Henry C. Metcalf, *Personnel Administration* (New York: McGraw-Hill Book Co., Inc., 1920), pp. 2–5.

[8] National Industrial Conference Board, *op. cit.*, pp. 83–101.

[9] *Ibid.*, p. 85.

employees or the social desirability of a more human approach to industrial relations was not the accepted basis for employee programs; the latter had to demonstrate a dollars-and-cents value. "Industry realizes the benefits of these welfare measures, which, if cooperatively participated in by the industrial worker, are conducive to better mutual understanding between employers and employees and produce such improved results; but industry realizes also that such measures must have a sound financial basis or they cannot be carried on. . . ." [10]

Philosophy of Personnel Administration. Since the turn of the twentieth century, there had been a growing concern over the effectiveness and productivity of labor, and World War I had accelerated the shift of managerial emphasis to a more efficient utilization of the human factor. A science of personnel administration, to increase the effectiveness of the human element in production, had developed out of these conditions. The first textbook bearing the title *Personnel Administration* was published in 1920. This new function of management was defined as ". . . the direction and coordination of the human relations of any organization with a view to getting the maximum necessary production with a minimum of effort and friction with proper regard for the genuine well-being of the workers." [11]

The ultimate objective of this new discipline was to increase production, and its success was measured by the extent to which it produced a more effective application of labor to production. In this respect, personnel was not different from other managerial functions; the main distinction existed in methods utilized to achieve maximum productivity. Personnel administration sought to achieve this goal by enlisting the workers' interests, good will, and cooperation. Each individual worker was to be treated as a human being

[10] Floyd H. Hazard, "Industry's Handicap of Fear," *Industrial Management* 65 (April, 1923), 4:204.
[11] Tead and Metcalf, *op. cit.*, p. 2.

with definite needs, desires, and aspirations. The purpose of the personnel executive was to insure that executive action be taken only after psychological and human considerations have been explored and evaluated. The personnel department "acts as the eyes, ears, and memory; as the head, hands, and brains of the management in handling its personnel." [12]

To promote the well-being of the worker requires a knowledge of the substance of human well-being and also of the mental and physical capacities of individuals. For this information the personnel executive was dependent upon the disciplines of psychology and physiology. Elements of human well-being were those "qualities in individuals which are native, fundamental, socially useful, and worthy of fuller release and development." [13] Given an adequate industrial environment, expression of these human qualities would reinstate the human personality of employees in industry. "The human tendencies which are seeking wider and wider expression and which bring harmony, release, and happiness are the positive characteristics of love of family, of association, of creation, of group approval. Personality is thus translatable into terms of fullness of life, forbearance, generosity, creative power, comradeship and love." [14]

The concept of instincts was deemed the most promising approach to understanding complexities of human relationships and comprised an important part of the rationale of personnel administration. Ordway Tead and Henry Metcalf, the first authors to present the scope and functions of personnel management, stressed satisfying basic instincts if maximum human satisfaction and production were to be achieved. Pursuing the same theme in 1921, A. M. Simons wrote: "The problem of human relations in industry is largely a psychological problem. . . . The study of human behavior through analysis of instincts and habits, and the examination of the mind by experimental methods—the two phases of psychology of

[12] Sam A. Lewisohn, *The New Leadership in Industry* (New York: E. P. Dutton & Co., 1926), p. 218.
[13] Tead and Metcalf, *op. cit.*, p. 12.
[14] *Ibid.*, p. 20

which personnel relations has the greatest need—are both new factors of investigation." [15]

Instinctive psychology was presented as the practical psychology for executives. Misconduct of labor was directly attributable to the failure of executives to direct the human drives of employees into proper channels. "The reason why the instinctive nature of workers so often leads to industrial disorders is because certain of the most powerful instincts are thwarted by their industrial environment. . . . The results are found in unrest, restriction of production, ill-will, radicalism, inefficiency, unhappiness, and disloyalty. Those are the outlets for the energies within balked instincts." [16]

These new insights into human behavior also held promise of mitigating the complete reliance upon authority to achieve the objectives of industry.

The human instincts, especially those concerned with industry, are not isolated, immutable forces, foreordained to some particular direction, but are interrelated, flexible, adaptive and, therefore, capable of responding in many ways. Upon this fact rests the confidence that, despite specialization, industry can be so organized and managed under skillful guidance as to utilize all the mental resources at its disposal. With industry thus managed, the fundamental objective of the present economic system, namely, to induce people to work with a will, should no longer be confused with the mere exercise of authority. [17]

One manager of industrial relations expressed the contribution of psychology as follows: "The purely professional 'psychologist' has

[15] A. M. Simons, *Personnel Relations in Industry* (New York: Ronald Press Co., 1921), pp. 33–34.

[16] Lionel D. Edie, ed., *Practical Psychology for Business Executives* (New York: H. W. Wilson Co., 1922), p. 57.

[17] O. F. Carpenter, "The Need for Enlightened Leadership in Industry," *Industrial Management* 71 (June, 1926), 6:371. For other references to the use of human instincts see Charles W. Clark, "The Foreman and His Development," *Industrial Management* 60 (August, 1920), 3:105–109, and Clarence N. Northcott, "The Human Factor in Industry-III, The Psychology, Instincts and Tendencies of the Worker," *Industrial Management* 62 (1921), 6:363–69.

made his chief contribution by helping executives to gain a better viewpoint of their relations with employees . . . industrial psychology has been and will continue to be one of the most fruitful sources of suggestions for improving industrial goodwill." [18]

Despite the popularity of the instinctive approach, there developed a tendency to question its adequacy. Instincts were logical abstractions that varied, depending upon the investigator, in number and kind. It was doubted whether they were well-organized mental patterns of behavior or habits of experience.[19] By 1927, one observer concluded: "We are not so sure today that man has to begin with any basic drives which cannot be modified by a different or new situation. *We are much more likely today to attempt an analysis of the situation in which he is working and living to determine specific causes of unrest and dissatisfaction than we are to appeal to any specific unsatisfied instinct.*" [20]

Workers were considered to have basic needs or desires, although not instinctive in nature, such as those for status, self-esteem, and pride in their work. However, one can conclude, as did Metcalf, that the "entrance of the psychological engineer in the industrial field is a clear indication of the new humanized philosophy of business which is surely taking shape." [21]

The promise of a manipulative psychology still held a great attraction for many industrialists. Henry S. Dennison, president of Dennison Manufacturing Company, stated, "The crux of management is how to make the men and women folks behave, or rather, how to make them behave as the manager thinks they ought to. The science behind the possibilities of business as a profession is psychology." [22]

[18] Roy W. Kelly, "Promoting Industrial Harmony," *Industrial Management* 69 (February, 1925), 2:89.

[19] Viteles, *The Science of Work* (New York: W. W. Norton & Co., 1934), pp. 357–58.

[20] C. S. Yoakum, "The Role of Impulse, Emotions, and Habit in Conduct," in *The Psychological Foundations of Management*, ed. Henry Clayton Metcalf (New York: A. W. Shaw Co., 1927), p. 36. Emphasis added.

[21] Metcalf, ed., *The Psychological Foundations of Management*, p. 10.

[22] Henry S. Dennison, "Management's and Labor's Interest in the Development of an Industrial Psychology," Metcalf, ed., *op. cit.*, p. 12.

Another industrial relations manager observed, "Fortunately for executives, psychology had advanced far enough as a science to offer a wealth of information for the understanding and controlling of men and women." [23] Tead, visualizing some of the implications of psychology, concluded: "If, as psychologists claim, a working knowledge of their science increases the possibility of *predicting* and controlling behavior, is there not a likelihood that managers will use psychology to strengthen their control over the behavior of their subordinates? . . . The answer is, clearly, Yes." [24]

For some executives psychology contained promises of manipulating the worker in his very thought and action, channeling all human drives into productive effort, and modifying employees to meet the needs of business enterprise. Such an application of psychology failed to appreciate that individuals learn, think, communicate, and respond differently to the industrial environment on subsequent occasions. Prediction and control were extremely difficult unless all variables in the industrial environment could be controlled.

Many personnel managers sought to produce an industrial environment conducive to harmony and cooperation by utilizing this science of understanding, predicting, and controlling worker behavior. However, they generally made a more enlightened application by seeking to develop motivations which would spontaneously generate employee efforts to achieve the results sought. Objectives of the enterprise were sufficiently inclusive to promote employee desires and aspirations within the organizational structure. Psychological concepts pointed to the same conclusion found in the rationale of personnel administration: ". . . the true means of permanently influencing others lie in the direction of fostering conditions in which people, in and through their own inner desires, come to seek the results which the leader also comes to desire." [25]

[23] Carpenter, *op. cit.*, p. 364.
[24] Ordway Tead, *Human Nature and Management* (New York: McGraw-Hill Book Co., Inc., 1929), p. 4.
[25] *Ibid.*

MODIFICATIONS OF EXECUTIVES' PHILOSOPHY OF PERSONNEL ADMINISTRATION

During the 1920's there was a noticeable change in industrial leadership and practices that facilitated formulation of a more enlightened rationale of personnel administration. With the continued growth in scale of industrial operations, there was a change in the form of industrial organization which compelled a search for better forms of internal structure. An increase in the number and size of departments and divisions was not sufficient to meet the problem and such new functional departments as planning, personnel, sales promotion, and merchandising were created to meet new complexities. Executives, requiring broader knowledge and training, were necessary to administer these expanding functions. Such innovations emphasized the coordination of line executives and staff specialists, and the conference as a coordinating device increased in usage. Consultation, persuasion, and inspiration increasingly replaced the technique of order-giving in the upper echelons of management. "It is the man who can lead rather than domineer who is now chiefly desired in executive positions." [26]

New Insights—Concern for Public and Service. Industrial leadership was also changing in other respects. Formerly, ownership and management were one and the same, and the owner-manager conducted his business as he saw fit, administering the operation in the interests of ownership; the laissez-faire philosophy of personnel had most often accompanied this form of management. With the growing number of corporate and trust forms of organization, conspicuous at the turn of the twentieth century, owners were replaced by managerial officials who did not have an appreciable financial interest in the company. Ownership was diffused among a number of stockhold-

---

[26] Henry S. Dennison, "Management," in Committee on Recent Economic Changes of the President's Conference on Unemployment, Edward E. Hunt, ed. *Recent Economic Changes* (New York: McGraw-Hill Book Co., Inc., 1929), II, 502.

ers who, through the directors, held salaried officials of the company responsible for its financial results. In many instances, an exclusive sense of responsibility to stockholders had led to oppressive practices and lack of consideration for employees. A trend notable in the 1920's, however, was for members of management to regard themselves as representatives not only of stockholders but also of labor and the public. An industrialist of fifty years' experience concluded, in 1925: "Management is thus coming to occupy the position of trustee, and to maintain its position it must serve the public with the greatest efficiency consistent with a fair return to labor; and with the return to capital necessary in order to keep it in industry. This change is not yet complete. It is a trend rather than an accomplished fact, but it is a very promising trend." [27]

Growing recognition of labor and public tended to modify slightly the predominant profit motive for some industrialists. In 1927 Eugene Benge, an observer of industrial trends, stated, "Probably one of the greatest steps forward in American industry has been this acceptance of the viewpoint that business exists to give *service* to Society." [28] A more positive statement of the relationship between service and profits was made earlier by the vice-president of Stratmore Paper Company, who said, "Service and not profits is essentially the reason of existence of organization, essential as profits are to increased service, and a motive of intense action." [29] Although most executives were not as inclined to sublimate the profit motive as indicated in the statement above, there existed a strong tendency to couple the service motive with that of profit. *This trend away from the all-impelling profit motive made it possible for industrial executives to devote more time, consideration, and expenditures to matters that improved the general well-being of employees; it facili-*

[27] Robert S. Brookings, *Industrial Ownership: Its Economic and Social Significance* (New York: Macmillan Co., 1925), p. 23.
[28] Eugene J. Benge, "Trends in Labor Management," *Industrial Management* 73 (February, 1927), 2:124.
[29] B. A. Franklin, "The Body, Soul and Spirit of Organization," *Industrial Management* 63 (March, 1922), 3:45.

tated the adoption of a more enlightened philosophy of personnel administration.

A New Economic Outlook. There was also a new managerial economic philosophy manifested during the 1920's. The relationship between the market and consumer had only been vaguely perceived since the typical producer had been completely preoccupied with producing and selling. Now, however, it was recognized that the purchasing power of the masses was an essential factor if demand was to be given effective expression. Consequently quantity, quality, lower prices, and more effective distribution were emphasized. Price was no longer set at what the traffic would bear, and the consumer was accorded newly found consideration. *Caveat emptor* as a business practice was waning.

The creation of mass purchasing power demanded a new approach toward both public and consumer, and labor was viewed in a different manner as these new economic insights emerged. Whereas previously little thought had been given to the problem of where people obtained their purchasing power, it was now perceived that wages constituted a significant force in its generation. Previously labor had been considered as a commodity to be obtained for as little as supply and demand dictated; labor was bought as cheaply as possible and sustained with the least possible expense. This concept, in addition to ignoring the human factor, did not acknowledge that workers comprised the largest and best market for industrial production. Now, however, it was generally accepted that the wage earner had a vital role to play in the cycle of mass production and mass purchasing.

Appreciation of the wage-earner's importance as a consumer of manufactured products has led to a new realization of his purchasing power and a strong desire to cultivate and maintain it, and the belief that inadequate wages react upon purchasing power and jeopardize the whole economic balance has gained wide acceptance. In short, an interdependence exists which requires that each element must do its part if industry as a whole is to enjoy the benefits of collective prosperity. The individual employer, to a greater extent than ever before, has apparently come to realize the influence of his own policy and his own actions upon the composite country-wide result.[30]

The broadening economic viewpoint now was holding forth a promise of lower prices to consumers and higher wages for labor as a means of enhancing the feasibility of mass consumption. While seemingly incompatible, these two objectives, lower prices and higher wages, were reconciled in a very novel way for most industrial leaders. Economies were to be achieved by machinery and methods rather than from labor and wages. Industrial waste, physical and human, was thoroughly studied by numerous firms in an effort to achieve these newly discovered economic objectives. The changed economic philosophy abandoned "the out-worn notions of unrestricted competition, of minimum wages and maximum prices, of restricted output and limited consumption to substitute the new gospel of mass production, high wages and maximum consumption." [31]

A New Executive Philosophy Formulated. As a new executive group divested of sole ownership and aware of expanding responsibilities emerged on the industrial scene, there appeared a concomitant appreciation of the need to cultivate cooperation between labor and management. Managements, partly as result of World War I, began to realize that the "greatest developable resource lies in the ability of the employees and is brought out through their happiness." [32] There was a growing recognition that fear as an incentive was inadequate for achieving higher productivity and that conflict should be replaced by cooperation as a basis for industrial relations.

[30] National Industrial Conference Board, *op. cit.*, pp. 23–24.

[31] Lewis E. Pierson, president of Chamber of Commerce of the U.S., quoted in Charles C. Chapman, *The Development of American Business and Banking Thought, 1913–1936.* (rev. ed.; New Lork: Longmans, Green & Co., 1936), p. 69.

[32] B. A. Franklin, "Elements of Successful Organization," *Industrial Management* 61 (April, 1921), 7:243.

Taylor had made cooperation a basic tenet in his philosophy of scientific management, and personnel administration also had adopted this as a principle in its rationale. Acceptance of this idea among top executives, however, had been slow. "His [the industrial executive's] greatest shortcoming is his failure to see the great value of labor's good will and cooperation. . . . What seems so difficult for the average employer to grasp is the simple fact that labor presents an administrative problem aside from its conflicting interests with capital." [33]

Cooperation was included as a basic law of employment relations in a report of the Employment Relations Committee of the National Association of Manufacturers in 1928. The sixteenth law was formulated as follows: "Best results in securing economical production are secured by obtaining the willing cooperation of workers with management." [34] Such cooperation was judged to be promoted by the education of employees in the aims, purposes, and problems of management. In addition, the provision of procedures in industry to permit employees to discuss with management problems affecting conditions of employment was considered instrumental in promoting cooperation.

The novel emphasis placed on cooperation between labor and management called for new conceptions on the part of management. Obviously cooperation could not be elicited by use of the fear incentive or by continued neglect of the human factor with its needs and desires for a fuller physical, psychological, and social life. Management saw the need for accepting the labor problem as an integral part of its task. Effective work promoted by a human labor policy was required. Employees gladly adhered to this plan because it included ". . . the best working conditions; a fair pay based on the reasonable cost of a decent standard of living and relative skill shown; and agreeable loyalty induced by methods which recognize length and faithfulness of service; and particularly an assumption

[33] Carpenter, *op. cit.*, 366.
[34] Noel Sargent, "Basic Laws of Employment Relations," *Factory and Industrial Management* 80 (November, 1930), 11:950.

that each worker is in some sense, by the very fact of his daily participation of effort toward success, a partial partner in the movement." [35]

Accompanying the growing realization of the importance of co-operation, *there was an emerging conception of employer moral and social responsibility for the employee.* Industrialists, slowly becoming conscious of the importance of the human factor, were dimly aware that the laborers, like themselves, were human and had similar needs and desires. This new emphasis on recognition of the individual and his personal development was expressed by Mr. Paul Shoup, vice-president of the Southern Pacific:

> The greatest responsibility of management toward employees is that of understanding and recognition of the fact that each employee is entitled to consideration on the basis of what he is and what he makes himself, and there must be such systematic comprehension as will give opportunity to men to advance upon their merits. . . . The situation is difficult, and I think in this respect more than in all others, management . . . has been imperfect in its achievement.[36]

New orientations demanded a new leadership and some industrial leaders were endeavoring to meet the situation. Many executives felt their leadership challenged by labor leaders; furthermore, revolution of the working masses in Russia was a veiled implication of what could happen if the working population were ignored. Executives were beginning to realize their responsibilities to employees.

Public concern over employers' social responsibilities had been expressed in legislation designed to protect the physical well-being of employees. However, an observer of labor-management trends concluded that employers engaged in medical services, accident prevention, sanitary inspections, and first-aid not merely because of legal requirements, aid to greater productivity, or the scarcity of labor, but because the "social viewpoint is present in the minds of most

[35] Franklin, "Fundamental Policies of Organization," *op. cit.*, p. 372.
[36] Quoted in Kelly, "Promoting Industrial Harmony," *op. cit.*, p. 91.

large employers of labor." [37] It was further concluded that as a corollary to the emerging service motive to society there ". . . has been the realization that the employer bears a social responsibility for each employee, especially if that employee has given life, limb or years of service. In addition to the compensation laws and health measures mentioned, there are workers' insurance plans, mutual benefit associations, pension plans and unemployment insurance as further indications of the concrete ways in which employers are acknowledging their social indebtedness." [38] Despite these manifestations of concern, a majority of employers were opposed to social insurance legislation; the great expense, harmful effects on character and habits, removal of stimulus to self-support and thrift, and diminution of incentives to initiative and cooperation were cited as reasons for their opposition.[39]

Further evidence of the broadened social viewpoint of business leaders was demonstrated by the number of codes of ethics formulated and published by various industries. The Department of Commerce pointed out, in 1927, "The last four or five years have witnessed the preparation and adoption of a great number of codes of ethics and standards of practice by trade organizations, both commercial and professional." [40] This awareness of proper trade relations and social responsibilities was reflected in the "Principles of Business Conduct" adopted by the Chamber of Commerce. Principles indicative of attitudes toward employees included:

Equitable consideration is due in business alike to capital, management, employees and the public.
Obligations to itself and society prompt business unceasingly to strive toward continuity of operation, bettering conditions of employment, and increasing efficiency and opportunities of individual employees.

[37] Benge, *op. cit.*, p. 125.
[38] *Ibid.*
[39] National Industrial Conference Board, *op. cit.*, p. 21.
[40] *Trade Association Activities*, Department of Commerce Series, No. 20 (Washington: Government Printing Office, 1927), p. 109.

Waste in any form—of capital, labor, services, materials or natural resources—is intolerable and constant effort will be made toward its elimination.[41]

It is significant that these principles reflect a growing awareness of responsibility toward labor; equitable consideration was to be given employees as well as other groups in industrial relations. Exploitation and waste of labor were repudiated, and the Chamber of Commerce committed itself to improving work conditions and promoting employees' personal development. It should be noted, however, that this code of ethics gave more attention to employee relations than did a majority of such codes. Edgar L. Heermance concluded after examining numerous codes of ethics, "The relations with the employees show a great many gaps, so far as the codes are concerned." [42]

Employer interest in the employee was slowly gaining ground. In a summary of the 1924 annual convention of the American Management Association it was noted, "Employers have a growing realization of the importance of finding out what the workman is really thinking about and what he wants." [43] Thus there seemed to be emerging a concern for the dignity of the worker, whose attitudes and inner feelings and desires must be considered in industrial operations. One industrialist made the following observation: "Probably the primary 'rub' applicable in our dealings with men is that they are men—men appealed to as we are by the same motives of profit, utility, fear, pride and pleasure. A worker wants more than just a day's pay. He desires justice, status, and opportunity as well. He wants life in its truest sense, and will work most efficiently for us

[41] Edgar L. Heermance, *Code of Ethics* (Burlington, Vermont: Free Press Printing Co., 1924), pp. 77–78.

[42] Edgar L. Heermance, "Standards of Business Practice," in *Business Management as a Profession*, Henry C. Metcalf, ed., (New York, A. W. Shaw Co., 1927), p. 174.

[43] "The AMA Annual Convention," *Management and Administration* 9 (March, 1925), 3:275.

when we accommodate our policies, plans and procedures to his natural habit and gait." [44]

Personnel administration, utilizing the contributions of psychology, had demonstrated the importance of the human factor and of non-financial incentives. Later one finds a few industrialists giving expression to these new conceptions. "Organization is after all, in essentials for highest attainment, much like the very ones who operate it, namely *human*, which is indeed very natural, since organization is the highest development of civilization to work out through its results the very needs, longings, desires, and inspirations of human beings." [45] Another general manager expressed the new viewpoint in the following terms: "Concede that every human being is entitled to a certain amount of well-being, to the pursuit of happiness, and to the opportunity to earn his livelihood, then an outstanding problem of industrial management is to reconcile these facts to the demand of efficient production. . . . A little thought along these lines will indicate the trend, the need for consideration of the *human nature* side of the problem as well as the monetary side." [46]

The above statements reveal that some executives were turning to a humanistic philosophy of labor, based upon the viewpoint that the minds of employees had an important bearing upon their willingness to cooperate and give their full service; it was industry's moral obligation to aid the individual in achieving these basic needs and promoting his development.

The new humanizing role of personnel administration was slowly being realized in some industrial circles.

The belief on the part of capital willingly or unwillingly acquiesced in, that labor is no longer a commodity . . . and the problems presented by the development and growth of new thoughts and aspirations on the part of labor . . . have forced the development in the managerial fold of a new department—sometimes called the Per-

[44] Joseph H. Barber, "Toward Science in Management," *The Management Review* 19 (December, 1930), 12:397.

[45] Franklin, "The Body, Soul and Spirit of Organization," *op. cit.*, p. 145.

[46] Dale S. Cole, "The Human Elements of Wage Incentive," *Industrial Management* 65 (January, 1923), 1:39–40.

sonnel Department or Department of Industrial Relations. . . . the desired objectives are . . . —a more complete understanding and harmonious relationship between the employee and that distant, unapproachable, intangible entity, the corporation or employer.[47]

Another executive expressed the purpose of the industrial relations department as follows: "Its [Industrial Relations'] aim is to tie men in their energy and service . . . to production by furnishing to its employees that assistance and happiness which through lack of opportunity, education, or initiative, they do not obtain readily for themselves (an appreciation of trusteeship), and . . . to gain this highest cooperation of the employees." [48] Industrial relations departments as promulgators of enlightened labor policies were viewed as a means of achieving cooperation. "Such policies involve . . . the development of all practical plans through which, within reasonable limits, the worker may attain such share of enjoyable living, development and social benefits as will tend to make him feel contented with his progress and desirous of delivering the maximum cooperation." [49]

Several well known industrial enterprises formulated employer-employee relations policies that reflected newly emerging viewpoints. In May, 1924, the Western Electric Company issued its statement of "Relations with Employees" under the following key headings:

To pay all employees adequately for services rendered.
To maintain reasonable hours of work and safe working conditions.
To provide continuous employment consistent with business conditions.
To place employees in the kind of work best suited to their ability.
To help each individual to progress in the company's service.
To aid employees in times of need.
To encourage thrift.
To cooperate in social, athletic and other recreational activities.
To accord to each employee the right to discuss freely with execu-

[47] Carleton F. Brown, "Industrial Relations," *Industrial Management* 64 (September, 1922), 3:185.
[48] Franklin, "Elements of Successful Organization," *op. cit.*, p. 243.
[49] Franklin, "Fundamental Policies of Organization," *op. cit.*, pp. 371–74.

tives any matters concerning his or her welfare or the company's interest.
To carry on the daily work in a spirit of friendliness.[50]

In 1925, the Bell Telephone System published its personnel policy that formulated "three fundamental lines of action." These were as follows:

1. Remove from every company, department and office every practice, policy, custom, routine, phrase and tradition which is inconsistent with each individual's feeling that he is a part of the enterprise or which harks back to the old master and servant conception, or to the conception that a contract is the only tie between the individual employee and the company.

2. Develop and encourage every proper practice, policy, custom, routine, phrase and tradition which will affirmatively tend to make each one feel that he is a part of the business, and therefore ready and anxious to assume all the responsibilities, both individual and joint, as well as to enjoy the privileges and compensations that go with the relationship.

3. Develop ways and means to contacts by which to discover the individuals or groups who have not reached the point of feeling that they are anything more than servants, hired men or contractors, and direct special and intensive effort toward finding ways and means of making them see . . . that employment in the Bell System presents an infinitely more satisfactory and self-respecting status if they will only accept it and live it.[51]

Both the above companies were among the forerunners of industrial firms seeking to promote sound personnel relations. The "humanistic" content of Western Electric's statement is reflected in the basic psychological needs appealed to in the implementation of such a program. Security needs would be gratified by adequate wages, safe working conditions, continuous employment, and aid in times of emergency. Although limited, attention is directed to social needs

[50] Thomas G. Spates, "An Analysis of Industrial Relations Trends," *AMA Personnel Series*, (1937), No. 25, pp. 16–18.
[51] *Ibid.*

through the provision of recreational activities and commitment to a spirit of friendliness. And finally, the program has an impact on egoistic needs as expressed in concern for proper placement and growth within the firm.

The Bell Telephone Company's policy is notable for its commitment to eradicate all remaining vestiges of the master-servant type of relationship and to eliminate the "economic nexus only" association with employees. Equally significant is the dedication to creating an identification of the employees' activities, responsibilities, and privileges with organizational goals and objectives.

An Evaluation of the Status of Personnel Philosophies. Although the previous statements are indicative of an advance in executive thinking, acceptance of the basic rationale and humanizing role of personnel administration was not characteristic of most industrialists. Numerous executives were giving expression to an enlightened approach to personnel problems, yet there was lacking any definite conception of their own duties and responsibilities which should naturally stem from such a rationale. "In only a very few instances was any attention given to inspiring in rank-and-file employees a sense of significance in their work. Numbers of executives seemed unable to understand this human need. A few others . . . had a vague feeling that some effort in this direction was desirable, although they usually had no definite idea of what to do or how to do it." [52]

The human element was acknowledged as the most important factor in industry, but managerial action indicated no sincere conviction. There was little awareness that the chief executive set the stage for enlightened human relations or determined the firm's rationale of personnel administration. "With a small number of exceptions, the recorded declarations of executives regarding their attitude toward employees were vague and general. . . . It is significant to note that such pronouncements as were made almost never involved

[52] J. David Houser, *What the Employer Thinks* (Cambridge: Harvard University Press, 1927), p. 80.

any clear-cut assumptions of obligation or that of executives in general to the conscious and definite development of workers." [53]

A popular policy was to let the personnel department handle all human problems. Such delegation arose from an ignorance that top management had ultimate responsibility for personnel relations and that it was a function that could not be delegated or departmentalized as could sales, production, and finance. There appeared little recognition that good human relations began with the chief executive and should be practiced by all managerial personnel. Consequently there was a lack of executive philosophy and personnel policies to guide subordinate executives in their relationships with employees. "Few industrial organizations were found with policies definitely placing upon subordinate executives any obligation for leadership and human development. There were likewise but few examples of emphasis upon the importance of training subordinates as an executive function." [54]

The failure of top management to provide sound training in personnel relations for those in managerial positions was also disclosed, in 1929, by two personnel officials who contacted approximately sixty-five executives. While it was noted that the serious attention of management to the development of supervisory or executive forces had occurred only within the last ten years, this movement left much to be desired. A majority of the companies surveyed favored training programs which included training in both the technical aspects of management and human relationships. However the authors concluded:

Despite the general beliefs . . . in the need of greater emphasis on the human elements of executive duties, it is by no means the general practice. The present status of subject matter in most executive training programs seems to indicate an actual stress on the mechanical, technical training. . . . we are led to conclude that the present opinion as to the importance of the human phases of executive functions is

[53] *Ibid.*, pp. 80–81.
[54] *Ibid.*, p. 81.

of such recent development that few actual training programs have put this theory to practice.[55]

Despite numerous enlightened statements by employers, there still existed a lack of understanding of the human factor, of motives, needs, and desires. Psychological principles pertaining to the complexity of individual emotional needs generally had not become a part of the typical executive's thinking. A majority of industrial executives still attached foremost importance to the financial incentive. J. David Houser observed, "It is surprising to find how widespread is the naive assumption that financial motives are the only ones activating workmen. So many executives reason, if they can meet these desires, they will have no more problems." The idea of wages as being the primary connection with employees was still prevalent. There was no indication, with very few exceptions, of an obligation for the "personal development of workers through a more intelligent participation in industrial activities or through stimulation of their sense of social usefulness." [56]

As observed previously, the basic philosophy of personnel administration tended to precede that actually adopted and applied in industry. The record of the development of personnel philosophies has been a record of the attempt of executives to assimilate that which had been expressed by pioneers in the field of personnel and its related sciences and disciplines. The extent to which industry has utilized the personnel executive in the formulation of production and personnel policies is an indication of whether a more human philosophy of personnel administration has been adopted. Because of training and a knowledge of the human factor, personnel executives generally were in a better position than anyone else in management to assure proper consideration of employee interests. One personnel executive stated the problem as follows: "Whether the industrial re-

[55] Harold B. Bergen and Garrett Lawrence Bergen, "Executive Training Programs," *American Management Association, General Management Series* (1929) No. 107, pp. 14–15.
[56] Houser, *op. cit.*, pp. 86, 141.

lations executive plays a major or a minor role in shaping policies is itself largely a question of policy." [57] Therefore the extent to which industrialists have perceived and utilized the personnel executive in policy formulation indicates to a large degree the awareness and desired emphasis to be placed on the human factor. Considerable time elapsed before the personnel executive was fully accepted and given a place in policy formulation committees; such practices were not extensive during the 1920's.

Although personnel executives generally had not achieved a position in the industrial hierarchy that would permit their full utilization in personnel activities, as a professional group they were uniting to promote and elevate their discipline. The National Association of Employment Managers, after three annual conventions, had been succeeded by the Industrial Relations Association of America (1919–1922) which undertook to expand the scope of its predecessor. In turn this group merged with the National Corporation Training Association of America to form the National Personnel Association. In 1923, the National Personnel Association changed its name to The American Management Association in recognition of the fact that personnel is a problem of general management; in 1929 a Personnel Division was created.

One can conclude from the previous examination of personnel concepts as actually implemented in industrial organizations that developments in the area of personnel philosophy had lagged far behind the professional contributions. The prevailing personnel philosophy was technique in its orientation, accompanied by strong authoritarian leadership. The technique philosophy is quite consistent with an authoritarian approach to personnel administration and has often been labeled as an authoritarian philosophy. A cursory glance at the personnel programs and techniques utilized might lead one to conclude that humanistic considerations had become paramount. However the possibility of better control over the work force was the primary motive for adopting the techniques and knowledge of psychology and personnel management. One of the basic assump-

[57] Paull, *op. cit.*, p. 155.

tions of the technique personnel philosophy was that job satisfaction would automatically result if employees were properly selected, trained, and compensated. The prevailing concept of labor supported by the technique rationale deemed each individual unique, a resource which should be conserved and utilized properly. Personnel administration was accepted as a managerial function, but there was no emphasis on providing a work environment conducive to gratifying social and psychological needs. The technique philosophy was devoted primarily to promoting efficiency but human values were given scant, if any, consideration.[58] Personnel practices were evaluated on an economic and competitive basis.

Such a viewpoint is analogous to that taken toward scientific management; the techniques and mechanisms were rapidly adopted but the underlying philosophy was ignored. The scientific management approach did not acknowledge good human relations as a worthy goal to complement the objective of maximum efficiency. Acceptable aspects of personnel administration were those offering means of control and manipulation. The techniques of personnel administration were compatible with authoritarian principles which sought to dominate and control employees but failed to recognize the individual or respect his rights.[59]

Experience with the Citizenship Concepts of Labor. Employee representation plans and works councils became a new implement of the open-shop drive toward maintaining unilateral control over the work force. A cursory examination of the growth in employee representation plans throughout the 1920's would seem to indicate a definite trend toward abandoning repressive, unilateral personnel practices.[60] Employer acceptance of these plans, however, resulted from a recognition of new purposes which they might serve. Although employees were represented by delegates chosen from among

[58] Lewisohn, *op. cit.*, p. 226.
[59] G. P. Hutchins, "Leadership—An Opportunity and a Challenge to Industrial Employees," *Industrial Management* 66 (August, 1923) 2:76–77.
[60] Lescohier and Brandeis, *op. cit.*, p. 350.

themselves to work jointly with management on matters pertaining to their general welfare, they were not identified with independent trade unions and, therefore, were subject to employer control.[61] Work councils and shop committees were substitutes for unions and became known as company unions.[62] Having been initiated, protected, and financed by employers, they offered no threat to unilateral managerial authority. This form of employment management was consistent with the open-shop principle adopted by the National Association of Manufacturers in 1904 and indicated a continuation of authoritarian leadership practices and methods in personnel administration.

Although most industrialists considered works councils a substitute for genuine collective bargaining, such plans indicated a recognition of employee demands that previously had been ignored.[63] Many employee representation plans, deficient when measured by the ideal standard of industrial democracy, did have desirable features. Machinery of varying effectiveness was provided for employee representation, and safeguards were frequently established to protect employees' rights. Some plans provided for old-age pensions and health, accident, and life insurance; provisions for acquisition of company stock and various profit-sharing schemes were characteristic of others. However, only a few industrial leaders attempted a sincere application of industrial democratic principles.

One finds in this maligned practice of industrial democracy the emergence of a citizenship concept of labor. This concept holds that employees are entitled to have a voice in determining the rules and regulations affecting their welfare. An employee's investment of his labor in industry conveys rights similar to those of community citizenship, each individual has inherent rights and is entitled to a voice in determining and expressing those rights. Although there was some recognition of employees' right to a voice in industry among em-

[61] National Industrial Conference Board, *Works Councils in the United States, Research Report No. 21*, (New York: 1919), p. 1.
[62] Lescohier and Brandeis, *op. cit.*, pp. 345–47.
[63] W. Jett Lauck, *Political and Industrial Democracy, 1776–1926* (New York: Funk and Wagnalls Co., 1926), pp. 160–62.

ployers having representation plans, this philosophy was not prevalent during the 1920's. For a majority of executives it was a means of minimizing labor strife, promoting harmony and cooperation, and yet maintaining unilateral, authoritarian control.

The Do-Nothing Personnel Philosophy. An additional expression of contemporary personnel practices and philosophy was made in a 1923 trade magazine:

The employer who conceives his duty done and his leadership fulfilled when he pays his people prevailing wage scales and carries out the factory and insurance laws, has neither social nor normal right to protest if his employees, in their turn, render little, or nothing more than fear of losing their jobs forces them to yield. They're both doing the irreducible minimum and *both are losers and society loses still more.*

If the employer . . . cannot feel many obligations to his people arising out of his control of their economic and social destinies, how in the name of Justice can the ordinary working man be expected to develop a transcendent ethical sense and to give his all—his heart, soul and body in return for a weekly wage based on the "labor market" with his security of employment dependent on the employer's will? [64]

This indictment of executive leadership not only illustrates new insights into the recognition of responsibilities, but also succinctly illuminates the do-nothing philosophy of personnel administration found both in the 1920's and today. It is an approach that responds only to pressures and emergencies and is void of long-range planning or constructive policies to prevent personnel problems before they arise; it is blind to the human factor in production.

The real difficulty of labor relations has been one of neglect. Executives have treated the question of human organization as a minor matter, not as a major problem. They have too often failed to realize that their responsibilities as assemblers and organizers of man-power are just as great as those in mechanical and financial matters. One who has the opportunity to observe the conduct of industrial opera-

[64] Hutchins, *op. cit.*, 2:76–77.

tions can see many concrete instances of unwillingness to focus attention on matters of human relations.[65]

Labor problems, therefore, were administered on a day-to-day basis and most often inconsistently. This approach failed to recognize human values or to assist employees in fulfilling their psychological needs within the industrial organizational structure. Furthermore, it was a characteristic of autocratic leadership that expected, even demanded, the obedience, loyalty, and cooperation of labor still basically considered a commodity; the only connection with workers was the cash nexus. Such an attitude exemplified a philosophy of neglect that invited stringent governmental regulation during the 1930's.

The do-nothing philosophy of personnel administration is notable, as the name implies, for its insulation from the primary forces contributing to better personnel relations. Changes, when made, have been precipitated by state or federal statutes affecting wages and work conditions. This philosophy is remarkable in the sense that executive leadership has remained impervious to public, community, and employee values and to the behavioral concepts contributed by scientific disciplines. A model of the do-nothing model of personnel philosophy is outlined below.

1. Leadership. The chief executive is an autocratic figure who finds his philosophical foundation for management in the freedom of contract and the right of private property. Rather than considering the interests of various groups encountered in the administration of company affairs, the chief executive is dedicated singularly to serving the interests of private property or personal ownership.

    Executive leadership is committed to protecting managerial prerogatives and exercising unilateral direction and control in both personnel and labor relations.

    Management is insensitive to changes in the sentiments and values of the public, community, and employees as they affect personnel relations. Executives are equally unresponsive to philosophical implications, behavioral concepts, and techniques of scientific disciplines in the area of employee relations.

[65] Lewisohn, *op. cit.*, p. 226.

The employer perceives his responsibility as completed and his leadership role fulfilled when he pays his employees a "reasonable" or "fair" wage or the legally required minimum and conforms to the minimum working conditions dictated by federal or state statutes. No obligation is perceived arising from control of the workers' economic or social destinies—the employer is doing his irreducible minimum. However, management expects, and even demands, the obedience and cooperation of employees.

2. Personnel Management. Personnel management is not accepted as a function of management but is confined to record-keeping, usually those records required by state and federal laws.

Management has no perception of the relationship between sound personnel relations and technical efficiency.

Since management does not consider personnel a managerial function, subordinate managers are not trained for their personnel responsibilities. Employee problems are administered on a day-to-day basis—and often inconsistently.

Unless organized by labor, policy is not stated, or if so, committed to writing, because conditions of employment may then be changed at any time by unilateral action. Expediency and indifference, rather than principle, prevails.

Management responds primarily to pressures and emergencies since it has failed to make long-range plans and to design constructive policies to prevent problems before they arise.

3. Concept of Labor.
Impersonal. Having repudiated or at best ignored its responsibility for employees beyond the legally required minimum, management has little respect for its employees or concern for their welfare. Management fails to perceive its employees as endowed with human attributes that should find expression in the work environment. Consequently, work is deficient in personal satisfactions; the psychological needs and aspirations of employees are given no serious consideration.

4. Incentives. Work is accomplished through the use of fear, threat of penalties, and punishment, such as discharge, demotion, and withholding promotions and wage increases—negative motivation.

Arbitrary managerial actions, favoritism and discrimination arouse uncertainty with respect to security of employment.

No attention is given to inspiring in rank-and-file employees a sense of significance in their work. Management fails to recognize human values or to assist employees in fulfilling their psychological needs within the industrial organizational structure.

5.   Labor Relations. A conflict rationale of labor relations prevails.

Management's collective bargaining strategy is directed toward maintaining its unilateral power and resisting the demands of labor regardless of their merit.

Management overtly strives to discredit and undermine the union and its representatives.

As noted in the model just presented, an impersonal concept of labor was utilized which was not presented in Chapter I. The reason for its appearance here is to make this labor concept reflect the dynamic developments disclosed. In light of the wave of humanitarianism that swept the nation at the turn of the present century and its continuing impact, the negative connotations associated with the terms "commodity" and "machine concepts" are such that a more neutral descriptive term is desirable. Furthermore, these concepts were more appropriate in an era dominated by trading activities and emerging mechanization. As noted previously, both commodity and machine concepts of labor were notable for their failure to consider factory operatives as individuals possessing rights and human aspirations which should receive the serious consideration of management in its daily employee relations. The basic managerial attitudes of some modern executives are identical with those prevalent when the designations of commodity and machine were more appropriate. Since such attitudes reflect a lack of concern for the human element, the term "impersonal concept" is more descriptive in view of historical developments.

An Evaluation of the Do-Nothing Philosophy. The foregoing do-nothing philosophy, as well as the rationales to follow, should be evaluated by some specific criteria. At present no such guidelines have been formulated by which one may gauge the potential effectiveness or adequacy of personnel rationales. A promising criterion does exist in the generally accepted classification of human needs as structured by A. H. Maslow and popularized by Douglas M. McGregor.[66] These needs are categorized as physiological, safety, social, egoistic, and finally self-fulfillment; the ego needs have been divided into two groups—self-esteem and other-esteem. The assumption of prepotency, in which the lower order needs must be partially gratified before the next or higher order need can become activated, has been excluded. The theorized extent of employee satisfaction for each category of needs, with the exception of the physiological which are assumed to have been met, provides a means for assessing the potential adequacy, or inadequacy, of the personnel philosophy being examined.

The do-nothing rationale with its minimal emphasis on all forms of employee relations, precipitates a work environment in which even the safety needs fail to find appreciable expression. Uncertainty and insecurity are prevalent in a work situation permeated by favoritism, discrimination, and unpredictable administrative practices. Expediency and indifference rather than sound principles prevail; consequently, the safety needs are activated but extremely frustrated. If the firm is subject to required governmental wage and hour provisions and minimal safety requirements, some of the economic and physical uncertainties may be alleviated. However, the employer perceives his responsibilities and leadership role fulfilled when he pays employees a wage he considers reasonable or fair, or which meets the legally required minimum and conforms to the minimum working conditions dictated by federal or state statutes. Failing to recognize human values or assist employees in fulfilling psychological needs within the organizational structure, the employer is doing his irreducible minimum.

The non-economic safety needs, however, will remain unsatisfied since the employee is in an extremely dependent position and motivation is accomplished through the use of fear and threat of

[66] A. H. Maslow, "A Theory of Human Motivations," *Psychological Review* 50 (1943), 370–96. See also Douglas M. McGregor, "The Human Side of Enterprise," *Management Review* 46 (November, 1957), No. 11, pp. 22–28, 88–92.

penalties—negative motivation. The worker is uncertain of where he stands with respect to his supervisor, his job performance, or his promotional opportunities. The social needs barely find limited expression at best, and then only because of the spontaneous informal actions which invariably occur, and which cannot be completely suppressed by immediate supervisors or management. Under such conditions the norms, sentiments, and behavior patterns of the group are likely to conflict with managerial goals and objectives.

Self-esteem, if attained, is likely to arise by accident from the job itself rather than any conscious effort by management to cultivate opportunities for fulfilling this need. No attention is given to inspiring in rank-and-file members a sense of significance in their work. Furthermore, status-prestige needs are ignored by the accompanying autocratic or authoritarian superior-subordinate relationships. Since top management does not consider personnel a managerial function, subordinate managers are not trained for personnel responsibilities. The leadership associated with this philosophy is unaware of personnel relationships that would convey recognition or appreciation and thereby enhance status or prestige needs. In summary we find, as one would expect, that the prospects are very poor for an employee finding appreciable fulfillment or satisfaction in a work environment in which the do-nothing philosophy prevails.

Additional Developments in Personnel Philosophy. One cannot say that only a technique or do-nothing philosophy of personnel administration was held by executives in the early twentieth century, for there was some evidence of a more enlightened leadership. The humanistic philosophy of personnel administration maintained that good human relations were not inimical to efficiency.[67] Applications of psychology in personnel management offered a means of securing a better understanding of employees' motives, needs, and aspirations, a means which promised the possibility of eliciting their cooperative efforts in objectives mutually advantageous to management and to labor; understanding rather than manipulation and

[67] Cole, *op. cit.*, pp. 39–41.

control was the objective.[68] This viewpoint considered labor and management as partners in the productive process. Humanistic patterns of leadership abandoned the leave-it-alone philosophy and sought to enlist the constructive cooperation of employees, maintain two-way communication, and work for the ego satisfaction of employees as well as management.[69] Policies were formulated to insure consistency, fairness, and the minimization of discrimination. Industrialists who adopted this philosophy of personnel administration, as well as its tools and techniques, were a small minority. However, an enlightened philosophy of personnel was taking shape and many of the applications of scientific management represented a movement toward an intelligent and planned industrial organization for the purpose of eliminating mechanical and human waste.[70]

SUMMARY

During the 1920's there was a significant divergence between the do-nothing and the technique philosophy of personnel administration; the latter approach demonstrated a measure of flexibility not shown during the first twenty years of the twentieth century. Rigid insistence upon maintaining the status quo gave way to a partial alignment with the social values of the public and to a much lesser extent with those of employees. The narrow individualistic attitudes toward business and social problems which had previously prevailed were slowly being modified. This new viewpoint was manifested by the acknowledgment that business existed to render a service to society and to a much lesser extent by an indication of moral and social responsibility for employees. The technique philosophy of personnel management was gradually modified by the concept that business had a responsibility for an employee's well-being. There emerged an awareness that the economic system had become so interdependent

[68] Franklin, "Fundamental Policies of Organization," *op. cit.,* pp. 371–74.
[69] Barber, *op. cit.,* pp. 395–401.
[70] H. A. Overstreet, "The Philosophic Foundation: Is a New Business Philosophy Forming?" in *Scientific Foundations of Business Administration,* Henry C. Metcalf, ed. (Baltimore: The Williams & Wilkins Co., 1926), p. 315.

that individuals were subject to conditions beyond their control. This attitude found expression in the growth of industrial insurance, unemployment compensation, old-age pensions, workmen's compensation, and working conditions better than the minimum required by law. Legislative measures to correct oppressive and abusive working conditions were now willingly implemented by many employers who before had given only grudging acceptance or minimal compliance. Protection against unanticipated emergencies also reflected some effort to bring the objectives and values of executive personnel philosophy more in alignment with those of the public. Employers, to some extent at least, were endeavoring to harmonize their economic and social obligations.

Personnel administration increasingly was accepted as a general function of management. The basic philosophy of personnel administration as a discipline was to promote maximum production by enlisting employee interest, good will, and cooperation; these objectives were achieved through providing a work environment conducive to meeting physical, psychological, and social needs. This rationale was not widely accepted by industrial executives, although there was a definite trend toward a more humanistic approach to personnel relations.[71] Some executives recognized that labor was human with needs and desires similar to their own, but little concrete action was predicated on these insights. Responsibility for the physical well-being of workers was more prevalent than acknowledged responsibility for promoting their psychological and social well-being.

There were the vague beginnings of an interest in labor participation reflected in the recognition of community of interests between employer and employee. Since cooperation was required to promote this mutuality of interests, success of a business enterprise was increasingly visualized as contingent upon the extent to which all employees were participating in an integrated manner. Worker welfare was perceived as interwoven with the welfare of business and industrial enterprise. This was indicative that philosophies founded on neglect and employee manipulation were slowly being modified.

[71] Metcalf, *The Psychological Foundations of Management,* p. 10.

V

PERSONNEL PHILOSOPHY ORIENTED TO
NEW PRESSURES, 1930–1939

During the twenties some employers had sought to harmonize economic and social objectives, but seldom had such goals been extended to promoting the psychological and social well-being of employees. While considerable progress had been experienced in improving employer-employee relations, such achievements were inadequate to stem public hostility and governmental intervention during the depression. In the chapter to follow, a survey will be made of the impact of severe economic and political pressures on the personnel function and philosophy. Perceiving the relationship between public opinion and governmental action, numerous industrial firms became extremely sensitive to the public as consumer, voter, and employee. Consequently an evaluation will be made of public relations and its association with employee relations and practices.

Furthermore, organized labor, having achieved legal status, required many firms to formulate or modify their position toward labor unions and also to determine the appropriate role between personnel and labor relations; the impact of such action on personnel rationale will be examined. Finally, the technique philosophy will be analyzed, a model of its content presented, and its merits and limitations considered.

PERSONNEL MANAGEMENT UNDER ECONOMIC
AND POLITICAL PRESSURE

In the 1920's considerable activity had centered around ascertaining the place of personnel management in the industrial structure and its acceptance as a managerial function. Considerable evidence seemed to indicate an acceptance of personnel administration, although many executives failed to perceive their responsibility for this new function and paid mere lip service to sound personnel relations. As the 1929 depression continued into the 1930's, there was some question whether the pattern of dispensing with the personnel function observed in the depression of 1920–1922 would be repeated. This was a test of whether the personnel point of view had become a part of executive thinking and action or whether it was simply a fringe function to be abandoned when economic conditions became unfavorable.

Personnel Function Tested and Proven. In the 1930's however, there was no abandonment of current personnel relations policies. Instead of jettisoning their personnel programs, managing executives were taking more interest in labor administration than ever before in the history of American business.[1] Previously, employers had made only a faint gesture toward providing employees with security against unemployment or unanticipated emergencies. Some companies sought to avoid wholesale and indiscriminate dismissal of employees as the depression lengthened. Many employers sought to divide available work among employees; others sought to provide relief for workers laid off; still others attempted to maintain wage rates in the face of declining prices and profits. An observer of personnel practices concluded: "This protection of continuity of employment and the increased attention being paid by management to maintaining the earning power of the workers is one of the most significant of the changes in industrial relations emphasis brought on as a result of the depression." [2] Such policies were remarkable when one realizes that few if any of these measures were attempted during the depression of 1920–1922; it represented a change in executive philosophy from neglect to one in which responsibility was being

[1] Edward S. Cowdrick, "Personnel Practice in 1930," *AMA Personnel Series*, No. 11, (1931), pp. 1–12.
[2] *Ibid.*, p. 6.

assumed for the worker. No longer was labor to be regarded as a commodity to be bought and indiscriminately released without any obligation felt by the employer toward the employee.

This change in attitude toward acceptance of responsibility for employees continued, and in 1934 one finds an executive making the following evaluation:

The next characteristic of the new era is the marked change in orientation toward the worker. There is almost spontaneous movement, accelerated from month to month, in the direction of shorter hours, improved conditions and increased security. It is not to be confused with the crystalization of progress in these matters attained as the results of legislation imposed, but rather it seems to be gathering force as an expression of a generally awakened sense of social obligation of the employer toward the worker. Not that this sense of obligation is felt by all or even most employers (we have not yet reached the millennium), but it may be likened to a wave or current of contemporary thinking which, irrespective of legislation, must of itself be reckoned with.[3]

Later, in 1937, one industrial relations director concluded that there was developing a recognition on the part of employers that workers had vested interests in their jobs. In addition, there was considerable interest in year-around stability of employment and the possibilities of annual earnings as distinct from wage rates. However, these were long-range trends which were just beginning to emerge in a depression-racked America.[4]

Even after the government entered the field via the Fair Labor Standards Act of 1938, employer interest continued in the economic security of employees. Industrialists were not content to sit back and comply with the minimum requirements for unemployment or retirement; instead, many sought to improve these measures by supplementary policies in private industry. This policy reflected an awareness of social responsibility for the individual worker.

[3] Harry Arthur Hopf, "Developing Office Management to Meet the Needs of the New Era," *Management Review* 23 (March, 1934), 3:69.
[4] Thomas G. Spates, "The Shifting Scene in Industrial Relations," *AMA Personnel Series*, No. 32, (1938), pp. 4–14.

Determination to do more than the legally required minimum represented a further departure from the do-nothing philosophy of personnel administration which held that the company should do no more for its employees than governmental, economic, or other pressures dictated. Now, however, rather than drift with no constructive policies or programs, numerous employers were taking a positive viewpoint and deeming governmental requirements as a minimum instead of an optimum necessary to achieve satisfactory work and personnel relations. Governmental intervention still left managements free to ascertain this optimum and many executives initiated long-range planning and policy statements to achieve maximum employee welfare and development.

Personnel administration became a more important function of management than ever before during the 1930's. Definite expression of its growing influence was evident by (1) concentration of personnel functions under one executive who had equal status with those in charge of manufacturing, (2) a trend toward placing chief personnel officers in charge of personnel policy-making committees, and (3) the practice of companies of disseminating personnel policies to employees and having supervisors utilize such policies as a basis for action.[5] During the 1920's, policy expression had been rare; emphasis had been more on personnel techniques that would promote labor efficiency. Now, however, managements were increasingly concerned with formulation of personnel policies that gave concrete expression to managerial objectives.

It is significant that crystallized policy statements were now being perceived as a foundation for good personnel administration. Expediency, coupled with considerable emotion and prejudice, previously had dictated the settlement of employee relations problems. Managements were beginning to feel a need for conscious, intelligent, and well-planned personnel policies. Although progress had been slow, the trend toward policy statements had been accelerated by two developments—economic and political.

[5] J. Walter Dietz, "New Trends in Personnel Policies," *Personnel* 16 (February, 1940), 3:97–106.

Economic and Human Objectives of Personnel. Economic pressures had reinforced the idea that good personnel administration promotes efficient production to an extent not appreciated during the prosperous years after 1922. Personnel executives found a receptive audience in a decade of depression when they continued to reiterate that the objective of personnel administration was to increase production, increase sales, and improve quality.[6] Personnel functions were sold on the basis of making an economic contribution to the industrial firm. C. M. Chester, chairman of the board of General Foods Corporation, concluded that a good personnel job produced efficiency, improved a firm's competitive position, and minimized strikes. Given all other industrial conditions as equal, more effective utilization of the human element, through personnel administration, gave an industry a competitive advantage.[7] As in the 1920's, this was placing the value of the personnel function on a strictly dollars-and-cents basis.

Fortunately, acceptance of the personnel function did not terminate with the mere adoption of its efficiency objectives; there was also a more generalized adoption of its human philosophy. Turbulent economic and political conditions stimulated executives to examine more closely than ever the treatment accorded the human element, and many concluded that industry had been guilty of neglect. The economic function had received primary attention whereas skill in handling human relations had lagged behind skills developed in the technical areas. The president of Republic Steel was frank to admit: "We have not always given due consideration . . . to the most efficient and sympathetic relationship between employee and employer." [8] Expediency and indifference had been substituted for principle, but employers were making a collective reappraisal of their practices.

[6] Harold B. Bergen, "Fundamentals of a Personnel and Industrial Relations Program," *Personnel* 13 (May, 1937), 2:46–54.

[7] C. M. Chester, "Management's Responsibilities in Industrial Relations," *AMA Personnel Series,* No. 36, (1939), pp. 3–14.

[8] T. M. Girdler, "Industrial Relations," *AMA Personnel Series,* No. 22, (1936), p. 3.

Personnel executives assisted in this re-evaluation of employee relations practices by continuing to point out the human aspect of their philosophy to those inclined to consider and assimilate their viewpoint. Thus, Thomas G. Spates, director of industrial relations of General Foods Corporation, stated that social justice and industrial peace could be attained by policies and methods of personnel administration which had been shown ". . . (a) to enhance the value of the individual to himself and society, (b) to encourage and perpetuate voluntary cooperation, and (c) to create and maintain a spirit of friendliness throughout the work relationships." [9]

The director of industrial relations of Proctor and Gamble Company reiterated that, in addition to achieving efficiency, sound personnel management sought to increase employee satisfaction and morale and also to protect the physical and mental well-being of employees. He further stipulated that increased efficiency could not be achieved at the expense of lowered morale or the physical impairment of employees.[10]

Many executives were more disposed to accept the personnel rationale during the 1930's than ever before. One vice president concluded that employee relations was one of industry's most complicated problems and that for "efficient and economical operation, a plant must have a happy, hopeful, and cooperative personnel." [11] The president of Nunn-Bush Shoe Company drew the following conclusion from his industrial experience: "The man on the production line is no better and no worse than the man who employs him. He is inherently fair; and he wants no more than a job in which he can be assured of the fairness of management and his reasonable share of what he produces. . . . It is only by making it possible for workers to have these things, so necessary to the maximum happiness of any

[9] Spates, *op. cit.*, p. 13.
[10] Bergen, *op. cit.*, p. 46.
[11] John H. Goss, "The Employee's Challenge—A Right and an Obligation," *Personnel* 13 (May, 1937), 4:123.

human being, that the full cooperation and good will of labor can be justly asked or attained." [12]

One can definitely assert that acceptance of the worker as an individual with specific needs and aspirations which must be met within the industrial structure became a prevalent viewpoint in the 1930's. Employees were given more recognition and status in industry as employee satisfaction and mental well-being were accepted by many executives as complementary objectives to the emphasis upon efficiency and profits. A humanistic philosophy flourished, founded upon a social consciousness and humanitarian point of view. Furthermore, the movement was predicated upon an acceptance of labor as human with a right to dignity, self-esteem, and respect as well as to fair wages, fair hours, and decent work conditions. There was a definite trend toward a "clear, clean-cut statement of management's intended standard of treatment in all human relationships within a business." [13] The philosophy of personnel administration held by many executives was beginning to overtake the rationale of personnel administration as a profession.

Political Pressures and Public Opinion. In addition to economic forces, political pressures also stimulated executives to re-examine their personnel policies and philosophy. The National Industrial Recovery Act of 1933 restricted the hours of work, established minimum wages, and sanctioned collective bargaining with labor representatives chosen by employees as requisite conditions for the establishment of industrial codes of fair competition. An industrial relations director, conveying the collective opinions of thirty personnel officials, concluded that these measures placed few detrimental limitations on management. "Perhaps this [N.I.R.A.] will also stimulate better and sounder management rather than limit it. In this connection, there is some feeling that the limitations on management

---

[12] H. L. Nunn, "A New Concept by Capital of Labor's Relationship in Industry," *AMA Personnel Series*, No. 32, (1938), p. 36.

[13] Dietz, *op. cit.*, p. 97.

action have been negligible in comparison with the stimulus provided the recognition of personnel administration as one of the most
vital and important functions of business management." [14]

A majority of industrialists, however, were quite glad to see the
National Industrial Recovery Act declared unconstitutional and
were greatly concerned when its Section 7 (a), which sanctioned collective bargaining with labor unions chosen by employees, was incorporated into the National Labor Relations Act of 1935. Company
unions were abolished and collective bargaining received public
sanction. The public had found employee representation programs
or company unions sadly wanting as a democratic means of giving
employees a voice in determining working conditions. Too many
employers had considered employee representation as a substitute
for sound personnel relations or as a means of thwarting unionization rather than as a means of facilitating communication with rank-
and-file workers.[15]

A majority of industrialists had made no effort to reconcile their
philosophy of personnel administration with the values of the public.
Continued disregard of public sentiment had resulted in a governmental labor policy that crystallized the public interest.[16] A director
of industrial relations concluded, *"Current emphasis upon the legislative and collective bargaining approach to industrial relations was
a direct consequence of past indifferences of employers to the human aspects of enterprise."* [17] As a result, there was considerable
soul-searching, and great efforts were made to set the industrial
house in order. Another industrialist viewed the situation:

> While a good many organizations have all too recently attempted
> to create pleasant relations with the employees because it seemed to

[14] H. B. Bergen, "Personnel Policies in the Light of the New Deal," *Personnel* 11 (August, 1934), 1:18.

[15] W. T. Holliday, "Employee Representation," *Personnel* 10 (May, 1934),
4:99–104.

[16] J. Walter Dietz, "Controlling Factors in Industrial Relations Administration," *AMA Personnel Series*, No. 27, (1937), pp. 36–48.

[17] Spates, *op. cit.*, p. 5.

be "good business," too few of them have tackled the problem with any degree of sincerity. The fear of public opinion and the dread of governmental intervention have accomplished more for the employee in the span of two years than ordinary weapons have won in the past decade. Much to their chagrin, some employers have discovered that they cannot buy loyalty, especially when the benefits they establish come as a result of external pressure.[18]

Industry was made aware of the inadequacy of a do-nothing philosophy of personnel administration based upon apathy and neglect. For many executives, their personnel rationale was responding again to pressure rather than developing as a result of intelligent, long-range planning of personnel relations. Employees had sought a voice in determining conditions affecting their welfare, but employers had responded with outright hostility and oppression against all efforts to bargain over wages, hours, and working conditions. A few employers had made gestures toward granting employees a more equal bargaining position by installing employee representation plans or company unions, but a majority of these programs were not undertaken with any degree of sincerity. Managements had utilized their superior bargaining position to suppress labor rather than to recognize labor's rights and promote the personal development of their employees. Industry had refused to accept the citizenship concept of labor which recognized employee rights to a voice in industry, but the government provided a statute that would facilitate its operation whether accepted voluntarily or not. Failing to respond to changed social and economic conditions, managements had been compelled by public sentiment, now crystallized into governmental legislation, to reconsider their handling of labor relations.

Reactions to Organized Labor. After congressional enactment of the National Labor Relations Act, two basic decisions confronted management now faced with dealing with unions chosen by their employees. The first consisted of determining what kind of working

---

[18] R. G. Harmon, "Is There a Future for Sound Industrial Relations?" *Personnel* 12, (February, 1936) 3:219.

relationship with the union should prevail; alternatives ranged from continued conflict and opposition, to an arms-length or legalistic form of recognition, to voluntary cooperation with union representatives. A second decision for many managements consisted of deciding if, or how, the personnel function was to be integrated with labor relations. Possible courses of action ranged from utilizing the personnel function to combat, weaken, or neutralize the union, to adopting a position of cooperating with organized labor and integrating its personnel and labor relations programs. Some managements, taking an intermediate position, developed extensive personnel programs and voluntarily expanded their fringe benefits, thereby vying with the union for the loyalty of the employees while avoiding direct or overt union-management conflict. This rationale resulted in dichotomizing personnel and labor management.

A few executives, although a definite minority, began to express a more friendly attitude toward the role labor was destined to play under governmental protection. One of America's most respected industrial leaders, H. L. Nunn, stated that management "must accept Labor's right to a voice and vote in every matter that vitally affects Labor's welfare." [19] Another executive stated that "management undertook the wisest thing it ever tried and began to sit around the table wtih the workers themselves and talk things over." [20] The president of General Electric stated: "In a democratic society such as ours, which is founded upon the inalienable right of human beings to determine the policies and leaders of our government, it cannot be questioned that a group of men, workers in a unit, should have the right to get together and speak as a unit for what they think would better their work conditions." [21]

Other executives also maintained a constructive view toward governmental intervention into personnel and labor relations. In an address to industrial leaders, Thomas G. Spates, stated: ". . . *You*

[19] Nunn, *op. cit.*, p. 30.
[20] D. H. Morris, "What Personnel Policies Are Included in a Comprehensive Industrial Relations Program?" *Personnel* 11 (August, 1935) 5:145.
[21] Gerard Swope, "Industry's Role in Society," *Management Review* 28, (May, 1939) 5:147.

can neither legislate nor contract out the spirit of friendliness which must prevail throughout the work relationship if human happiness in the daily task is to be assured. In other words there is no successful substitute for good personnel administration." [22] A similar viewpoint was expressed by the vice-president of Scovill Manufacturing Company: "No government-written labor policy can accomplish for everyone the kind of security and everyday self-confidence which comes from knowing definitely from one's own employer what are one's rights and obligations while in his service and how we can all get into team work with him." [23]

These opinions were evidence that some managements were determined to pursue a more humanistic program of personnel administration. A personnel function partially determined by governmental labor policy was not deemed sufficient in itself to implement the recognized objectives of personnel administration. Mere legal compliance and disavowal of responsibility for additional constructive personnel practices would have been consistent with the do-nothing philosophy of personnel. Many executives were moving away from this viewpoint and visualized governmental intervention as providing only a framework for personnel and labor relations which left considerable latitude for developing industrial cooperation and harmony.

The philosophy of opposition toward unions was altered only slightly during the 1930's. Few industrialists would admit as true the statement made by Virgil Jordan, president of the National Industrial Conference Board, when he said, "The one respect in which, it seems to me, management is most backward in the industrial relations field, is in the development of constructive contact, intercourse, and cooperation with labor organization." [24] Jordan failed to perceive that management's lack of a constructive labor relations policy was not due to neglect or accident. Industry's basic policy toward

[22] Spates, *op. cit.*, p. 13.

[23] Royal Parkinson, "Another Kind of Security Desirable?" *Personnel* 14 (August, 1937) 1:43.

[24] Virgil Jordan, "Management's Role in Preserving the Enterprise Order," *Management Review* 26 (February, 1937), 2:41.

organized labor had been one of planned opposition from the time organized labor activities had appeared, and its leadership was premised upon maintaining unilateral control over labor. In general, industry had failed to give the human factor adequate consideration and opposed the intervention of any independent labor union that sought to do so. Most industrialists felt that business was administered to promote efficiency and that lacking unilateral control this objective could not be achieved.

Under compulsion of the National Labor Relations Act, there was a reluctant acceptance of unions but no change in the managerial philosophy of opposition for most executives. Rather, there was a strategic retreat while employers sought to rid themselves of unions by demonstrating that the company could do more for its employees than could the union. Other employers went to the opposite extreme by tightening up on employee relations to prove the union had precipitated worse conditions. Taking a legalistic approach, many managements provided only what the rules demanded and insisted that employees follow shop rules to the letter.

The Personnel Function and Labor Relations. In their efforts to weaken unions, employers sought to compete with them for the loyalty of employees. "In the final analysis the crisis we are facing today in industrial relations is in reality a question of competition by management against outside agencies for the loyalty and confidence of their own employees." [25] A technique philosophy of personnel is incompatible with rival or dual loyalties, and many executives sought to maintain their unilateral control of relationships by devious methods. To meet the challenge and threat of legally sanctioned unions, many companies installed hastily devised personnel departments or sought to improve existing ones. The implication of Henry L. McCarthy, a former chairman of the Chicago Labor Relations Board, was apparent when he stated before a group of industrialists: "In

[25] Thomas G. Spates, "An Analysis of Industrial Relations Trends," *AMA Personnel Series*, No. 52, (1937), p. 20.

my experience with the Labor Board it has been borne in upon me a thousand times that there is only one basic cause for labor troubles, and that is poor administration of personnel. No employer who has developed and maintained an intelligent program of personnel administration has ever been hailed before the Labor Board. Further than that, such employers do not have labor troubles nor do they have to worry about the so-called labor agitation. Their battle is won before they start." [26]

It was during this era that personnel administration became analogous to fire-fighting techniques rather than becoming a well-planned administrative function based upon a humanistic philosophy. In the minds of many, personnel administration came to be identified with anti-unionism. One personnel executive later summarized such activities of industry and the ensuing results as follows:

> Personnel programs were inaugurated during the thirties because many managements saw in them a device for preventing unionization. When the unions organized anyway, as they usually did, enthusiasm for personnel management in these companies often reached a pretty low ebb.
> In some companies when unions organized the employees faster than the companies could organize personnel departments, management often reasoned that since personnel management seemed to obviate the need for unions, a liberal use of personnel techniques would keep the union weak and docile.[27]

It is apparent that the motivating rationale of personnel programs inaugurated under such circumstances was not to enhance the physical, social, or psychic development of the laboring force but to maintain unilateral control over employee relationships. This rationale was a continuation of the technique philosophy of personnel which previously had utilized works councils and employee representation plans to dominate all work relations. Significantly, the personnel

[26] Henry L. McCarthy, quoted *ibid.*, p. 19.
[27] Wade E. Shurtleff, "Top Management and Personnel Administration," *AMA Personnel Series*, No. 144, (1952), p. 5.

function was accepted with all of its gadgets, techniques, and welfare activities, but the inherent personnel philosophy was ignored.

Industry demonstrated once again that the personnel function with its scientific methodology might be employed to implement diverse philosophies. On the one hand, personnel administration could be, and was, used to exploit, coerce, or deter employee rights in the interests of efficiency, profits, and unilateral control. Conversely, this management function was utilized to enhance employee personal development, integrity, and dignity within the industrial organization.

PERSONNEL RELATIONS:
BASIS FOR PUBLIC RELATIONS

Although there had been some emphasis upon public relations during the 1920's, the depression decade became an era of relentless public relations for industry. Public relations activities gained momentum after 1935 and reached their peak intensity prior to the commencement of hostilities in Europe. An article in *Fortune* magazine stated, "The year 1938 may go down in the annals of industry as the season in which the concept of public relations struck home to the hearts of a whole generation of businessmen." [28] Public relations became an accepted personnel function and good employee relations was accepted as the first step in the creation of enlightened public opinion.

Businessmen were operating in a hostile climate of public opinion that had sanctioned governmental intervention in labor relations. Consequently, there was a collective consciousness of a lack of adjustment to new social and economic conditions; increasingly business sought to inform the public of its basic beliefs and to explain the identity of interests between business and the community. Through public relations media, executives attempted to inform the public of existing labor-management relationships and the recog-

[28] "The Public Is Not Damned," *Fortune* 19 (March, 1939), p. 83.

nition of its social responsibilities. As a condition of relatively independent business survival and long-run self-interest, it became mandatory that industrial policies be more in harmony with public values and standards.

Noting the expansion of American industry and the nation's dependence upon its goods and services, James H. McGraw, president of McGraw-Hill Publishing, concluded: "It [American industry] has established so close a relationship between business and the citizenry, between business and government, that every American corporation has become a matter of public concern. It is becoming apparent that the affairs of corporations in the future will be conducted as in a goldfish bowl for all the world to see." [29] Any attempts to hide internal conditions were deemed futile because employee relations had become a matter of public concern. "We are all consumers, and we are all conscious of good and bad personnel relations in companies which seek our patronage. . . . Somehow, people will learn what your personnel relations are." [30] H. P. Liversidge, president of the Philadelphia Electric Company, observed that human relations in the plant shaped the attitudes of public, customers, and employees; and if such attitudes were unfavorable, profits would be reduced. He concluded:

So I believe public relations work is strictly common sense in business, which must be the case if we are to justify it. At the same time I cannot refrain from expressing my inner conviction that in addition there are more compelling grounds for justification. The achievement of proper public relations calls for exercise of the highest business statesmanship. The times challenge us to demonstrate that the system of private enterprise can produce the greatest good for the greatest number of people. [31]

Many industrial executives were not merely talking of expanding

[29] James H. McGraw, Jr., "The Concept of Public Relations," *Management Review* 27 (November, 1938), 11:362.

[30] Chester, *op. cit.*, 10.

[31] Horace P. Liversidge, "The Common Sense of Public Relations," *Management Review* 28 (June, 1939), 6:183.

public relations, they were advocating specific programs to achieve this objective. Typical were the courses of action outlined for industry by McGraw-Hill:

First: Establish better relations with its employees, by the improvement of its labor policies as they affect the safety, wealth, comfort, earning power, security, ambition, and education of the worker.

Second: Improve its relations with its customers and prospective customers by interesting them in its policies as they relate to its social responsibilities and the social benefits that come from its products and services.

Third: Build a closer relationship with its security holders by making them more conscious of the social aspects of its policies, its activities, and its products.

Fourth: Become a better citizen, a neighbor in every community where it operates, by more actively participating in local affairs and by making its policies and practices known to everyone interested.[32]

Significantly, the program suggested above begins within the plant and radiates outward to the family, community, and public. To implement public and employee relations, employee editions of annual reports were published and open-house day held to permit families and friends of employees to visit the plant.

The Public-Consumer-Employee Identity. As a result of the emphasis upon public relations, industry developed a new concept of labor. Employees were perceived as part of the consuming public whose good will employers were endeavoring to cultivate. It was a "consumer" concept of labor that accepted employees and consumers as one and the same. "We have learned that business depends not only upon those who furnish the capital, those who produce, and those who manage, but even more upon those who buy. We have learned that those who buy are overwhelmingly the same people as those who produce." [33] Another industrialist, also recognizing this

[32] McGraw, *op. cit.*, pp. 362–63.
[33] Harry Arthur Hopf, "Juggling and Management," *Management Review* 26 (August, 1937), 8:254.

identity, stated, "The responsibility of foresight and conservation put a special challenge to management in its relation to workers and consumers. Both these groups are one. . . ." [34]

The consumer generally was given careful and thoughtful consideration, since he ultimately determined the demand for a company's product. To a certain extent, however, the attitude of business had often been to let the buyer beware. This attitude had proved less acceptable and compatible with social and economic changes during the 1920's and 1930's. Since the employee was also a consumer, he was entitled to solicitude and concern similar to that given the consumer. Goodwill of the employee had to be obtained as well as that of the consumer, because both were capable of retaliatory or defensive measures if exploited or abused. A combination of the consumer concept of labor and the concept that good employee relations were the foundation for public relations further stimulated the acceptance and practice of a humanized philosophy of personnel administration.

One of the most interesting developments in the movement to cultivate good public relations was the realization that it was not simply an outside job; it was a task that began within the plant.[35] As one public relations official put it, "First in any program to better public relationships, come the employees. Good public relationships result in the end from good inside relationships." [36] If the objectives of public relations were to be achieved, there must be a sound program of personnel administration. To achieve this purpose, it was necessary to "disseminate to the public information concerning the personnel policies and methods of the company for the purpose of building public good-will for the company." [37]

Therefore the emphasis upon public relations stimulated employer promotion of good work conditions and sound human relations. Many firms were compelled to exert a degree of attention that previ-

[34] Jordan, *op. cit.* p. 41.
[35] McGraw, *op. cit.* p. 362.
[36] Paul Garrett, "Public Relations Techniques," *Management Review* 28 (February, 1939), 2:38.
[37] Bergen, "Fundamentals of a Personnel and Industrial Relations Program," p. 46.

ously had been lacking, the new programs thus expediting the institution of corrective measures. Furthermore, public relations called for the formulation of policies that heretofore had not existed or, if so, had not been reduced to writing. Increasingly, personnel policies that stated managerial objectives were clearly defined and distributed to both employees and the public.

Gone was much of the complacency of industrial relations found prior to the depression and which was characteristic of the technique and do-nothing philosophies of personnel administration. The employee-be-damned and public-be-damned attitudes were no longer tenable. The turbulent depression years had prompted many industrialists to take stock of existing practices and policies; they were found inadequate and many executives sought to "bring their policies into line with the demands of public opinion." [38]

The Social Responsibility Viewpoint Spreads. Public relations also became a medium for acknowledging industry's social responsibilities, which were predicated upon the acceptance of motives other than profits. The service motive received some recognition by industrialists in the 1920's and in the depression decade was proclaimed by an increasing number of executives. The waning importance of exclusive concentration on profits cannot be overemphasized. It marked the decline of the individualistic philosophy of industrial administration which was devoted exclusively to profit maximization. As long as this remained the only objective of industry, consideration of human values, whether within the plant or in the community, was neglected. It was pointed out that "industry must accept its responsibility for the national welfare as being an even higher duty than the successful operation of private business." [39]

This new emphasis, however, did not rule out the profit motive, because profitable industrial operations were necessary in a nation that functioned under a profit system. Rather, the profit motive was

[38] "The Public Is Not Damned," p. 86.
[39] Dietz, "Controlling Factors in Industrial Relations Administration," p. 37.

related to the achievement of a broader range of objectives. One industrial executive summarized this new viewpoint when he exclaimed, *"By prospering, a well-managed company best serves the community."* [40] Summarizing the role of profits, Gerard Swope, president of General Electric, concluded: "Industry, with all its specialization, is developed primarily to serve the material requirements of society, with the least time and effort of human beings and under the best possible working conditions. This is the main function of industry in society—not the acquistion of profits." [41] Edward R. Stettinius, Jr., as chairman of the board of the United States Steel Corporation, also noted that the general welfare demanded new responsibilities of industry. "No longer can industry plow a single furrow towards a strictly commercial objective; instead, it must manage its affairs with due regard to the whole field of human relations. Industry must strive to adjust its operations to the highest purposes of life." [42] The managing partner of Hopf, Kent, Willard and Company expressed this new attitude as follows: "Management, for its part, must be alive to the implications of a broader philosophy of social justice. *The new touch stone of success of management is not alone what percentage of profit did the business earn, but how sound are its labor and consumer relations."* [43]

A new philosophy of social justice took shape during the 1930's. It was based upon recognized responsibilities toward employees and public as well as to stockholders and represented a better balance of interests of groups affected by the industrial organization. Whereas the interests of owners and stockholders had previously been the primary concern of the managerial function, the welfare of consumers and employees was receiving an unprecedented degree of attention. Although this sense of trusteeship did not guarantee a humanistic philosophy of personnel administration, it indicated an appreciation of the human factor and a further departure from man-

[40] Chester, *op. cit.*, p. 7.
[41] Swope, *loc. cit.*
[42] Quoted in Edward L. Bernays, "Private Interest and Public Responsibility," *Management Review* 28 (April, 1939), 4:111. Emphasis added.
[43] Hopf, "Juggling and Management," p. 255.

agement for the purpose of profits only. This new viewpoint was necessary because many of the personnel programs and practices necessary to implement an integrated personnel function were difficult to justify concretely on a dollars-and-cents basis.

The concept of service to the general welfare, both public and community, that was consistent with sound human relations was compatible with a humanistic rationale of personnel. Service to the nation at the expense of the employees who made the material necessities possible would have been a farce. Executives were slowly but surely developing a philosophy of personnel administration which was consistent with the goals and values of the community and employees.

A SOCIAL PHILOSOPHY
OF PERSONNEL ADMINISTRATION

Personnel management traditionally had emphasized relations with individual employees, and group relationships were considered mainly in terms of unions, collective bargaining, or employee representation. The Hawthorne investigations, however, pointed out the limitations to the purely individual approach to personnel relations and demonstrated that the social structure of an organization must be considered if cooperation between management and the employees was to be obtained.[44] The practice of dealing primarily with individuals reflected the individualistic philosophy of management and the influence of industrial psychology, based on individual differences, upon personnel administration. Previously, personnel management had confined itself almost exclusively to the satisfaction of physical and psychological needs of employees. Personnel management had sought to secure employee cooperation for the maximization of production by enlisting worker interest and goodwill in achieving the firm's objectives, but there was less awareness of social needs or the importance of social relations within the work group.

---

[44] F. J. Roethlisberger and William J. Dickson, *Management and the Worker* (Cambridge: Harvard University Press, 1940), pp. 551–604.

New Insights from Hawthorne. Work was found to serve two mutually dependent functions—economic and social. The economic function was familiar to executives but they had little or no conception of the social aspects. Industry was found to consist of informal work groups in which the individual employee had a social position. Each job has its own social values and a rank in the social scale; the worker adopted the behavior pattern consistent with the job's social position. Having assimilated the general values and attitudes of the group, employees were largely regulated and controlled by group sentiments. Therefore, to understand employee behavior, it was necessary to consider the worker's social environment. Such an orientation to the analysis of the behavior of the employee, his satisfactions and dissatisfactions, was entirely new in industry where the individual had been the primary focus of attention.

Of special significance to management was the conclusion that economic incentives might not be effective if inconsistent with group values. Employees would act contrary to their own economic advantage by following production norms established by the work group, although they might be capable of greater output. In essence the economic incentive was found less effective than the social. Furthermore, technological changes instigated by management would be resisted, although to the employee's economic advantage, since such modifications might threaten an individual's social position within the group or alter the group's social standing within the organization. Contrary to the traditional approach, the organization of production and work should utilize the forces of the informal organization. Managements had relied heavily upon economic incentives for higher labor output, but they were now compelled to expand their concept of employee motivation.

In order to promote cooperative employee behavior and effectuate the human responsibility of management, it was necessary to maintain effective two-way channels of communication throughout the organization. Management had to be informed of employees' thoughts and actions, and, in turn, employees needed to be informed of managerial expectations and proposed courses of action. An integral part of planned communication was employee consultation; this would indicate that workers were important members in the organization and their views welcomed and duly considered. Participation provided employees an opportunity to contribute to company development and minimized resistance to technological changes. Participation by workers, or a voice in determining their own welfare, had been resisted by managements, but the Hawthorne investigations found consultation crucial for achieving cooperation. Instead of a one-way flow of communication from top to bottom, frequently based on a take-it-or-leave-it basis, the studies indicated that supervisors should keep in contact with employees, listen to their suggestions and complaints, and explain departmental affairs.

The Hawthorne investigations also demonstrated a need for a new type of leadership by supervisory and managerial personnel. Unfavorable employee behavior such as restricted output and failure to follow instructions were found to be symptomatic of underlying dissatisfactions or grievances; good supervisory practice required the obtaining of a complete picture of the situation in order to ascertain the hidden causes of such behavior. Morale definitely was related to good first-line supervision, which, in turn, was contingent on the utilization of practices providing for the motivation and well-being of work groups. Morale was correlated with personal contentment, social satisfaction, and managerial practices as they affected the individual.

In essence, it followed that management was partially a social skill. Socially sound leadership required the use of communication and consultation at the group level. Problems of vital interest to employees should be taken up with them before decisions were made. This practice would serve to acquaint the group with economic or efficiency aspects of work problems and would provide an opportunity for employees to solve problems in a manner consistent with their values. Thereby, work groups would be able to make a worthwhile contribution and share a greater degree of responsibility for achieving established objectives.

Results of Mayo's studies also indicated the need for development of social skills in managerial and supervisory training programs. Suggested content for such a program was an understanding of the social structure of the firm and work groups, informal groups within the organization and their implications for technological change, the necessity for good two-way communications, and employee consultation and participation. Being greatly concerned with the human factor, supervisory personnel were to utilize a sound human approach. Training programs were needed that were oriented toward a better understanding of the human element and toward cultivation of social skills to promote cooperative employee behavior. The Hawthorne experiments had demonstrated the importance of adequate supervision under scientifically controlled conditions; but, more importantly, they revealed many of the characteristics of good supervision.[45]

The studies conducted at the Western Electric Company by Elton Mayo and his associates marked the inception of the human relations movement and served as a foundation for further research. Additionally, these investigations provided a social concept of labor that supplemented the economic and egoistic perceptions of employee needs. Consequently, the individualistic approach to personnel administration was complemented by new insights into the group or social aspects of work, giving a more balanced perspective of employee motives and the work environment.

The "action-designated assumptions" of human relations as formulated by William G. Scott, professor of management, are considered mandatory by personnel experts for a human relations philosophy from which operating objectives and policies may be derived.[46] These assumptions are summarized as follows:

1. Good human relations practice is the product of the manager's

---

[45] Elton Mayo, *The Human Problems of an Industrial Civilization* (New York: Macmillan Co., 1933), p. 87.

[46] William G. Scott, *Human Relations in Management: A Behavioral Science Approach* (Homewood, Illinois: Richard D. Irwin, Inc., 1962), pp. 54–57.

using experience, intuition, and interdisciplinary generalizations to guide him in the action he takes.

2. Employee participation which involves workers in the decision-making process on their job is often essential to higher productivity and greater human satisfaction. Democratic leadership is necessary for establishing a permissive environment in which participation can flourish.

3. An employee's behavior is a product of a "job-oriented role," as determined by the job or company (formal), and an "informal group-oriented role", as determined by his work associates.

4. Communication is essential to organization effectiveness and largely a human problem.

5. Teamwork is an indispensable element of management practice for organizational survival and is a matter of both management and employees striving to obtain the same objectives.

6. Man is diversely motivated—economically, psychologically, and socially.

7. The plant or office is a social system that must be maintained in balance or equilibrium by the executive.

8. Executive skills in human relations practice can be developed.

Executive Reactions to the New Human Relations. Some of the implications of the Hawthorne investigations had begun to infiltrate industrial thinking as early as 1934, and a few personnel executives were evaluating personnel problems in terms of the investigations' conclusions.

Today, management must develop better ways of training the supervisory staff in interpreting to the employees the personnel policies, plans and problems of the company and in translating to the top executives the misunderstandings, complaints, grievances, and irritations of employees. This two-way channel of information must be developed more effectively than it has in the past. The foreman and other members of the supervisory force must also be aided in developing better personal leadership skills. . . . The efficient foreman of today must not only get production but he must get this production under modern employee relations.[47]

[47] Bergen, "Personnel Policies in the Light of the New Deal," p. 20.

Acceptance of consultation and participation in personnel management was slow, and in 1936 Harold Bergen, director of industrial relations at Procter and Gamble, concluded that most executives had failed to recognize the "growth of democratic ideas in industry and the desire of employees to be consulted on matters which closely affect their interest." [48] One of the greatest tasks facing personnel executives was to convince top management that time spent in consultation was well spent and tended to strengthen good personnel relations.

Participation ran counter to the prevailing philosophy of management, but a more democratic climate was discernible. Under the pressure of hostile public opinion and governmental intervention in employer-employee relations, industrial leaders began thoroughly to scrutinize their leadership practices; some industrialists interpreted such events as a mandate for more democratic leadership.[49] One industrial relations director observed, "We are witnessing the passing of the industrial autocrat." [50]

A few executives began to consider democracy, which was highly desirable in government, to be suitable for industry. The president of Nunn-Bush Shoe Company stated: "Every real American abhors the thought of having a dictator over our government. He should also abhor the thought of dictators in industry. Arbitrary industrial decisions of industrial men should be looked upon as destructive to the social good." [51] Nunn added that although his opinion was definitely in the minority, other executives were also giving consideration to making industry more democratic. P. W. Litchfield, president of Goodyear Tire and Rubber Company, took the following position on democracy in industry:

Fair and equitable representation for all component parts of the state is the essence of democracy in government. Carry that funda-

[48] Bergen, "Fundamentals of a Personnel and Industrial Relations Program," p. 49.
[49] Bernays, *op. cit.*, pp. 110–11.
[50] Bergen, "Personnel Policies in the Light of the New Deal," p. 25.
[51] Nunn, *op. cit.*, p. 36.

mental into business and it insures fair consideration for the three basic elements of business—the workers, the stockholders, and the consumers.

With any deviation from such a concept of equality, we find ourselves in the realm of autocracy where a dominating group gains disproportionately through the exploitation of the remaining groups. It would seem to me, therefore, that management should strive for the establishment of a democratic basis of operations. Management's success in this may well determine the future course of our nation, because it does not seem likely that democracy could endure in government should any form of despotism prevail in business.[52]

The industrial climate was slowly becoming more suitable for utilization of Elton Mayo's principles of communication and consultation. Spates of General Foods Corporation concluded in 1937 that the application of democratic principles to business administration was a definite trend in industry. A system of consultative supervision exists when "a two-way channel of communication is maintained up and down through the line organization; and the point of view of supervisors and employees is taken into account before, rather than after, decisions are made that materially affect their interests."[53] Still another executive proclaimed consultative supervision as the keystone of good industrial relations.[54]

There was also a growing appreciation of the social aspects of work. Chester I. Barnard, president of the New Jersey Bell Telephone Company, noted that recognition of labor as a social factor had not been deemed a critical element in production but that a change was under way.[55] F. J. Lunding, senior operating assistant to the vice-president of Jewel Food Stores, concluded: "Today success is difficult to attain unless the social functions and the social aspects of the job are attended to. The executive must not only know

[52] P. W. Litchfield, "A Labor Relations Program," *Management Review* 26 (June, 1937), 6:184–85.
[53] Spates, "The Shifting Scene in Industrial Relations," p. 11.
[54] Chester, *op. cit.*, p. 13.
[55] Chester I. Barnard, "The Significance of Management," *Management Review* 27 (September, 1938), 9:290.

how to manufacture and distribute a product at a profit, but he must also be skillful in the handling of human relations." [56]

Mayo's social philosophy of personnel administration was not extensively accepted by industrialists during the 1930's because the prevailing philosophy of personnel administration was still technique oriented and executive leadership was strongly authoritarian. Management still insisted upon unilateral control and, therefore, failed to accept participation and consultation as requisites to good personnel relations. Like industrial psychology, the principles and concepts of the Hawthorne investigations were considered to be compatible with authoritarian forms of direction and motivation. For some industrialists, the principles of human relations and social skills promised a scientific means of manipulating work groups and controlling their attitudes and behavior. Techniques of communication, both up and down, were cultivated without regard to Mayo's rationale, and participation consisted of selling employees decisions already made. Thus consultation did not necessarily indicate that management had relinquished any measure of its authoritarian approach or changed its basic philosophy. Consultation was often tactfully utilized to induce employees to agree with management and yet think they had participated in determining matters affecting their welfare.

Technique Philosophy of Personnel Administration. The reception of Mayo's social concepts during the thirties and the developments previously observed drew more attention to the technique personnel philosophy. Technique rationale, which had been evolving over the past thirty years, was structured primarily around procedures for implementing the objectives of personnel administration and was founded upon authoritarian forms of leadership and manipulation to preserve unilateral direction and control.

Of the basic forces that were instrumental in the evolution of the technique personnel philosophy, none is perhaps of more sig-

[56] F. J. Lunding, "Building an Effective Executive Organization," *AMA Personnel Series*, No. 31, (1937), p. 5.

nificance than the changes occurring in executive leadership. During the period from 1900–1930, there was a decided shift from the autocratic leadership pattern of the laissez-faire period to an authoritarian one in which unrestricted executive power was gradually diminished by state and federal legislation. Another parallel development was a shift in executive leadership from personal ownership to the professional management. This change in leadership was accompanied not only by a modification of the rigid insistence on maintaining the status quo in personnel and labor relations to a more flexible position, but also by increasing sensitivity to public values, often culminating in the acceptance of social responsibility and trusteeship.

In addition to political and public influences, the technique rationale was given impetus by economic necessity which, to a considerable extent, hastened the utilization of tools and techniques made available by scientific management, industrial psychology, and personnel management. Many of these techniques facilitated proper employee selection, placement, and evaluation, thereby increasing the proper utilization of human resources and employee satisfaction. Such advantages, in conjunction with numerous welfare measures, were often perceived as an effective means of preventing unionization or of at least confining the union to a weak, ineffective position. Whether unionized or not, however, the technique philosophy had become the basic rationale for many executives. A model of this technique personnel philosophy follows:

1. Leadership. The typical executive is an authoritarian figure whose philosophical foundation for management resides in the freedom of contract and the right of private property, even though in many enterprises he acts on the behalf of absentee stockholders rather than personal ownership. However, top management regards itself as a representative not only of the stockholders but also of labor and the public—a sense of trusteeship. Sound public, consumer, and personnel relations are frequently complementary goals to the objective of profit maximization.

Although insistent upon maintaining managerial prerogatives and exercising unilateral direction and control, management is acutely aware of potential social and legal pressures if they fail to maintain a favorable image in the eyes of the public. The status quo is no longer defended with the tenacity previously displayed.

The techniques provided by the social sciences and scientific management are adopted and utilized in the solution of personnel and production problems; however, the philosophy and behavioral concepts from these sources are generally ignored. Scientific knowledge and skills have been applied primarily for promoting efficiency, manipulation, and control, and for adjusting the employee to organizational demands.

Technical efficiency and personnel relations are perceived as interrelated, but the personnel concept is extremely narrow.

In personnel relations, management has relied upon authority to achieve cooperation rather than having provided an organizational environment conducive to soliciting the interest, drive, and initiative of employees.

Minimal reliance is placed upon employees within the organization since they are perceived as incapable of contributing little more than their physical services to achieve company objectives. Therefore, management depends primarily upon the initiative and judgment of managers at the top of the hierarchy or staff officials and has relied upon close direction and a rigorous system of controls to attain goals.

2. Personnel Management. Top management accepts the ultimate responsibility for personnel relations, and personnel management is accepted as a proper function of management.

Personnel policy is formulated and properly communicated to insure consistency, fairness, and the elimination of discrimination. In addition to being a sound personnel practice, this procedure and the personnel program in general are perceived as essential to good public relations.

The personnel program contains the essential elements of personnel management, accompanied by the requisite techniques, many of which fail to contribute to sound human relations.

The ethical, philosophical, and behavioral foundations of personnel administration have been ignored. Consequently, personnel management is mechanistic, i.e., emphasis is placed upon personnel practices and procedures rather than upon people within the organization.

3.   Concepts of Labor.

Uniqueness. The employee is considered unique, i.e., possessing different physical, mental, and personality characteristics that may be matched with job requirements, thereby facilitating the achievement of higher productivity and profits.

Since one of the greatest developable resources lies in the abilities of employees, this resource is protected by an adequate work environment and utilized with discretion.

If employees are properly selected, trained, and compensated, job satisfaction will automatically follow.

Consumer-public. Each employee is a consumer of industrial products and a member of the general public to whom industry acknowledges specific social responsibilities. Furthermore, poor employee relations invite the hostility of both consumers and the public, as well as employees who are essentially members of these groups.

Partnership (optional). Emphasizing the financial side of the employment and the importance placed upon economic motives, stock ownership and/or profit sharing are devices used to secure an identification with company objectives, cultivate cooperation, and develop the mutual interests of employees and management.

4.   Incentives. The motivational approach is founded upon an individualistic conception of personnel and is centralized around economic motives.

Employee relations are recognized as an important social responsibility but one that is discharged primarily by programs centered about economic incentives which, in addition to adequate compensation, include hospital and medical services, sickness and accident insurance, life insurance, and pension fund contributions.

Supervisory direction relies upon authority to secure production and compliance with work and other managerial directives.

Restrictive or close supervisory leadership provides detailed working instructions and close checks on performance. Therefore, the employee is placed in an excessively dependent relationship with his superior.

Supervisory direction fails to convey recognition and appreciation of the broad range of human needs that seek expression and which would lead to greater employee growth, development, achievement, and independence.

Work group cohesion and informal groupings are perceived

as a threat to supervisory authority and in opposition to formal goals and objectives.

5. Labor Relations. A legalistic labor relations policy prevails whereby management rigidly follows the legal requirements governing labor-management relations; however, no positive advantages are perceived as emanating from employee representation or collective bargaining.

In order to maintain its position of power and preserve its prerogatives, management endeavors to work around the union, even on matters that are of joint interest. Furthermore, the union is not regarded as an acceptable channel of communication.

The company works to build "company-mindedness" among all employees through recognition of the employee as an individual. This individualistic approach is extended to competition with the union for the loyalty of employees.

A dichotomy exists between personnel and labor relations; i.e., personnel activities are utilized as a means for neutralizing the union's effectiveness and/or preventing its further growth. Management is engaged in covert feuding with representatives selected by its employees, and at the same time it is attempting to cultivate employee goodwill and cooperation through its personnel program.

Evaluation of the Technique Rationale. As with the do-nothing philosophy, the technique rationale will also be evaluated in terms of its ability to precipitate an organizational setting which will facilitate the satisfaction of safety, social, self-esteem, status-prestige, and self-actualization needs. The technique personnel philosophy, with emphasis on written policy and its consistent administration of activities, does much to facilitate gratification of employees' safety needs. Employment security and financial rewards, including extensive fringe benefits, are basic tenets which enhance economic security. However, the dependent relationship, especially that of supervisor-employee, prevents the gratification of safety needs to the extent possible and psychologically desirable. Restrictive or close supervision and the concomitant employee subordinate relationship precipitates a climate of potential threat and deprivation. Since the employee is subject to wage, promotion, and transfer evaluations, his psychological security leaves much to be desired. Such limitations may be further compounded by such communication problems as management's failure to inform the employee of where he stands with reference to performance and promotion possibilities.

If the firm's employees are represented by a union, some of the barriers to the gratification of safety needs are lowered since organized labor has dedicated itself to the protection of employees against arbitrary and discriminatory supervisory or managerial practices. Consequently the employee feels less dependent upon management; his safety needs are augmented by the union's presence, even though the tone of labor relations is a legalistic one.

As a result of both pressure by organized labor and independent top executive action, many managements have accepted social responsibilities for employees. This is manifested by a concern for the physical safety, economic security, and job security of workers. Consequently, the opportunity for fulfilling the safety needs of employees is further augmented. However, despite the presence of a mixture of positive and negative influences, the overall results are such that the safety needs are relatively satisfied.

In the technique personnel philosophy, social needs are not utilized as part of the motivational framework in establishing personnel relations. Management perceives the work group, both formal and informal, as opposed to company goals and objectives. At best management strives to cultivate bonds of belonging or association with the company by acquainting employees with the firm's products and consumer needs served by his productive efforts. Some companies, by means of an orientation program, seek to facilitate job adjustment by a buddy system or other means of introducing the employee to his foreman, work associates, and work area. However, such efforts are extremely gross in terms of utilizing basic social forces and needs to increase employee satisfaction.

Consequently, social needs are partially met by interactions at an informal level, occurring without direct, or in spite of, managerial efforts. Job design or work flow may require a high level of interaction, thereby facilitating social relationships. Workers will engage in a certain amount of non-work social activities at such times as during coffee breaks and rest periods. Thus, ignorance, lack of concern, or formal opposition to the social phenomenon of work does not fully block gratification of some social needs.

Since the technique rationale emphasizes the human abilities of each employee and utilizes personnel tools to bring about a closer coincidence of job requirements and individual capacities, the self-esteem of the employee is enhanced by the development of self-confidence, achievement, competence, and knowledge. Job competence likewise becomes a mean for winning the respect and recognition of associates, which enhances the worker's status and prestige.

However, conflicting forces are present that operate against the expression of status-prestige needs. Since this ego need is related to "other-esteem," or respect from others, the supervisory climate is of extreme importance. Supervisory direction which fails to convey recognition, appreciation, or respect, the reliance upon authority to secure cooperation, and the emphasis upon close supervision and control place severe limitations on additional ego gratification from task performance. Consequently, although employees find some ego gratification, a large gap remains between the status-prestige needs and their actual gratification.

An additional force working against the expression of self-esteem and status-prestige needs, if the employees in the enterprise are organized, is the potential lack of balance in employee and labor relations. If management's attention and concern have been devoted almost exclusively to collective relationships with its employees, to the extent of ignoring its relationship with employees individually, management has failed to build the confidence and goodwill of employees through the recognition of individual status and self-esteem. Therefore, an overall work environment obtains in which the safety and self-esteem needs are relatively satisfied, the status-prestige and social needs are only minimally gratified, and the self-actualization needs are not activated.

SUMMARY

The pressures of public opinion and a governmental labor policy compelled many industrial executives to adopt a more humanistic philosophy of personnel administration. The necessity for such compulsion was indicative of the extent to which a do-nothing or technique rationale of personnel management had dominated industrial practices prior to 1930. Industrialists had been insensitive to community and employee values, but unprecedented political, economic, and social upheavals precipitated a reevaluation. Public relations became a basic personnel function as employers sought to demonstrate the identity of interests between business and the community. Furthermore, sound human personnel relations were made the basis for public relations as managements became conscious of the need for public goodwill.

An unprecedented number of employers accepted responsibility for the economic and psychological welfare of their employees. Evidence of this was seen in the evaluation of personnel executives to a level equal to that of production managers and in the former's subsequent utilization on policy committees which considered employee values and interests before executive action was taken. Additionally, there was a proliferation of written policies stating management's intended standard of treatment toward employees. Such policies defined employee rights and protected employee interests. Intelligent and comprehensive policies were increasingly deemed to be a basic foundation for sound personnel relations. In committing such objectives to writing, executives were abandoning personnel management by expediency, which could be shifted daily to meet personnel problems in a manner most advantageous to management.

In addition to the above development, there was a growing tendency to consider consultation, but to a lesser extent participation in the decision-making function, compatible with industrial operations; executives, however, were slow to visualize and implement their responsibilities stemming from this new orientation. The social philosophy of Elton Mayo's Hawthorne investigations revealed the necessity for consultation and participation at the rank-and-file level, but this viewpoint was not widely accepted. Many executives who were sincerely concerned with the welfare and the human aspirations of employees failed to recognize or to accept the growth of democratic ideals in industry. Even administrators who embraced a humanistic philosophy of personnel administration which recognized the need for ego satisfaction and personal development of the individual employee could not accept democratic procedures as a serious or promising method in personnel relations.

The employee was approached with newly found consideration as employers accepted a consumer concept of labor. Not only was the worker entitled to treatment as a human being with specific rights, but he was also a consumer and a member of the public to whom industry was acknowledging responsibilities. Sound consumer and labor relations increasingly were made complementary goals to the objective of profit maximization. Executives were inclined to consider themselves as trustees who must properly balance the rights and interests of the public, stockholders, and employees. Whereas management had previously been associated with ownership, it was now becoming synonymous with a trusteeship which identified with the long-run continuity and public welfare objectives of industry. Neither the employees nor the public should be exploited solely for financial interests.

VI

THE HUMANISTIC ERA OF
PERSONNEL PHILOSOPHY—PART I

Having determined how personnel philosophy was affected by
economic and political pressures in a decade of depression, we enter
a humanistic era, so called because of the extensive acceptance of
old as well as some new principles of motivation and behavior.
Paternalistic and technique personnel philosophies were still much
in evidence, but the period being considered—1940 to 1960—is
most notable for the rapid and widespread utilization of psychological insights into human behavior manifested on the job.

Developments in the humanistic era were so extensive that two
chapters must be devoted to documenting and evaluating the most
significant events. The present chapter will examine the impact of
industry's newly perceived social responsibilities upon a philosophy
of management and, in turn, the latter's relationship to a humanistic
personnel philosophy. Newer concepts from the social sciences—
group dynamics, employee participation, and democratic leadership—will be examined for their relevance to the humanistic rationale. Finally, the present chapter will examine the implications of a
cooperative approach to labor-management relations and the impact
of this viewpoint upon personnel philosophy.

PHILOSOPHY OF MANAGEMENT
AND THE HUMANISTIC VIEWPOINT

During the 1930's, industry developed a consciousness of social
responsibilities, a realization of motives and objectives other than
profits; good public, community, consumer, and employee relations

170

became complementary industrial objectives. The philosophy of social responsibility had grown partly because business leaders of their own conviction had promoted it and partly because of governmental legislation and union pressure. Growth of this social justice concept was not a passing phenomenon of the 1930's but continued to spread throughout industry. A humanistic personnel philosophy for executives to employ had developed most rapidly in the context of social responsibilities. These responsibilities were slowly integrated into a creed that stated management's obligation to all directly and indirectly concerned with industry. Therefore, in the expressions of managerial philosophy, one frequently finds separate sections devoted to personnel, the public, and stockholders, and to the relationship of these groups to profits. In the 1930's, such statements were isolated and not very specific, and there were few attempts to integrate these into one basic philosophy; such integration primarily took place after 1940.

Social Responsibilities—Context for a Humanistic Philosophy. The groups to whom managements owed responsibilities were seen as interdependent. One finds numerous rationales of management that include all parties involved. A typical example is the following expression of managerial obligations which includes the company's personnel philosophy:

The goal of management is the optimum development of the opportunity to serve society, specifically the customers, the investors, the employees, and the community of the Charles Beck Machine Corporation.

To serve customers by:

1. Continually enhancing our knowledge of their and allied fields.
2. Analyzing their requirements, and providing products best adapted to their needs.
3. Producing products of maximum value, at the lowest practical prices.
4. Providing technical assistance and service facilities at all

times in order to maintain maximum performance of our products.

5. Carrying on continuous research and development on new and existing products.

To serve investors by:

1. Obtaining the highest profit potential.
2. Realizing over-all long-term growth, expansion, and diversification.

To serve employees by:

1. Encouraging and fostering individual advancement and high employee morale.
2. Giving each job meaning and dignity.
3. The appreciation that the employee's standards of living, security, and welfare are intimately linked with the welfare of the company.

To serve the community by:

1. Carrying the company's fair share of community financial responsibility.
2. Encouraging employee participation in worthwhile community endeavors and organizations.
3. Encouraging employee membership and participation in related technical and trade associations.

The attainment of these objectives will insure maximum realization of business leadership as a public trust.[1]

Management had found that employee relations were vitally linked with public, community, and consumer relations, and as businessmen sought to apply their sense of social responsibility, it began with the worker. Hines H. Baker, executive vice-president of Humble Oil and Refining Company, reflected the prevalent viewpoint in 1948 when he stated: ". . . employee relations are fundamentally the results of the way a company 'lives.' If it is motivated by a desire to render a worthwhile service and seeks to treat all with whom it deals, including its employees, in a fair way, the company has laid the basis for good employee relations." [2]

[1] Stewart Thompson, "Management Creeds and Philosophies," *AMA Research Study* (1958), No. 32, pp. 100–101.
[2] Hines H. Baker, "Employee Relations and Top Management Planning," *AMA Personnel Series* (1948), No. 117, p. 9.

The relationship among profit motive, social responsibility, and personnel philosophy is disclosed by the following statement:

> Economic and social responsibilities are discharged by one and the same set of policies and practices. It is the manner in which we discharge our profit responsibilities that will decide how well we discharge our human responsibilities. Not to discharge the social responsibility is poor business; only people who are intelligently and decently treated will produce at their best. Not to discharge the economic responsibility is poor citizenship, since the promises of our American society will not be met if business fails.[3]

Community relations were similarly intertwined with company personnel policy and philosophy. Since the promotion of better employee relations is a basic tenet of personnel philosophy, good community relations assist in achieving these objectives. A survey of 196 companies indicated that the concept of being a good neighbor in the community had become increasingly important.[4] Most industrial firms reported that they believed a good reputation in the community was good business; it enhanced employee morale and general public relations, it provided better recruiting opportunities, and it often assured increased sales. Typical of many firms, the American Seating Company maintained that its community responsibilities and employee relations rationale had many principles in common.[5] Such emphasis upon community and public relations parallels the importance placed upon the consumer-public concept of labor by many managements today. It denotes a cognizance of the employee as a neighbor in his community, as a citizen, as a customer, and possibly as a shareholder.

A survey in 1945 of public relations in industry by the National Industrial Conference Board disclosed the "complete acceptance of

[3] Charles R. Hook, Jr., "Profits and People: The Personnel Function of Management," *AMA Personnel Series* (1950), No. 132, p. 4.

[4] Bureau of National Affairs, Inc., "Management's Good Neighbor Policies: Survey of Company Community Relations Programs," *Management Review* 43 (February, 1954), 2:75–77.

[5] Harry J. Kelly, "Basic Company Philosophy," *AMA Personnel Series* (1954), No. 159, pp. 36–39.

industry's responsibility for developing and maintaining good public relations." [6] Satisfactory management-employee relations were considered the most important single phase of public relations programs, customer relations second, community relationships third, and relations with stockholders were fourth in importance. This did not indicate, however, that industry as the trustees of stockholders, employees, and the public were not striving to give equitable consideration to all groups concerned; it was a matter of which one should be stressed under existing economic and industrial conditions. One company that placed stockholders last in importance in its public relations program stated: "If pleasant, appropriately publicized relations are maintained with our employees, residents in the community, the public at large and our customers, the stockholders' interests are being served." [7]

The recorded objectives of public relations programs, as revealed in the board's survey, are significant because they promote some of the same objectives as do stated philosophies of personnel administration. Major objectives were "keeping satisfactory employee-management relations, indicating the company's contribution to the general welfare, building confidence in the company's product, and promoting a belief in the free enterprise system." [8] Not only were public, community, and stockholder relations viewed as being related to healthy management-employer relations, they were integrated in many recorded management philosophies. Management's position tended to become that of a trustee seeking to maintain a balance between the various affected interests. Significantly, almost every aspect of such a trusteeship affected employees. This seems another definite indication of the trend for management to place the responsibility for personnel management on an equal plane with its obligations toward other groups.

[6] National Industrial Conference Board, "Industry's Public Relations Job," *Management Review* 34 (July, 1945), 7:245.
[7] *Ibid.*
[8] *Ibid.*

Personnel Philosophy in the Context of Managerial Philosophy. Some managerial philosophies are very detailed and lengthy as they state company beliefs and responsibilities to consumers, public, and employees. Rather than present the complete personnel rationale of any one company, since they tend to be repetitious, a sample of statements pertaining to employees as contained within broader management philosophies will be presented.

CROWN CORK AND SEAL COMPANY, INC.

Establish the view that our greatest assets are our human assets and these must be developed as a matter of moral obligation and material advantage.

Reward, encourage progress, fully inform, train and develop, and properly assign all employees in order that their lives and work be given meaning, dignity, satisfaction, and purpose both on and off the job.

H. J. HEINZ COMPANY

A sound organization structure in which each position is clearly defined is essential to the attainment of our objectives.

We will maintain personnel policies embodying continuous concern for the adequacy of compensation, including insurance, retirement and other employee benefits, and working environment.

Inspiring leadership and effective teamwork are essential.

CLUETT, PEABODY AND COMPANY, INC.

We must continuously raise the level of our administrative and technical skills and create the kind of environment in which all of our employees can develop and prepare for greater responsibilities. This constant improvement and growth on the part of individuals will cause the Company to grow and provide better jobs for more people and greater earnings for our stockholders.

Management must think in terms of people—first, last, and always—and must act in a way that will strengthen rather than weaken the individual dignity of every man and woman in the organization.[9]

PROCTER AND GAMBLE

Successful business—one that earns regular profits.

The chance for the employee to become a capitalist himself (by

[9] Thompson, *op. cit.,* pp. 104, 107, 116.

becoming a part-owner of the business, or accumulating bonds, savings, etc.).[10]

GILLETTE SAFETY RAZOR COMPANY

Adjust all complaints of every kind promptly and fairly.

Assure each employee the right to discuss with management any matter concerning his welfare.[11]

The above abbreviated statements from personnel philosophies clearly convey the importance placed upon the human factor and the policies requisite to implementing such viewpoints are outlined in broad terms. Equally significant, these rationales reflect some of the basic components of a humanistic philosophy as well as several underlying concepts of labor. Basically individualistic in orientation, these humanistic philosophies are founded upon the "unique" or "individual differences" concept of labor. Success of the business is recognized as being partially contingent upon the different capabilities of individuals comprising the work force. Employers implement the unique concept of labor by modern employment techniques, training, and promotion. Consequently, employee morale is enhanced, job satisfaction increased, and at the same time, higher productivity is usually realized for the company.

Additionally, the humanistic personnel philosophy rests firmly upon the humanistic concept of labor which approaches the problem of production from a human point of view and upon concern for the psychological welfare of employees. Therefore, those organizations quoted above seek to aid employees in achieving the latter's needs, desires, and personal aspirations. Recognizing the fact that employees are entitled to considerate and understanding treatment, management endeavors to assist them in achieving self-respect, a sense of personal worth and dignity, status, and a feeling of "belonging" within the totality of the industrial operation.

The foregoing rationales also are consistent with the tenets for a

[10] William G. Werner, "Sixty-Two Years of Profit Sharing at Procter and Gamble," *Management Review* 39 (October, 1950), 10:601.

[11] Paul L. Davis, "Are Personnel Policies Different in a Non-Union Plant?" *AMA Management Report* (1957), No. 1, pp. 72–73.

personnel philosophy outlined by J. S. Parker, vice-president of the General Electric Company:

Perhaps the first requirement of a workable personnel philosophy is that it accord with national traditions. In addition, it should permit employees to satisfy their work-oriented needs, allow for individual differences, encourage self-development, and bolster self-respect. It should encourage rising productivity and business efficiency while at the same time upholding the dignity and rights of individual employees. It should recognize the contribution of business to our socio-economic system and, of course, be compatible with the institutions of a free country and the ways and spirit of free men.[12]

Because the focus of such a philosophy is upon the individual employee, who is more conscious of his own needs, rights, and obligations than anyone else, it is psychologically sound. It is sound from the standpoint of morality, since it "is morally right to uphold the dignity of the individual, to respect his rights, and to be responsive to him as an individual." [13] Finally it is economically sound, because individual attitudes are the primary determinants of the skill and efforts an employee gives to his work, except when impeded by union rules or other group restrictions. In personnel relations, the fundamental economic and human unit is the individual. "We would all agree that the individual is at the root of all human problems in business. And one ultimate aim of management's personnel function is the increase of individual productivity through individual satisfaction and motivation." [14] The humanistic philosophy of personnel administration is considered successful because it is based upon the "recognition of employees as individuals possessing human attributes and frailties, and, as such, entitled to treatment in accordance with the dignity and finesse that this distinction justifies." [15]

Implementing the Humanistic Philosophy. Obviously in light of

[12] J. S. Parker, "The Individual in Industry: An Investment in the Future," *AMA Management Report* (1958), No. 24, p. 52.
[13] *Ibid.,* p. 53.
[14] Hook, *op. cit.,* p. 8.
[15] Davis, *op. cit.,* p. 73.

a high degree of industrial specialization, increasing the individual's satisfaction and motivation presents a formidable task, but numerous managements have undertaken to cope with such difficulties by a program of human relations that facilitates the implementation of a humanistic concept of labor. A survey by the Bureau of National Affairs of 180 personnel and industrial relations officials revealed that these executives felt that management could create a perception of job importance by making sure each employee understands not only the relationship of his job to others in the department and the company, but also how his task affects succeeding tasks or the end product.[16] Such action should be supplemented by conveying the end uses of the product to the employee and the community in an effort to instill pride in his contribution.

A human relations program as structured by the BNA survey respondents would also include devoting attention or giving recognition to the individual employee; this task would begin with an employee's proper selection. Following appropriate selection, the objective of worker recognition would be accomplished by providing an opportunity for promotion and self-development; recognition of individual merit, coupled with fair and just performance ratings; informing employees of new developments and changes; and finally by providing an opportunity to contribute ideas that would be carefully considered by management. Additionally, a possible change of work assignments, including job rotation and/or job enlargement, was judged an effective means of enhancing worker interest.

Finally, work was to be made interesting and psychologically rewarding; each supervisor would demonstrate a personal interest in the employee as a human being. This objective was to be achieved by training foremen in human relations. As stated by one respondent of the survey: "When the supervisor . . . shows this interest clearly and consistently—in daily job contacts, application and explanation of policy, individual coaching and rating interviews, action on grievances, etc.,—the work, whatever it is, will become interest-

16 Fred H. Joiner, "Making Employees' Work More Interesting," *Personnel* 29 (January, 1953), No. 4, pp. 309–13.

ing by becoming integrated with the employees' personal goals of growth and achievement." [17]

The Role of Supervision in a Humanistic Philosophy. The study summarized above and a myriad of other investigations since Elton Mayo's Hawthorne studies have pointed to the foreman's role as a key one in good human relations. The viewpoint has been accepted by many executives that "it is the constructive day-to-day relationship between immediate supervision and employees which determines the amount of satisfaction that an employee derives from his work situation." [18] Supervisors, accordingly, need and have received training not only in the mechanics of production, but also in the areas of human relations.[19] The nature of the workaday relationship has a place of paramount importance in the humanistic personnel philosophy, often being most effective in distinguishing it from an authoritarian one. An arbitrary use of authority is not practiced; leadership consists of motivating rather than driving. Some of the characteristics of supervision consistent with the promotion of employee productivity and satisfaction were disclosed in a survey of 114 companies.[20] Executives who favored more general instructions and major emphasis on objectives and results outnumbered two to one those who favored detailed working instructions and a close check on performance. Significantly, and a basic requisite for general supervision, was the disclosure that nine-tenths of the respondents endorsed a policy of decentralized authority, with maximum initiative and responsibility given to supervisors at all levels, as the setting required to promote greater productivity. Nearly 80 percent of the executives indicated their companies were pursuing such a decentralization policy.

---

[17] *Ibid.,* p. 312.

[18] Garrett L. Bergen, "War's Lessons in Personnel Administration," *AMA Personnel Series* (1954), No. 94, p. 31.

[19] H. W. Anderson, "Supervisory Personnel Program of the General Motors Corporation," *AMA Personnel Series* (1944), No. 78, pp. 3–5.

[20] Bureau of National Affairs, "Raising Employee Productivity, A Survey of Company Practices," *Management Review* 48 (February, 1959), no. 2, pp. 29–31.

In addition, there has been a persistent growing recognition of the foreman's role in facilitating the full and free flow of information and ideas between employer and employee.[21] Managements are cognizant of the necessity for lower supervisory levels to channel upward the workers' viewpoints and problems if their companies' human relations programs are to remain sensitive to changing conditions and are to achieve the desired results. Foremen and departmental supervisors are admonished to get into the communications stream as active participants; employees not only want to be informed of events and conditions which affect them and their families, but they have a right to this information.[22]

Group Dynamics and Humanistic Philosophy. Concomitant with the increasing emphasis placed upon the foreman's leadership role, there has developed a considerable body of research pertaining to the social nature and structure of the work group supervised. Commencing with the Hawthorne investigation, numerous studies in social psychology and group dynamics have demonstrated the importance of group or social phenomena to an understanding of organizational behavior and the important contribution work groups, as a social unit, may make in facilitating the achievement of departmental and company objectives. In 1949, Alfred J. Marrow, president of the Harwood Manufacturing Company, made the following observation:

Within the present decade, however, there has developed a growing interest in the importance of interpersonal relationships in industry. . . . The individual is no longer to be studied as an isolated unit but in relation to his environment as he interacts with those about him. The industrial organization is considered as a unit, governed by laws of social interaction. And if we would treat properly the personnel ills which beset us, we must first determine the social

---

[21] J. J. Evans, Jr., "Interchanging Ideas Between Management and Employees," *Personnel Series* (1941), No. 46, pp. 8–19.
[22] Kelly, *op. cit.*, p. 38.

structure of our industrial organization . . . by so doing we create a healthy social unit.[23]

Some executives are cognizant that the success of an enterprise is partially dependent upon how well each of the number of small groups comprising the organization does its job. Additionally, the effectiveness of the small group is seen as dependent upon the group's supervisor, the relationship between individuals within the group, and finally, upon the external influences on the group from top management, other groups, the union, and community influences.[24]

Significantly, the key figure in achieving a balance among these relationships and securing an alignment of group and management objectives is the supervisor. There also exists an awareness that the tendency of work groups to form a cohesive unit may affect productivity according to the Bureau of National Affairs survey cited earlier. A majority of executives, nearly 4 to 1, considered the tendency of employees to "stick together" as a useful means of raising productivity rather than as a obstacle.[25] However important a concept for industry it may be, group cohesiveness, with its implications for productivity, is only one facet of group dynamics. And, at the present time, there is little concrete evidence that managements have seriously looked upon their organizations as social structures composed of various sub-groups or have attempted to utilize group forces effectively.

This blind spot in management's portfolio of human relations principles is revealed in several ways. First, there appears to be a lack of awareness of the individual employee's social needs; this is revealed by the frequent omission of any mention of social needs whenever an effort is made to catalogue human needs or what the

[23] Alfred J. Marrow, "Human Factors in Production," *Personnel* 25 (March, 1949), 5:342.
[24] Guy B. Arthur, "A Scrutiny of Personnel Practices," *Personnel Series* (1947), No. 111, pp. 6–15.
[25] Bureau of National Affairs, "Raising Employee Productivity, A Survey of Company Practices," 29–31.

worker wants from his job.[26] Secondly, if social work group phenomena were accorded serious importance, one would expect to find a sizable portion of supervisory human relations programs devoted to understanding and dealing with work group problems, since such managerial personnel are most intimately involved in such group dynamics. However, it is doubtful if this has been the case. One observer has drawn the following conclusion:

While there was and still is a remarkable range in the content, methods, and settings of these programs, nearly all of them have centered around improving supervisory skills in dealing with people—either as individuals or in face-to-face groups. They are frequently directed at teaching the supervisor how to work with an employee as an individual, occasionally at working with employees as members of a small group, but only rarely at understanding and working within the complex social system of the larger corporation or factory. Another way of saying this is that the courses have drawn heavily from psychology, to a lesser extent from social psychology, and usually not at all from sociology.[27]

In addition, the literature found in personnel journals reflects the lack of serious efforts to integrate the social concepts of the behavioral sciences into the body of knowledge of personnel management. Such an examination is found primarily in textbooks or specialized, professional journals and seems to indicate that many of the newer concepts have not become a significant part of personnel managers' or executives' approach to analyzing daily employee problems, at least to the extent that philosophical tenets have been predicated

[26] For a representative listing of human needs and personal aspirations as seen by industrialists, see the following: Richard C. Smyth, "Practical Philosophy of Labor Relations," *Personnel* 27 (September, 1950), No. 2, p. 103; C. L. Huston, Jr., "Design for the Future Industrial Relations," *Personnel* 20 (July, 1943), No. 1, p. 27; Harry A. Bullis, "Personnel Is People," *Management Review* 38 (June, 1949), No. 6, p. 306; Ralph J. Cordiner, "Breakthrough to the Future," *Management Review* 45 (August, 1956), No. 8, p. 681; James J. Nance, "Top Management Views the Job Ahead in Industrial Relations," *AMA Personnel Series*, No. 124, p. 38.

[27] Floyd C. Mann, "Studying and Creating Change: A Means to Understanding Social Organization," in Conrad M. Arensberg, et. al., *Research In Industrial Human Relations* (New York: Harper & Brothers Publishers, 1957), p. 149.

upon the newer social concepts or insights. "The use of the coordinated efforts of well-integrated work groups to achieve organizational objectives apparently requires greater leadership skills and a different philosophy of management than that generally prevailing today." [28]

Most managers are still inclined to look upon the individual as an economic unit, whose behavior is influenced and controlled primarily by economic considerations and individual differences, rather than as an individual strongly motivated and influenced by his immediate work groups. Other executives would not deny the importance of group relations, but are deeply convinced that individual personal relations should be the primary subject of human relations.[29] And while it appears that a better understanding of employee relations has been made possible by considering the primary work group, it has tended at the same time to generate some confusion. "*The vacuum lies in the need for integrating the received truths of individualism with those of group relations among workers at work.*" [30] Another executive reflected the confusion between individual and group motivations when he said: ". . . there is a wide difference of opinion even among progressive management about what the individual does want and need from business, about what makes him tick and produce effectively. Most of us would agree, however, that the answer lies somewhere between the concept of the worker as an 'economic man' interested only in his pay check and that of the school of Elton Mayo." [31]

Group Dynamics—Participation and Democratic Leadership. Closely integrated with and paralleling much of the research pertaining to the social phenomena of industrial organizations has been

[28] Rensis Likert, *New Patterns of Management* (New York: McGraw-Hill Book Co., Inc., 1961), p. 38.

[29] Fowler McCormick, "American Business and Its Human Relations." *AMA Personnel Series* (1947), No. 106, pp. 3–8.

[30] Rensis Likert, quoted in George S. Odiorne, "The Clique—A Frontier in Personnel Management," *Personnel* 34 (September, October, 1957), 2:40.

[31] Hook, *op. cit.,* p. 8.

study of the concept of work group participation and the democratic leadership requisite for its promotion. Studies by Harvard and Michigan universities, as well as numerous other investigations in social psychology, have demonstrated the important contributions work groups, as a social unit, may make to an industrial organization, especially by taking part in the decision-making process. Such group participation, accompanied by democratic leadership, creates a permissive environment conducive to the personal involvement of employees when problems appropriate for its utilization arise. When problems amenable to participative solution present themselves, the foreman, as group leader, initiates the session by stating the problem, acknowledges all contributed comments without expressing agreement or disagreement, solicits the ideas of reticent employees, and accepts the attitudes and feelings of all group members as necessary for reaching an objective, acceptable solution. Therefore, rank-and-file employees engage in the decision-making process and their decision, not the supervisor's or management's, sets the course of action to be followed.[32] Such an approach to problem solution is the opposite of authoritarian leadership, which is characterized by unilateral decisions emanating from the top and flowing downward. It should also be noted that participation in the decision process is *not* just consultation in which the employees' opinions are solicited before a decision is reached, but the final decision is made by a member of management, not the employees.

Group participation is significant in an examination of personnel philosophy because it represents one manifestation of the citizenship concept of labor. The potential usefulness of such a labor concept resides in the ability of worker involvement to bring about a coincidence of company and personal goals, a basic objective of many managements. However, despite a general acceptance of some human relations principles, the concept of participation by work groups, which recognizes the employees' right to contribute to their ideas and abilities to the solution of common problems, has received

[32] Norman R. F. Maier, *Psychology in Industry* (2nd ed.; Boston: Houghton Mifflin Company, 1946), pp. 137–77.

little acceptance by executives who formulate philosophy and policy.[33] Sufficient time and validation of industrial experience apparently have not yet justified this system's inclusion into top management's consideration of policies and procedures. No philosophies of management or personnel rationales examined in the present investigation have explicitly stated a belief in employee participation. The democratic process, via participation, has not become a tenet of personnel rationale because of its incompatibility with strongly entrenched authoritarian principles. There still persists a strong tendency for individualistic concepts to predominate and while some appreciation of social or group factors appears evident in managerial thinking, little use has been made of employee group decisions.

Norman Maier, professor of psychology, states that most training in human relations is at the first level of supervision, since this group is an all-important determiner of employee morale. The supervisor is trained to secure cooperation and production by stimulating group participation and maximum satisfaction of workers' ego needs. Many such programs fail, however, because top executives fail to practice the same kind of human relations in dealing with their subordinates that they encourage supervisors to utilize with rank-and-file employees. Top management's attitude has tended to exclude itself from those actions required in the practice of good human relations and participative management.[34]

As a partial explanation for the limited use of democratic leadership, it has been suggested that there is a cultural lag between accumulated scientific knowledge and practice. Certainly this has been true of personnel administration in practice despite numerous studies in human relations.

Management ideology is traditionally authoritarian, and the official leaders at all hierarchical levels have been expected to be bosses. The democratic pattern of leadership, on the other hand, requires

[33] Reinhard Bendix, *Work and Authority in Industry* (New York: John Wiley & Sons, Inc., 1956), p. 319.
[34] Norman R. F. Maier, *Principles of Human Relations* (New York: John Wiley & Sons, Inc., 1952), pp. 1–3.

abandonment of the one-way edict, the take-it-or-leave-it philosophy which seems to be the essence of bossing. The new leadership at the working level embodies two-way communication, participation, consultation, and ego satisfactions.[35]

Another suggested reason for executives' failure to accept a democratic philosophy is that: ". . . the development of cooperation and participation to the degree proposed by Mayo and Lewin is not only something that American management lacks the skill to promote, but is also something management fears, since such a degree of cooperation and participation might bring on problems for both workers and executives that require more in terms of time and energy than they are prepared to devote to them." [36]

Industrialists have sought the elusive formula which would induce employees to cooperate in achieving the firm's objectives, and in doing so have become aware that cooperation was feasible only if the industrial process met the worker's needs. However, participation has not been extensively employed to give employees a sense of belonging, importance, or self-esteem. There appears to be considerable confusion as to how management can establish the proper relationship between itself and the individual employee and also the primary work group of which he is a member. Until the uncertainties between individualism and group relations are reconciled, there will be great hesitancy in utilizing the democratic process of participation. Consequently, no strong movement has yet developed toward adopting a more democratic rationale of personnel administration.

Herbert Eby, vice-president of personnel and industrial relations of Schenley Industries, Inc., indicated his misgivings about the human relations movement: "I sincerely believe that over the past decade we have had an overdose of 'human relations'—too much pampering of employees, as if our factories were quasi-social insti-

---

[35] John M. Pfiffner, "A Pattern for Improved Supervisory Leadership," *Personnel* 24 (January, 1948), 4:272.
[36] Eugene Emerson Jennings, "The Authoritarian Cultural Lag in Business," *Journal of the Academy of Management* 2 (August, 1959), 2:119.

tutions rather than business organizations. *Human relations has become a fetish which companies undertake in order to 'keep up to date.*' " [37] To the extent that companies have gotten into the human relations movement in order to keep up with others, there has been no basic change in viewpoint, and one would hardly expect to find the concepts of human relations incorporated in personnel philosophy or policy. Instead, the utilization of human relations is merely a cloak to temper a technique philosophy of personnel administration and yet make it appear consistent with accumulated scientific knowledge, as well as with employee and public sentiment for democratic ideals. Employers have adopted the language and a few techniques of human relations but not the social philosophy of Elton Mayo.

An Authoritarian Organizational Framework. Contrary to what one might expect, the humanistic, like the technique, philosophy of personnel administration is founded upon authoritarian principles and is implemented within an authoritarian structure. In the typical industrial organization, all authority flows from the top downward and is delegated so as to enforce, at lower organizational levels, policies and decisions which have been made by those in the upper echelons. Staff organizations have multiplied in order to impart specialized information to groups at or near the top of the managerial hierarchy who exercise the judgment and skill requisite to achieving company objectives. Quality decisions are thereby more likely assured. Consequently the employee's opportunity to contribute his native capacities to enterprise objectives is often thwarted by imposed authoritarian leaders and by the transfer of skill and responsibility to technicians.

Within the authoritarian organizational framework, however, one finds distinct differences between companies operating under a humanistic philosophy and those under a technique philosophy of personnel administration. While authority clothes the superior with the power to command subordinates to engage in activities necessary to

[37] Herbert O. Eby, "A Business-like Approach to Labor Relations," *AMA Management Report* (1958), No. 24, p. 65. Emphasis added.

achieve enterprise objectives, such authority is not used in an auto-cratic manner when a humanistic personnel philosophy sets the climate for work activities. An atmosphere prevails whereby, when conditions permit, subordinates are directed by means of persuasion, suggestion, requests, consultation, and, to a much lesser extent, participation in the decision-making process. While authority as utilized in the technique philosophy—bossism and direct orders—usually results in obedience, under the humanistic rationale or approach it results in cooperation. Although obedience insures minimal compliance, cooperation results in a job well done, since an approach to work direction has been used that taps the mainsprings of human motivation and satisfaction.

Furthermore, with a technique rationale of personnel, elaborate systems of control are established to guarantee that production is achieved efficiently and with a minimum of mistakes and delay. Little reliance is placed upon others in the organization, especially rank-and-file employees. ". . . There is sometimes a tendency to regard management's competence as a result not of experience and training, but of inherent superiority. This tacit conviction may be carried to the point where employees are believed to be incapable of understanding management's view, and therefore incapable of contributing more than their physical effort to achieve the company's purposes." [38]

The humanistic philosophy, on the other hand, recognizes that employees have abilities and potentialities that may be utilized in achieving the organization's objectives via more self-direction and self-control. While this seldom leads to group participation in the decision-making function at the employee level, it does much to augment feelings of achievement, self-respect, and identification with the company.

The achievement of such powerful human motivations and satis-

[38] Clinton S. Golden and Virginia D. Parker, *Causes of Industrial Peace* (New York: Harper and Brothers Publishers, 1949), 29–30.

factions throughout the entire organization starts with the very philosophy of management; the decentralization that recognizes the dignity and capacity of each individual. It is implemented in the structure of the organization, and of each position in the organization so that each position has its own responsibility and authority. It is implemented in the climate that prevails—and that is deliberately created—in the organizational components and in each man-to-manager relationship.[39]

It is significant that an authoritarian structure and administrative practices do not prevent the practice of a humanistic rationale of personnel administration, although perhaps setting definite limits to the human satisfactions that might accrue from it. Economic security is increased, job satisfaction enhanced, and employees accorded dignity and status. There is less abridgment of employee rights. Advocates of a humanistic philosophy generally take the following position: "Industry must remain basically authoritarian—at least for a long time to come. But that admission still leaves a lot of room for exploring the areas which can be made more democratic and individually satisfying." [40]

LABOR RELATIONS AND PERSONNEL PHILOSOPHY

As already shown, union management relations frequently have had a stormy developmental history. Traditionally the basic labor relations philosophy of many managements has been one of opposition toward organized labor and an insistence upon unilateral control as being consistent with the principles of private property and free enterprise. Furthermore, when ownership was separated from managerial control, management often justified its position by insisting that its obligations to stockholders would not permit bilateral arrangements unless the stockholders endorsed such action. Additionally, industry has considered it administrative folly to work cooperatively with a third party that had no responsibility if control

[39] Cordiner, *op. cit.,* pp. 671–85.
[40] Walter H. Wheeler, "A Challenge in Human Relations," *Management Review* 40 (March, 1951), 3:112–13.

were shared.[41] With such viewpoints as these dominating managerial thinking and behavior, a combative or conflict philosophy of labor relations was frequently observed.

A Cooperative Approach to Labor-Management Relations. From this context of conflicting forces and views, however, there emerged a philosophy of labor relations founded upon union-management co-operation. This denoted a significant deviation from the conflict and legalistic rationales based primarily upon legal compulsion and maintenance of the status quo. James De Camp Wise, president of Bigelow-Sanford Carpet Company Inc., summarized the transition as follows:

> . . . the philosophy of management toward industrial relations was largely unchanged in this country until the 1930's. In most cases the philosophy management was, until the 1930's, one of resentment toward unions, of non-acceptance of unions as organizations that served a useful function in our society. . . . Enactment of the NIRA in 1933 and the Wagner Act in 1935 forced recognition of the principle of unionism upon management in a very practical sense. Management's resentment of this change was at first marked. Gradually the philosophy of a large segment of management changed. At some time between active resentment over passage of the Wagner Act and its considered approval of the Taft-Hartley Act, a large segment of management recognized the need for a new philosophy.[42]

Much of the alteration in labor philosophy was attributed by De Camp Wise to the change in the composition of the managerial group. There had been a gradual separation of management from ownership, and the professional manager had emerged who possessed a broader background and a different conception of the managerial function. The modern executive served as a trustee of the interests of stockholder, public, and employees.

Coincident with the modification of labor policy, there was a re-

---

[41] John G. Turnbull, "A Study of the Management Prerogative Issue," *Personnel*, 25 (September, 1948), 2:106–24.

[42] James De Camp Wise, "Positive Management Action in Human Relations," *AMA Personnel Series* (1949), No. 124, pp. 22–23.

appraisal of the role of personnel administration. The newer viewpoint was

> ... sound personnel administration is neither advocated nor practiced for the purpose of thwarting the growth of unionism. Second, there is not the slightest degree of incompatibility between sound personnel administration and collective bargaining through the chosen representatives of employees. . . . The record clearly shows that collective action helps to achieve and maintain many of the objectives of sound personnel administration. Far from detracting from the magnitude and importance of the personnel function, the process of collective action adds to both by revealing defects in organization and administration, and increasing the incentives for constructive action.[43]

Many personnel programs were initiated during the depression to prevent unionization or, if that failed, to keep the union placated or weak. Consequently personnel administration became identified in the minds of many as anti-union in philosophy and function; after 1940, however, numerous personnel officials sought to correct this viewpoint.

One such personnel executive, seeking to correct the anti-union position associated with personnel administration, admonished, "We need to emphasize that personnel management is not antagonistic to union representation, it is complementary." [44] The Radio Corporation of America has acknowledged the interrelation between union and personnel functions by making union recognition and acceptance a tenet in its personnel philosophy.[45] Herbert Eby of Schenley Industries advocated "full and sincere recognition of the employees' choice of bargaining representatives." [46]

The above comments are directed at the legalistic rationale of labor relations, characteristic of the technique personnel philosophy, that utilizes the personnel function to oppose the union or as a means

[43] Spates, "The Competition of Leadership in a Welfare Economy," p. 9.

[44] E. H. Van Delden, "Toward A New Personnel Philosophy," *Personnel* 26 (November, 1949), 3:175.

[45] A. F. Watters, "Background of the RCA Program," *AMA Personnel Series* (1953), No. 154, pp. 11–13.

[46] Eby, *op., cit.,* p. 66.

of competing with the union for the loyalty of employees. Under such conditions there exists a dichotomy between personnel and labor relations. Similarly, many unions elect to align themselves against the personnel function.[47] Consequently there is a continual struggle to secure and hold the employees' loyalty, with personnel administration being utilized as a means to this end. The personnel program is structured, or so it is thought, to contain all the means for satisfying employees' needs and securing their loyalty. ". . . An opportunity exists for industry—the opportunity to fulfill by its own policies and their administration the fundamental desires of the workers in such a way that no executive need ask the question, 'Has our men's loyalty been lost to the unions.' " [48]

An alternative personnel viewpoint by management considers both individual and group relations, as structured by collective bargaining, equally important. Labor relations do not exclude employee relations. This trend toward the integration of personnel and labor relations philosophy will probably increase since managements are beginning to realize that cooperation with the union as well as with individual employees is necessary to secure greater efficiency and higher productivity. Employees cannot be expected to cooperate if their union and its representatives are under continual attack by management. Personnel relations attempting to promote cooperation with employees but utilizing conflict in its union relations is too inconsistent to win general acceptance.

A more cooperative rationale toward unions was reflected in the comment of John A. Stephens, vice-president of industrial relations of United States Steel Corporations: "A labor relations philosophy, we believe, must have as its objective improvement in the efficiency of the business involved. It must be sincerely accepted by those who work within it. It should comprehend principles and practices to encourage employee and union understanding, enthusiastic and coop-

[47] Solomon Barkin, "A Trade Unionist Appraises Management Personnel Philosophy," *Harvard Business Review* 38 (September, 1950), No. 5, pp. 59–64.
[48] Huston, *op. cit.*, pp. 24–31.

erative effort to improve the business." [49] Significantly, this position was based upon an understanding and regard for the rights and responsibilities of the union and dedicated to cooperation. Additionally, conflict as a basis for union-management relationships was repudiated, as was maintaining a legalistic stand at all costs on abstract principles such as management prerogatives.[50] This position was indicative of a cooperative rationale and definitely a departure from the conflict and legalistic philosophies of labor relations. A similar rationale was expressed by F. M. Rich, general manager of Indiana Harbor Works, Inland Steel Company: "We also believe that the existence of properly managed unions is a necessary part of our American system. Our policy has been, and is, to work with the union on a fair, humane, and businesslike basis. We want to achieve mutual understanding and respect, which will, in turn, bring cooperation." [51]

A significant tenet of the cooperative labor relations philosophy is the recognition that the employee as a union member need not feel antagonistic toward management, that workers need not be classified either as pro-union or pro-management. Rather, some top managements take a position similar to Raytheon Manufacturing Company. "The company believes that employees can have dual loyalties, just as a foreman must have loyalty to his employees as well as to the management. This duality need not present serious conflict or create adversaries." [52]

A labor union, considered as a group, does not preclude sound employer relations with individuals; both are deemed necessary for cooperation and harmony. As John Stephens of U.S. Steel indicated, "We want good relationships with individual employees, with employees as a group, and with their union. . . . We see labor-

[49] John A. Stephens, "Labor Relations in United States Steel," *AMA Series* (1955), No. 164, p. 35.

[50] *Ibid.*, p. 46.

[51] F. M. Rich, "A Businessman's Management Philosophy," *Journal of the Academy of Management* 2 (August, 1959), 2:95–96.

[52] Leslie E. Woods, "Ten Years of Labor Peace at Raytheon," *Personnel Series* (1957), No. 172, pp. 37–45.

management relations in two dimensions, the individual and the group." [53] The philosophy of Schick, Inc., closely resembles that of U.S. Steel with respect to integrating labor and individual employee relations. One of the objectives requisite to the achievement of its labor relations philosophy is: "To have generally satisfied employees and to secure and maintain the respect and confidence of employees and their representatives. This objective is perhaps the most important, since all the others are dependent upon it." [54] At Schick, Inc., personnel administration is a major managerial function that aids top management in achieving its basic philosophy.

The Radio Corporation of America has a personnel philosophy that clearly depicts both group and individual employee relationships. It is predicated on the following beliefs:

1. The belief that the loyal cooperation of our employees is of basic importance to the success and progress of our business.
2. The maintenance in all units of competent personnel administration.
3. Employment on the basis of qualifications, without regard to race, color, or creed.
4. Promotion from within as determined from such factors as character, dependability, skill, intelligence, and physical fitness.
5. Payment of wages at levels comparable to those paid for similar classes of work in the areas in which our plants and operations are located.
6. *Where employees choose to bargain collectively, a policy of dealing willingly and frankly with their authorized representatives.*[55]

Investigations of factors contributing to industrial peace, based upon thirteen case studies, revealed as one of the primary causes an acceptance of collective bargaining and of the union as an institution. Collective bargaining was felt to have positive values and definite advantages accrued from bargaining with a well-disciplined union. In addition, top management accepted personnel administration as having equal importance with the financial and technical

---

[53] Stephens, *op. cit.*, p. 46.
[54] Smyth, *op. cit.*, p. 103.
[55] Watters, *op. cit.*, p. 13. Emphasis added.

functions of business. Furthermore, an attitude toward individual workers that reflected a concern for their welfare and a recognition of their needs and feelings was found to be another significant cause of industrial peace. A management philosophy founded upon sincere acceptance of collective bargaining, responsibility for personnel administration, and the human needs of employees contributed to industrial peace and harmony under collective bargaining.[56]

Additionally, it should be noted that the cooperative rationale of labor does not imply the complete absence of conflict, as there are always bound to be differences of interests. Taking a positive approach, management strives to separate the areas of conflict from those of non-conflict and concentrates on those problems involving mutual interests. This approach is facilitated when

1. Both organizations respect each other's sincerity and live up to their respective responsibilities.
2. Both organizations deal in principles, not expediency, with both concerned about solving mutual problems and meeting employee needs.
3. Both organizations are strong—but if one is stronger than the other, the stronger exercises appropriate self-restraint.
4. Both organizations recognize that fundamental to the success of each is the success of both.[57]

Therefore, the cooperative philosophy assimilates the diversity and similarity of interests into the management of employer-union relations and strives to deal with such interests constructively. The Esso Standard Oil Company, in a statement of its principles, takes the following position.

Mutual Acceptance: We believe that employees, their union, and management need to accept each other as individuals and as groups and need to respect each others' functions and responsibilities.

Common Interest: We believe that employees, their union, and management are bound together by a common interest—the ability

---

[56] Golden and Parker, *op. cit.*, pp. 29–30.
[57] Edward L. Cushman, "You Must Bargain for Yourself," *Personnel Series* (1956), No. 166, pp. 36–43.

of their unit to operate successfully and that opportunity and security for the individual depend upon this success.[58]

At Esso, union and management goals, especially long-range ones, are not incompatible, and the common interests of all parties provide a foundation for cooperation that will go far beyond the minimum legal requirements.

However, the cooperative rationale which embraces the development of mutual acceptance, responsibilities, and interests is not the most popular approach to labor relations by industrial executives or union officials. There is a reserved, reluctant acceptance of the institution of unionization by a majority of managerial officials, but there does appear to be a definite promise of a more constructive, possibly cooperative, viewpoint. A study of managements' attitude toward the presence of unions in 1948 revealed that: "There were examples where managements said they would prefer to get rid of any and all unions and there were others where the hope was expressed that unions would eliminate numerous undesireable practices. But by and large, there appeared to exist a feeling that unions—for better or worse—were here to stay, and methods must be found for constructive relationships, regardless of abridgement challenges." [59]

One reaction to organized labor occasionally has precipitated unexpected consequences. In response to union demands, management has decided to build an organization for handling union matters and, subsequently, has concluded that labor relations is all management need be concerned about in the personnel area.[60] Efforts of the personnel function have been channeled primarily toward compliance with labor laws and collective bargaining strategy. Such action has implicitly or explicitly assumed that adherence to governmental labor relations was sufficient to implement the basic objectives of personnel administration. Over a period of time this may persist as a

---

[58] *The Way We Work Together,* New York: Esso Standard Oil Company, 1954, in Keith Davis, *Human Relations at Work,* (2nd ed.; New York: McGraw-Hill Book Co., Inc., 1962), p. 65.

[59] Turnbull, *op. cit.,* p. 113.

[60] Garrett L. Bergen, *op. cit.,* p. 31.

legalistic approach to labor relations or may result in the evolution of a cooperative basis of interaction. In either case, the one-sided emphasis on labor relations has de-emphasized the supervisory-employee relationships and other personal satisfactions; management has been negligent in building the confidence and goodwill of employees through the recognition of individual status and self-esteem.[61]

SUMMARY

The period after 1940 was marked by a more extensive acceptance by management of social responsibility and the development of a sense of trusteeship. Public, community, and consumer relations became a composite concern of many managements and, significantly, the obligations avowed to these parties began with the worker and a sound program of personnel relations. Consequently, numerous enterprises acquired a more balanced perspective of their economic and social responsibilities.

During the 1930's many firms had made explicit and public for the first time the policies and practices governing employee-employer relations. The sequel to this for a few industrial executives consisted of an exploration and formulation of the firm's basic philosophy underlying such personnel policies. Statements of management philosophy generally were organized around the parties with whom the enterprise was directly or indirectly associated—stockholders, public, consumers, and employees. Therefore, the personnel rationale was often expressed as an integral part of management philosophy.

Taking newer form and content after 1940, the humanistic personnel philosophy approached production problems from a human point of view and with concern for the psychological welfare of employees. It was recognized that employees strove to achieve organizational goals and subgoals only to the extent that the firm served their needs as aspiring human beings. Therefore, management sought to assist the employees in achieving their needs, desires, and personal

[61] Van Delden, "Toward a New Personnel Philosophy," *op. cit.,* p. 175.

aspirations by restructuring the job and work environment. Supervision consisted of direction by persuasion and suggestion, motivation by the solicitation of personal interests, and general instructions, with major emphasis upon objectives and results. Considerable reliance was placed upon self-direction and self-control which enhanced employee feelings of achievement, self-respect, and identification with the company. While consultation was frequently employed, the participation of workers in decision-making regarding problems confined to the level at which they were employed was not accepted as a means of achieving a better alignment of managerial and employee goals. Additionally, the humanistic philosophy did not seriously consider the organization as a social structure composed of various subgroups or attempt to effectively utilize group forces.

To some extent the period was one in which attempts were made to assimilate the contributions of behavioral sciences. The concept of individual differences had previously received general acceptance, and there prevailed an appreciation of the complexity of human behavior. While there was some recognition of the psychological needs that could be served by work activity, the greatest omission resided in not appreciating the social needs of employees. Group cohesiveness was viewed with mixed reaction, i.e., as both a constructive and destructive force. There was little evidence which would indicate management was constructively or formally endeavoring to utilize work group dynamics for the achievement of enterprise goals or subgoals. The participation of work groups in the decision-making process and its requisite of democratic leadership conflicted with the prevalent mode of authoritarian leadership and consequently received little adoption. Personnel philosophies were basically individualistic in orientation.

VII

THE HUMANISTIC ERA OF
PERSONNEL PHILOSOPHY—PART II

The ideals and beliefs held by business and industrial leaders in the 1940's and 1950's were explored in considerable detail throughout the last chapter. Concepts pertaining to both personnel and labor relations were examined for their relevance to the human side of production as well as to the extent of their acceptance by top management officials.

The basic tenets of the humanistic personnel philosophy now have been developed in sufficient detail to justify a descriptive model of this rationale. Following the humanistic model, an evaluation will be made of the personnel function as seen by top executives and personnel officials. The emphasis placed upon the personnel function remains as the primary criterion of serious intent to practice the pronounced ideals and philosophies.

SIGNIFICANCE OF THE HUMAN FACTOR IN A HUMANISTIC
PERSONNEL PHILOSOPHY

As industry has elevated the human factor, executives have learned to think in terms of human relations as well as economics and technology.[1] Many industrialists have come to realize that the "activity of dealing with human resources is, without reservations or qualifications, the most important responsibility that anyone in a managerial position bears." [2] It has become a widely accepted prin-

[1] Thomas F. Patton, "Our Greatest Asset—People," *AMA Management Report* (1957), No. 1, pp. 9–15.
[2] Lawrence A. Appley, "The Significance of Personnel Administration in the Modern Corporation," *AMA Personnel Series* (1947), No. 11, p. 3.

ciple that employees will strive to meet the objectives of an organization only to the extent the company serves their needs as aspiring human beings.[3] Consequently, industrial leadership has dedicated itself to earning the loyalty, cooperation, interest, and goodwill of employees by persuasion rather than drivership and motivation by fear. ". . . Successful persuasion implies responsibility for dealing with people to their greatest advantage. A man will work for you and help you, if he thinks that by doing so he will get ahead. It means that business at all times should elevate the human factor above all others in its pattern of operation." [4]

In adopting a humanistic philosophy of personnel administration, managements have sought to practice the right kind of personnel relations by thinking of the worker as a human being, respecting his dignity and rights in order to develop a spirit of cooperativeness and mutuality of interests. Sound personnel relations are deemed not only a condition of efficient business operations and profit potential, but as desirable in the general social interest. "The inclusion of good human relations in the portfolio of management skills is not of value merely to the individual organization—it is essential as a broad management philosophy if we in this country are to ensure the future existence of our economic and social system." [5]

In addition to being desirable in the general social interest, the humanistic philosophy is seen as justified on religious and ethical grounds. One group of businessmen concluded that giving employment policies a sound ethical basis was the most important problem confronting America.[6] Today there is mounting evidence that an ethical evaluation is being made of personnel relations which may eventually serve as a firmer foundation for a better philosophy of personnel administration. "Concern for the individual is sound, also,

[3] James C. Worthy, "Freedom Within American Enterprise," *Management Review* 39 (June, 1950), 6:302.

[4] Harry A. Bullis, "The Road to Business Leadership," *Management Review* 39 (June, 1950), 6:302.

[5] James De Camp Wise, "Positive Management Action in Human Relations," *AMA Personnel Series* (1949), No. 124, p. 23.

[6] Robert Wood Johnson, "Human Relations in Modern Business," *Harvard Business Review* 27 (September, 1949), 5:521–41.

from the standpoint of morality. It is morally right to uphold the dignity of the individual, to respect his rights, and to be responsible to him as an individual." [7] Requisites for industrial harmony are found to reside partially in the following: ". . . it takes an underlying faith in the spiritual nature of man, in his divine right to dignity of individuality. . . . Such faith generally stems from religion. No organization of society—whether it be a nation or industrial plant— can succeed, which sacrifices this fundamental on the altar of materialism. . . . You can't separate Christian ethics from human relations." [8]

Significantly, humanistic personnel relations are no longer just a matter of good business or in the social interest only; they are perceived as ethically and morally right. The ethical note injected into personnel relations may further solidify the practice of sound employee-management relations. Certainly it offers a foundation for existing personnel relations that is consistent with community and employee values and therefore more likely to create industrial harmony and cooperation.

A HUMANISTIC PERSONNEL PHILOSOPHY

An outline of the humanistic rationale is in order. This philosophy represents the culmination of an approach to personnel administration which was initiated by psychology and personnel management and which had slowly taken form and substance over the last forty years. The solution for human relations problems is seen as existing not only in the whole field of management techniques, such as personnel administration and labor relations, but equally so in the field of knowledge about human beings, both as individuals and groups, as found in psychology and other social sciences.[9] Psychology had

[7] J. S. Parker, "The Individual in Industry: An Investment in the Future," *AMA Management Report* (1958), No. 24, p. 53.

[8] Walter H. Wheeler, "A Challenge in Human Relations," *The Management Review* 40 (March, 1951), 3:112–113.

[9] Fowler McCormick, "American Business and Its Human Relations," *AMA Personnel Series* (1947), No. 106, pp. 3–8.

contributed the concept of individual differences, demonstrated the complexity of human behavior, and emphasized the importance of psychological needs; sociology had revealed the existence of informal relationships between members of the work group, the limitations placed by the work group upon the supervisor's relation to that group, and the possibility of stimulating employees in jobs of restricted scope by intelligent control of the work situation.[10] Although leaving much to be desired when measured by the most recent contributions of our social sciences, the humanistic philosophy represents the most advanced approach to personnel relations as measured by its potential for fulfilling human satisfactions.

The humanistic model of personnel philosophy is outlined in the following paragraphs.

1. Leadership. The typical executive is an authoritarian, guiding an authoritarian structure, who finds a philosophical foundation for management in the rights of private property and the freedom of contract. However, management's legal status as employer or owner of the premises does not result in an arbitrary exercise of these rights. Such rights, and concomitant authority, are exercised wisely, judiciously, and with considerable appreciation of the human factors involved.

   Top management has dedicated itself to earning the cooperation, interest, and goodwill of employees by persuasion rather than drivership or motivation by fear. Persuasion is effectuated by accepting and discharging the responsibility for dealing with employees to their greatest advantage and by developing motivations which spontaneously generate employee efforts.

   Dealing with human resources is accepted as one of the most important responsibilities that anyone in a managerial position bears. This viewpoint is accepted as a moral obligation and the personnel function is shared by all managerial personnel.

   Additionally, having a sense of trusteeship, the chief executive regards himself as a representative of the stockholders, the public and labor. Sound public, consumer, and personnel relations are deemed complementary goals to profit maximization. This trusteeship has been expressed in personnel philosophy as an acceptance of social responsibility for employees.

[10] Ellis C. Maxcy, "Understanding People in Work Relationships," *Personnel* 18 (May, 1942), 6:371–76.

Healthy personnel relations are not incompatible with profits; rather, sound personnel relations encourage rising productivity and business efficiency. A balanced personnel program is considered not only a condition of efficient business operations and profit potential, but also desirable in the general social interest.

Both the principles of behavior and techniques of the social sciences are employed to cultivate harmonious personnel relations. While the techniques have been adopted and often used extensively, they are only a means of achieving management's personnel objectives. The implications and established principles of human behavior have been absorbed to some extent and find expression in a personnel philosophy that determines the tone of daily work relationships. Management's objective has been to provide a work environment conducive to providing each employee with an opportunity to gratify his economic, psychological and, to a lesser extent, social needs which promote his personal growth and development.

2. Personnel Management. The top executive accepts the ultimate responsibility for personnel relations, and personnel management is accepted as a proper function of management.

Management impresses upon everyone in a managerial or supervisory capacity that he has personnel responsibilities and must implement the attitude, policies, and procedures set forth by management in their daily relationships with employees.

The personnel manager is an active participant when policies are formulated that touch upon human relations; he is expected to aid in the examination of the human ramifications of proposed policies or courses of action. Consequently, human values are given top priority and considered before, rather than after, action is taken.

Personnel policy is formulated and properly communicated to insure consistency, fairness, and the elimination of discrimination.

The personnel program contains the essential elements of personnel management, accompanied by the appropriate techniques. Such a program, however, is only part of a broad approach to the adjustment of the individual to his job, his development, and gratification of his human needs.

Governmental labor policies are regarded as a minimum basis for many personnel practices and therefore leave considerable latitude for developing the optimum as management strives to build cooperative and harmonious employee relations.

3. Concepts of Labor.

Humanistic. Management approaches the problems of work from the human as well as the production point of view and manifests a concern for the employee's psychological and economic welfare. Since technical efficiency is seen as dependent upon sound personnel relations, management strives to secure the worker's interest, goodwill and cooperation by treating the employee as an individual with definite needs, desires and aspirations. Basic psychological needs of self-esteem, achievement, security, belongingness, and self-actualization are considered as attainable within the business organization. Expression of those human qualities which develop the human personality of employees are encouraged by an organization environment that enables the employee to fulfill his own needs while supporting the enterprise in achieving its objectives. Employees strive to meet company objectives because to do so serves their needs as aspiring human beings.

Social. Management recognizes that work has a social function—that the employee has social as well as egoistic needs. While recognizing that social needs of employees are necessary concomitants to job satisfaction and find expression through informal work groups, no formal activities are undertaken to foster the formation, functioning, and continued existence of such groups that would further facilitate development of the total personality.

Uniqueness. The employee is considered as unique, i.e., possessing different physical, mental, and personality characteristics that are matched with job requirements, thereby promoting work adjustment and satisfaction and higher productivity.

Management is cognizant that one of its greatest developable resources lies in the abilities of its employees, who should be utilized with discretion and protected by a sanitary and safe work environment.

Proper selection, placement, and training are methods of detecting and utilizing the employee's individual capacities and promoting job adjustment.

Consumer–public. Each employee is a consumer of industrial products and a member of the general public to whom the enterprise acknowledges specific responsibilities. Good personnel relations are the foundation for public and consumer relations.

Partnership (optional). Stockownership and/or profit-sharing are used to secure an identification with company objectives.

4. Incentives. The humanistic personnel philosophy contains a predeliction for individualistic forms of motivation and an implicit awareness of social motivations. Although leaving much to be desired, this rationale achieves a modicum of balance in aiding employees attain economic, psychological, and social needs.

Sound employee relations are sought by a program designed to achieve a balance between economic and psychological needs. While not minimizing the economic factors of work activity and considering these as a basic requisite for an honest appeal to other motives, nonfinancial incentives are extensively utilized.

Having a basic faith in the employee's capacity and willingness to direct his own behavior, as well as his capacity to assume responsibility, management strives to arrange conditions and methods of operation so each employee can achieve his own goals by directing his efforts toward organizational objectives.

Relying upon the employee's self-control and self-direction, management seeks to provide guidance and opportunities for growth and development.

Supervisory direction is based upon persuasion and the expression of employee self-interest to secure cooperation, productivity, and compliance with work and other managerial directives.

General or supportive supervisory leadership provides general work instruction and places primary emphasis on objectives and results. Therefore, the employee is provided opportunities for achievement, development, and independence.

Supervisory direction manifests a concern for the dignity and integrity of the employee by recognition of his inner feelings, desires, and aspirations.

Work group cohesion and informal groupings are deemed constructive forces aiding the supervisor to achieve managerial goals and subgoals.

5. Labor Relations. When employees choose to bargain collectively, management deals willingly and frankly with their authorized representatives and with understanding and regard for the rights and responsibilities of their union. Consequently management works with the union on a fair, humane, and businesslike basis—a cooperative philosophy prevails.

Properly managed, responsible and democratic unions are not incompatible with the American economic system; the union is accepted as a permanent factor in the operation of the enterprise.

Positive advantages accrue from bargaining with a strong and well-disciplined union; consequently, management encourages workers, directly or indirectly to support their union.

Labor-management relations are a product of consultations and cooperation rather than unilateral imposition and of working with rather than around the union. Management separates areas of conflict and nonconflict as an approach to the furtherance of cooperation.

Management recognizes the compatibility between sound personnel relations and collective bargaining; labor relations do not preclude the need for personnel management.

Employee cooperation can not be won if their union and representatives are under continual attack by management; therefore, management strives to secure and maintain the respect of both employees and their union.

Management maintains the viewpoint that it is possible for employees to be loyal to both the company and their union— dual loyalty; consequently, there is no competition with the union for employees' loyalty.

Evaluation of the Humanistic Personnel Philosophy. By applying the classification of human needs previously utilized for evaluative purposes, one can anticipate the extent to which the humanistic rationale meets these needs. Within the framework of this personnel philosophy, safety needs are extensively gratified because the threat and deprivation of such needs in the supervisory-subordinate relationship are minimized by a formal concern for the employees' psychological welfare. A supportive supervisory and organization environment is cultivated which will contribute much to the dignity and integrity of employees. Employees are informed of company matters that impinge on their welfare and also of performance and promotional possibilities.

Safety needs may be satisfied by the existence of labor unions, which provide management with an additional stimulus to give continual attention to fairness and consistency of its actions. Therefore, while the company climate provides a sound setting for the gratification of safety needs, it is further reinforced by the presence of a labor union. The employees' safety needs are further fulfilled by programs designed to protect their economic and job security—a partial expression of management's social responsibilities. Consequently, the total work setting provides greater opportunities for employees to realize their safety needs, both economic and psychological.

Although some managements couple their humanistic personnel philosophy with a cooperative approach to labor relations, they have not neglected to promote confidence and goodwill by recognition of individual status and self-esteem. Relationships with individual employees have not been sacrificed in favor of managing the collective relationships with employees through labor relations. The beneficial effects of this more balanced approach to individual and collective relationships is reinforced, since concern for the individual is not tinged with the covert struggle for the employee's loyalty as opposed to the union; a healthier personnel relations environment exists.

Recognition of the social needs of employees are implicit in the humanistic rationale, but do not find expression in a formal program sponsored by top management. The need for belonging or association is recognized to extend beyond that of merely being related to the company; it resides more directly in the immediate work group. Although group cohesion is deemed a constructive force in the attainment of productivity and managerial goals and subgoals, few formal procedures, such as training foremen extensively in the social phenomena of work activity, to constructively utilize and perpetuate group forces are undertaken. However, given a more permissive work environment for the expression of social needs and the irrepressible formation of spontaneous interactions on the job, the social needs are partially gratified, although informally.

Ego needs, both self-esteem and status-prestige, are provided greater latitude for expression, because in addition to matching the man and his job the leadership climate seeks cooperation by persuasion rather than by authoritarian means. Self-confidence, achievement, competence, and knowledge needs find expression through supportive supervision and the reliance upon more self-direction and self-control. Likewise, while management cannot provide an employee with self-respect or the respect of his fellow employees, it does strive to create conditions which will encourage and enable him to find such satisfaction for himself.

At best, personnel relations established under a humanistic personnel philosophy fail to gratify to any significant extent the needs for self-fulfillment. While there has been more emphasis upon decentralization and delegation, this has not had a strong impact at the rank-and-file level, which has been our primary emphasis in the present investigation. Furthermore, while more self-direction, self-control, and general supervision have made possible the activation of self-actualization needs, extensive opportunities for participation have not been provided to encourage employees to direct their creative energies toward organizational objectives; likewise employees have not been granted a part in decision-making on problems that affect their welfare at the level at which they are employed. However, more peripheral forms of participation are used, such as consultation and committee assignments of various kinds. For many employees, participation is attainable only via union membership, which provides an opportunity to take part in some activities influencing their work environment.

An overall evaluation of the humanistic philosophy leads one to conclude that the safety, social, self-esteem, and status-prestige needs are relatively satisfied, but the need for self-actualization, although activated, remains frustrated.

GROWTH OF THE PERSONNEL
FUNCTION AND PHILOSOPHY

The 1930's had been a period of expansion for the personnel function. Diminishing profit margins had focused the attention of top management upon the possibility of personnel administration's promoting employee efficiency. This division's handling of individual employee problems pertaining to spreading the work, layoffs, and keeping an experienced work force intact had been of invaluable service. Furthermore, relationships between employers and employees had become more complicated with the passage of new federal and state laws, the legal sanction given collective bargaining, and the subsequent growth of strong labor unions. Consequently, the personnel function became more complex; individuals specially trained in this discipline were of more assistance to the general managerial function than ever.

World War II provided supplementary forces emphasizing the importance of personnel administration which were responded to under more favorable economic conditions than those experienced during the depression. Garrett L. Bergen, personnel manager of the retail division of Marshall Field and Company, made the following observation: "What the war had done is to bring personnel policies and practices into focus. Under stress, the real impact of personnel administration, good and bad, has shown up as never before. . . . The war has certainly integrated personnel administration with the management of the business. *It has been brought to our attention in headline form that personnel management is management.*" [11] The personnel function increasingly was recognized as a responsibility of the top executive. No longer was it viewed as an area that could be departmentalized or divorced from general management. Sam A. Lewisohn, president of the Miami Copper Company, stated, "Personnel departments should be regarded as a sort of limb of the management—as an extension of the management itself." [12]

Top Management Evaluates the Personnel Function. Personnel administration experienced continued growth during World War II and did not diminish appreciably even after the termination of hostilities, according to a 1952 survey of 250 company presidents and an equal number of personnel officials. Seventy-six percent of the company presidents stated that their personnel programs were more extensive than in World War II, and only 7 percent indicated any

[11] Garrett L. Bergen, "War's Lessons in Personnel Administration," *AMA Personnel Series* (1945), No. 94, p. 26. Emphasis added.

[12] Sam A. Lewisohn, "Management's Responsibility for Human Relations," *AMA Personnel Series* (1944), No. 79, p. 5.

reduction. Ninety percent anticipated further growth. In determining why personnel administration had been accepted, many indicated that it was simply the right thing to do; others stated that it paid in dollars and cents. Some noted both the foregoing reasons, while a substantial number felt they had been forced to utilize personnel administration because of the growth of unions but subsequently realized other advantages. Of considerable significance was the fact that a majority of company presidents felt the benefits of personnel administration were too intangible to measure very precisely in financial terms and such accountability was no longer necessary. Traditionally executives had been skeptical of personnel administration and had insisted on concrete evidence that it was paying its way or justifying its cost; many executives still insist upon such justification. However, the survey concluded: "Without exception, the company presidents queried say that they believe a sound personnel program can improve individual productivity and make a definite contribution toward more productivity per payroll dollar." [13]

Evidence of the emphasis placed upon the personnel function was revealed when 70 percent of the company presidents indicated "personnel executives should rank along with manufacturing and sales executives." [14] Few deemed it a matter of prestige but as a requisite, because personnel administration was sufficiently important to justify such a position.

Increased participation of personnel executives in policy matters was observed during the 1930's, and this trend was accelerated after 1940. A study of management procedures in policy determination over a ten-year period, in 1938 and again in 1947, revealed the following:

One of the outstanding developments in the determination of industrial relations policies in the past ten years has been the increasingly influential role of the chief personnel officer. The change is evident in two ways: (1) the greater number of industrial relations

[13] Wade E. Shurtleff, "Top Management and Personnel Administration," *AMA Personnel Series* (1952), No. 144, p. 5.
[14] *Ibid.,* p. 6.

officers who are individually responsible for decisions on major or minor personnel policies; and (2) the more frequent appointment of the personnel officer to top policy-determining committees.[15]

The higher status of personnel officials and their increased utilization in policy formulation demonstrated that top management had accepted responsibility for personnel relations and the necessity of introducing the personnel rationale into policies and practices affecting employee welfare.

Personnel Executives Evaluate Their Profession. Concurrent with the elevation and acceptance of personal administration, personnel executives began to evaluate their profession. There was a critical attitude toward the prevailing emphasis upon techniques and a definite recognition of the need for more attention to personnel philosophy. This self-analysis was partly due to the desire of personnel officials to improve their discipline and partly attributable to the increasing attention being given the personnel rationale by chief executives. Managements had largely ignored personnel policies in the 1920's but devoted considerable time and energy to their formulation in the 1930's. Now, however, some executives were going one step further and advocating the explicit statement of philosophy lying behind such policies. Guy B. Arthur, Jr., vice-president and director of the American Tread Company, stated: "Another management must which has not received universal acceptance is written company policies. The first step here is to put down in black and white the objectives of the organization, including the company's basic philosophy as it affects the human resources." [16]

Some personnel officials had been unaware of the philosophy of personnel administration or negligent in communicating the personnel philosophy, if known, to management or in assisting them to formulate one. They had concentrated on techniques. A former in-

---

[15] Helen Baker, *Management Procedures in the Determination of Industrial Relations Policies* (Princeton: Princeton University, 1948), p. 57.

[16] Guy B. Arthur, "The Status of Personnel Administration in Management," *AMA Personnel Series* (1946), No. 102, p. 39.

dustrialist stated: ". . . personnel men as a group have been prone to think of personnel in terms of techniques rather than as a movement toward a basic management philosophy. . . . Personnel people have been depending upon techniques to accomplish results without reference to a basic philosophy to determine whether these results are socially desirable." [17] Numerous personnel techniques failed to contribute to sound human relations and, in many industrial organizations, were even utilized as a substitute for good human relations. The philosophy of many personnel and top management executives was succinctly summarized as follows:

> The assumption is that if employees are properly selected, well-trained, adequately paid, and fairly supervised, job satisfaction will automatically result, production and efficiency will be high, and all will be right with the world. The personnel administrator guided by this philosophy therefore has a relatively simple task in planning his program. All he has to do is catalogue the necessary elements of "sound employee relations"—which he can find spelled out in detail in any good book on personnel—and then set up the necessary systems, the "good personnel practices," to see that each element is properly provided for.[18]

An inordinate emphasis upon the techniques of personnel by its practitioners has, even today, limited the healthy growth of effective human relations. This "mechanistic personnel management" has ignored its own ethical and philosophical foundations and its emphasis has been upon techniques rather than people within the organizational structure. It is "dangerous because, on the surface, it permits a glib acceptance of principles which are not understood, and therefore cannot be applied." [19] This "gadget" approach to personnel was popular because it was, and still remains, consistent with the technique philosophy of personnel administration. It has, of course, as by-products the favorable results of promoting job adjustment by

17 E. H. Van Delden, "Personnel Looks to Its Future," *Management Review* 39 (September, 1950, 9:522–24.

18 James C. Worthy, "Changing Concepts of the Personnel Function," *Personnel* 25 (November, 1948), 3:167.

19 Michael G. Blansfield, "Personnel Management Too Mechanistic?" *Personnel Journal* 34 (February, 1965), 9:346.

selection and placement, but fails to create a work environment that would further facilitate the desirable fulfillment of a much wider range of employee needs.

There was ample justification for the accusation that personnel officials were technique-conscious rather than attentive to the philosophy inherent in their discipline. Leaders in the field had been in the forefront in formulation of personnel rationale and practices while others sought to approach this ideal. "The significant fact, however, is that with each passing year standards governing personnel activities are more generally adopted and specific techniques gain wider acceptance. Inevitably the individual personnel executives come progressively closer to what they should be—specialists in human engineering, in the management of people who make up the 'human equation' in industry." [20]

Prior to World War II, personnel administration had been a young discipline striving for professional status and recognition as a proper managerial function. Attainment of such a status, however, did not necessarily indicate that the personnel profession had become more active in promoting a sound personnel philosophy. Often just the reverse occurred. "Too many personnel officers have become yes men to executives who persist in putting human values at no better than second place. . . . They have become so completely integrated and absorbed into the "management team" as to lose sight of the very special and different nature of the personnel function of general management." [21]

While the foundation for good personnel management consists of a "chief executive, sincerely interested in a long-range personnel program, and actively engaged in sponsoring such a program," [22] one should not overlook the fact that it is this same top executive who determines the personnel philosophy of his organization, not

[20] Charles A. Drake, "Developing Professional Standards for Personnel Executives," *Personnel* 19 (March, 1943), 5:646–47.

[21] Thomas G. Spates, "Personnel's Influence Diminishing?" *Personnel Journal* 35 (December, 1956), 7:246–49.

[22] Harold B. Bergen, "Fundamentals of Personnel Administration," *Personnel Series* (1941), No. 46, pp. 3–7.

the personnel executive. The caliber of a personnel official is contingent upon the emphasis top management desires to place upon personnel relations. If an executive has a technique philosophy of personnel administration, he will tend to fill the personnel job with an individual who entertains a similar rationale, or confine one having a higher level of potential to an ineffective sphere of operation. Production and financial positions have been filled only after long and tedious searching, and it seems unlikely that the personnel executive could not have been sought in the same manner if the personnel function were accorded equal status.

Managements had been partly responsible for the failure of personnel executives to devise a working philosophy. They had insisted upon financial justification of personnel programs, and personnel officials had tended to forget the philosophy and idealism inherent in their discipline in an effort to "prove personnel techniques of value to cost-minded managers." [23] This, however, did not excuse personnel executives for their failures. One official pointed out: "Before personnel administrators can even think of becoming professional they must develop a philosophy to guide them in all their actions." [24] Personnel administration had a philosophy almost from its very inception, and a more correct evaluation would have been that its philosophy should be assimilated and brought up to date since the Hawthorne investigations, studies at the Survey Research Center of the University of Michigan, and the contributions of the social sciences had opened up new vistas in personnel relations.

Personnel executives had become more conscious of a need for a revised philosophy, and the following "American Code of Personnel Administration," which crystallized the personnel point of view, was published in 1948.

1. The practice of high standards of character and morality so that the institution stands as a source of inspiration which endows all other personnel practices with qualities of honesty and integrity.

[23] Van Delden, *op. cit.*, p. 523.
[24] Wilbert E. Scheer, "Is Personnel Management a Profession?" *Management Review* 45 (April, 1955), 4:238.

2. Provide everyone on the payroll with a written statement of principles of personnel administration, consistent with the philosophy upon which our nation was founded, and act on these principles courageously in every situation.

3. Good leadership, motivated by high standards of administration rather than by expediency and exploitation.

4. Organization concept and structure consistent with long established standards affecting authority, responsibility, planning, coordination, control and channels of communication.

5. The designation of a well-qualified person in the highest level of general management to specialize in solving the problems of people, and to help see to it that all the practices of the code are made effective.

6. The practice of satisfying the desire for participation, by means of consultation and explanation, both up and down, through all echelons of organization.

7. The practice of keeping everyone on the payroll informed on all matters affecting their interests.

8. Encouraging freedom of expression of points of view and attitudes without fear of reprisals.

9. A total work environment that appeals to the self-respect and dignity of the individual.

10. Sympathetic consideration of people's trials and tribulations, particularly supervisors who too often are not given time or the place to go to air their gripes.

11. Steadiness and certainty of employment.

12. A plan of promotional opportunity.

13. Equitable wage and salary structures that recognize differences in job and position requirements, as measured by such factors as knowledge, skill, difficulty and responsibility.

14. A training program designed to help everyone perform, in the best known ways, the tasks that are assigned for the attainment of stated objectives.

15. Recognition, particularly through individual evaluation, so that it may be said of each person on the payroll: He is prepared with what to go where.

16. A spirit of friendliness which is the essence of all good human relations and which should be diffused throughout the organization.[25]

25 Thomas G. Spates, "The Competition for Leadership in a Welfare Economy," *AMA Personnel Series* (1948), No. 124, pp. 6–7.

This code of personnel administration is significant in that it brings together the more traditional tenets, such as steadiness of employment and promotional plan, with some of the newer concepts. Consequently one finds statements pertaining to participation, communication, and even the total work environment. While such a philosophy reflects an awareness of individual and, to a much lesser extent, of group or social needs of employees, it is essentially a conservative statement when measured by the criteria of recent social science contributions. One finds more of the traditionally accepted concepts of personnel management and industrial psychology; however, no expression is given to the newer concepts of democratic leadership, group decision, or the social organization of work activities that have been examined by social psychologists, sociologists, and human relations investigators.

The lack of a more detailed development of group or social aspects of work does not indicate an unawareness of this facet of human relations; it represents a special bent of professional personnel people—concern for the individual. In terms of providing the basic satisfactions employees may derive from their work experience, the author of the above American Code of Personnel Administration has stated that managerial officials must commit themselves to the achievement of the two major goals of personnel administration: "to establish and maintain mutually satisfying interpersonal relationships among the members of each organizational group, and to encourage the growth of the individual personality of every employee." [26] Significantly an additional requisite for gratifying employee work experiences is that of specializing in the "problem of people as individuals, recognizing their needs and understanding their attitudes." [27] As observed throughout the present study, emphasis and focus of attention upon the individual is not a recent turn of events but the traditional approach to personnel relations and

[26] Thomas G. Spates, "The Spiritual Gap in American Labor Relations," *Management Review* 45 (March, 1956), 3:178–79.
[27] *Ibid.,* p. 178.

problems. This is true not only of most personnel officials but also of top management executives.

SUMMARY

The years since 1940 represent a crystallization of many forces set into motion during the 1920's and especially the 1930's. The depression period and World War II had illuminated both the assets and limitations of personnel administration, and the net effect was to elevate the personnel function and increase its acceptance as a responsibility of top management. Concurrently, the personnel manager or executive increasingly came to occupy an influential role in policy determination.

The newly emerging interest in personnel and managerial philosophy by top management was paralleled by a similar concern of personnel practitioners. Personnel officials had demonstrated little awareness of the philosophy of personnel as a discipline but were slowly perceiving their failure to do so. The great majority had been directing personnel programs without reference to a basic, explicit philosophy which would indicate whether their efforts were socially and humanly desirable or undesirable. With the gradual acceptance of personnel as a general top management responsibility, personnel officials as a group felt less insecure and hard-pressed to justify their existence. Concurrently, a conscious need evolved for a philosophy to guide their work and support their claim to professional status.

The personnel philosophies of top line executives and personnel officials were similar in one respect—both were fairly conservative positions when evaluated in light of the vistas being opened by the social sciences. Nonetheless, the humanistic philosophy, which became quite prevalent after 1940, was significant in terms of its potential for satisfying employee needs by a more appropriate integration of human and technical factors of production.

VIII

TRENDS IN PERSONNEL ADMINISTRATION
TOWARD A NEW PHILOSOPHY

Today there is an unprecedented amount of interest in the philosophy of business enterprise, and this emphasis is likely to increase rather than diminish. Managements are endeavoring to base their operations on sound principles founded upon ethical and social goals which may be endorsed by themselves, the public, consumers, and employees. There exists an appreciation that such a philosophy must be consistent with the "American way of life" and with the basic needs of free, democratic human beings. Managers, as they become better trained in the many facets of industrial enterprise, will seek assistance in formulating a basic, long-range philosophy of human relations. By virtue of training and position in the industrial organization, personnel executives are in an excellent situation to assist in this objective and to function as agents for the preservation of our economic and social way of life. This presents both an opportunity and a challenge. Unless personnel officials are to become relatively unimportant personnel technicians doing small chores for a people-conscious management, they must increasingly become working philosophers.[1]

What direction will this emphasis upon personnel philosophy take? Our modern industrial culture has produced a strange anomaly in that employees function under a democratic system during their non-working hours, but are subjected to an authoritarian environment within the industrial organization. Consequently, the individual is frustrated by imposed autocratic leadership and by the transfer of

[1] C. A. Efferson, "Charting the Course of Personnel Administration," *AMA Management Report*, No. 24 (1958), pp. 22–30.

responsibility to staff personnel who frequently render work activity unstimulating and meaningless. However, the American system has produced such widespread dissemination of knowledge and information that it is unlikely employees will be satisfied to remain voiceless in matters pertaining to their welfare; they will exert pressures on management for an industrial structure that permits participation in the solution of problems affecting their jobs.

Since the 1930's, management has sought more diligently than ever to make personnel rationales compatible with employee values; it is anticipated that this trend will continue. As the sentiment in favor of participation becomes more widespread and vocal, executives will respond by adopting a more democratic philosophy of personnel administration.[2] This will include recognition of employees' aspirations for union affiliation, since the lesson is slowly being learned that an employee may have dual loyalties and yet work cooperatively in achieving company objectives.[3] The employee has both individual and group aspirations that must be reconciled with his total work environment. It is the responsibility of personnel officials to ". . . prove that the basis for good production for satisfied workers is a triangle of good relations which consists of recognition and acceptance by *management* of the interests and needs of the worker as an *individual* as well as in a *group*." [4]

The continued emphasis upon management development will hasten the adoption of humanistic and democratic personnel philosophies. In managerial development it is implicit that personnel executives will be accepted as leaders only if they show evidence of special competence and leadership. Increasingly, the full scope of the personnel program is being applied to all levels of management and not just to rank-and-file.[5] Such attention will gradually elevate

[2] Walter H. Wheeler, "A Challenge in Human Relations," *The Management Review* 40 (March, 1951) 3:112–13.

[3] Herbert O. Eby, "How a Company Can Develop Union Responsibility," *Management Review* 44 (January, 1955) 1:38–40.

[4] E. H. Van Delden, "Toward a New Personnel Philosophy," *Personnel* 26 (November, 1949) 3:177.

[5] Dale Yoder, "Looking Ahead in Employment Relationships," *AMA Management Report* (1958), pp. 31–39.

the caliber of supervisory personnel and enable the company to better promote sound human relations. Personnel administrators must work with management to establish and elevate standards of management qualifications and practices, since morale and job satisfactions of employees are dependent on sound supervisory practices.

An elevation in quality of managerial personnel will facilitate "reversal of the trend toward centralization of the personnel function in one department." [6] The objective is that each line supervisor be a completely integrated personnel man. This is a wholesome development; managers and supervisors have often endeavored to separate human problems from those of production. Executives have become aware that personnel administration is a top, middle, and bottom management function with the primary responsibility lying at the top. Personnel administration is no better than the sum total of the everyday handling of human problems throughout an entire organization.

As top executives give more attention to personnel philosophy and as personnel officials evaluate their rationale, greater emphasis will be given the problems of influencing attitudes and promoting employee satisfactions rather than the further perfection of techniques. With the trend toward equalization of wage rates and benefits, a company's ability to attract and hold competent personnel and increase their productivity will be contingent upon good personnel administration. Under our present system of job security, new ways must be found to motivate employees; techniques will not accomplish this objective. Finding new methods to aid employees in gratifying their numerous psychological and social needs within the organizational structure will be a continuing challenge now and in the future.[7] There are endless opportunities to assist employees to achieve a richer, more wholesome and satisfying life in an industrial society which recognizes human resources as its most valuable asset. The key for a better tomorrow consists in the full development of

[6] Wade E. Shurtleff, "Top Management and Personnel Administration," *Personnel Series,* No. 144 (1952), p. 4.

[7] Lawrence A. Appley, *Management in Action,* (New York: American Management Association, 1959), pp. 376–77.

the human potential, and it is in this area that personnel executives can make their greatest contribution toward achieving industry's human objectives.

As less time and attention are given to the technical aspects of the personnel function, efforts will be made to resolve the conflict between individual motivation and group relationships. At present there appears to be a lack of understanding as to how the informal group can be properly integrated into the formal organization or a balance achieved between cooperation and competition. In essence this consists in bringing about a better alignment of the individual concepts of psychology with the concepts of group relations. The employee is both an individual and a member of the group, but these two relationships require a certain balance. Reconciling individual motivation with group dynamics and relating informal groups within an organization to the formal structure are two of the most crucial problems facing management.[8]

Traditionally, the industrial approach has been to reconcile or adjust the individual employee to the demands and structure of industry. The challenge of tomorrow will be to adapt the mass production process to man.[9] Efforts will be exerted to ascertain what type of industrial organization and internal administration will best meet human requirements. Further specialization for achieving efficiency conflicts with the objectives of developing the human factor in a manner conducive to promoting dignity, status, and self-esteem. Automation may further aggravate this problem, since it tends further to separate the employee from the final end product, and may diminish the feeling of personal accomplishment. The problem of maintaining work interest has been and will continue as a challenge to personnel administration.[10]

A number of personnel officials expect a "reversal of the trend

[8] Garrett L. Bergen, "Fashions, Fallacies and Fundamentals," *AMA Personnel Series*, No. 132 (1950), pp. 31–40.

[9] Herbert O. Eby, "A Business-like Approach to Labor Relations," *AMA Management Report*, No. 24 (1958), pp. 61–69.

[10] Paul D. Arnold, "Human Relations in a 'Hard Sell' Period," *AMA Manufacturing Series*, No. 124 (1954).

toward treating the employees as an organized group rather than as individuals." [11] This, however, does not mean a return to the old union-busting activities; rather, it denotes an awareness that union relations do not eliminate management's need to establish an adequate relationship with the individual. Labor relations, i.e., group relationships, received unprecedented attention after passage of the National Labor Relations Act in 1935 and tended to minimize the emphasis placed upon personnel relations, as the efforts of management were now directed toward grappling with new labor laws and collective bargaining. However, time has permitted the development of new insights and a more balanced perspective. An executive with considerable experience in labor relations summarized this new viewpoint as follows:

> . . . *labor relations is but one small phase* of the employee relations problem. When a management is unexpectedly faced with union demands, top management suddenly discovers that it must build an organization for handling union negotiations and concludes that this labor relations problem is all that management need be concerned with. *It is the constant day-to-day relationship* between immediate supervision and employees which determines the amount of satisfaction that an employee derives from his work situation.[12]

This emerging emphasis upon establishing better contact with the individual employee is consistent with the movement to make each supervisor an "integrated personnel man." Furthermore, it demonstrates the imperativeness of reconciling individual motivation with group relations; otherwise an adequate integration of individual and group components will not be sought by methods most conducive to promoting cooperation and employee satisfaction.

The foregoing trends reflect the anticipation of providing employees a stronger voice, via the decision-making process, in workaday affairs and the concomitant modifications of leadership necessary for its implementation. In addition, these trends also convey a

---

[11] Shurtleff, *op. cit.* p. 4.
[12] Garrett L. Bergen, "War's Lessons in Personnel Administration," *AMA Personnel Series,* No. 94 (1945), p. 31.

concern for the better utilization of group forces and motivations inherent in many work environments. The two variables are not unrelated but rather reflect a need to achieve a better balance between the needs of the worker as an individual, the needs of the work group of which he may be a member, and also the responsibilities of management to achieve the firm's goals.

Considered collectively, the foregoing forecast of changes in personnel administration anticipates a willingness of employers to reconcile the individual with his total work environment, or the total adjustment of the worker to his job, work group, supervisor, company objectives, and his union. Significantly, this indicates that the total personality of the individual in his industrial context is being considered and that the fulfillment of all human needs promises to be greater. Concern for the whole man, for the entire range of his needs, requires the reconciliation of the worker to his position so as to give full and balanced attention to the physical, psychological, social, and moral aspects of his personality. This development will be augmented by the professed concern of some top executives for the dignity and integrity of employers and also the employees' rights and sense of justice.

TOWARD A NEW PHILOSOPHY

With the foregoing trends of personnel function and philosophy in mind and a desire to capture in a formal expression some of the concepts from social psychology and human relations that have received little explicit adoption, a total personality personnel philosophy was structured. The model is somewhat eclectic because many of its tenets are found in existing personnel rationales and also somewhat idealistic in that a part of the content is based primarily upon research conducted by various scientific disciplines and has not been proven by extensive industrial experience. The "ideal" content appears to be desirable from the standpoint of meeting human needs, but, at best, remains implicit in current expressions of management.

As we have observed, the two most currently controversial concepts of labor appear to be the citizenship and the social; neither as yet appears to exert a significant influence on rationales of personnel. The *citizenship* concept which grants a voice in the decision-making process to rank-and-file employees runs counter to strongly entrenched authoritarian administrative practices. Many enterprises have been reluctant or remiss to extend authority to make decisions on anything but the most elementary matters even to first line supervision. While many managements have a philosophy of decentralized decisions, such a practice has not been extended to employees—the group comprising the focal point of this investigation. For many employees the only way to secure a voice in matters affecting their workaday lives is via forms of participation available through their union. Evidence suggests that this may have been one of the motives for the forming of or affiliating with a union. Although there is voluminous literature in the social sciences on the advantages that accrue from democratic management and the requisite leadership necessary for its promotion, industry has been reluctant to initiate participation with its implications of citizenship into either practice or philosophy.

Also of doubtful status is the influence of the *social concept of labor*. While the social scientists and human relationists have explored group dynamics and the informal group almost unceasingly since the investigations by Elton Mayo and his associates at Hawthorne, little evidence is available to indicate that such contributions have made a significant impression on administrative practice or philosophy. Much of the research has been cast in terminology foreign to the business world and is fragmentary, presenting difficulties in extracting generalizations useful in day-to-day relationships. At the present time, there appear to be considerable misgivings as to how the informal group may be effectively identified and integrated into the formal organization. Additionally, many are perplexed as to how one should integrate or reconcile the needs and values of the group with those of the individual so as to achieve both managerial and employee objectives.

The total personality personnel philosophy is an explicit utilization of the social and citizenship (participation) concepts of labor which are now absent, or at best, implicit in personnel relations as now practiced. In contrast to other personnel rationales, the total personality approach seeks to promote, develop, and maintain by formal means the social structure and participation of work group units. In giving expression to these two concepts of labor, the total personality relations philosophy reflects several current behavioral concepts as found in psychology, sociology, and other scientific disciplines and have been included for the purpose of achieving a better adjustment of the worker to his industrial environment and job.

Not only is concern for the social facets of work considered a requisite for better overall worker adjustment, the position is taken that employees are interested in participating in decisions affecting their immediate welfare, that employees have the capacity to make good decisions, and that employees can be of invaluable assistance in attaining managerial objectives. In essence, this is the citizenship concept of labor which maintains that democratic ideals and practices characteristic of civil government are applicable to the internal operations of business enterprise.

A New Framework for Personnel Philosophy. Obviously, the subject matter or content of personnel philosophy may have been organized in many different ways. While previous rationales were structured around the factors comprising the framework of analysis utilized in examining their development, many alternative frameworks are possible. Whatever one's preference for organizing personnel philosophy, it should convey management's beliefs pertaining to following basic relationships: the company and the individual; the supervisor and the work group; the individual and his supervisor; the individual and his job; the company and the union (if organized). These basic relationships are more complicated than one might gather from the list shown above, since each of the basic relationships will interact and influence, in varying degree, each of the others. The framework for the personnel philosophy which is to be presented will be comprised of the above relationships.

Objectives of the total personality personnel philosophy, presented below, are not too different from most other rationales.

1. To attain as effectively and economically as possible the production necessary to maintain the competitive and continuously profitable position of the company by conserving the human factor of production and by obtaining maximum cooperation between management and its employees.

2. To intelligently plan and provide an organizational work environment that enables each employee to achieve the satisfaction of physical, economical, psychological, and social needs, and, in addition, to give appropriate and balanced consideration to each broad area of needs.

The first objective is consistent with both technique and humanistic personnel philosophies, but the second is uniquely characteristic of the total personality model. Additionally, the latter objective reflects the basic assumption underlying the model being structured and accounts for its uniqueness—the employee must be reconciled with his total work environment. This denotes management's concern for the whole man, for the entire range of his needs, and requires the total adjustment of the worker to his job so as to give full regard and expression to the physical, psychological, social, and moral aspects of his personality. Needless to say, this is a large order and provides any enterprise concerned over its personnel relations with a challenging task. The total personality personnel philosophy which follows is offered as a promising means for attaining the above objectives.

THE TOTAL PERSONALITY MODEL
OF PERSONNEL PHILOSOPHY

I. Company and Employee Relationships.

A. Leadership Climate.

Although the philosophical foundation for management rests upon the rights of private property and freedom of contract, leadership is eclectic; that is, authoritarian when necessary but democratic when conditions permit. Based upon the decentralization of authority and decision-making, executive leadership formally encourages employees to function as a social unit by participation in decisions appropriate to the level at which employees work.

Positive leadership prevails that is directed toward earning cooperation, interest, and goodwill through the possession of human understanding, fairness, and consideration for the dignity, self-respect, personal interest, and security of employees.

Sound personnel relations are not incompatible with profits, but encourage rising productivity and business efficiency.

Relationships with each employee are governed by the highest standards of conduct and ethics; the personal satisfactions of employees is one of the measures of company success.

B.   Motivational Climate.

Management is committed to the promotion of a work environment that gives balanced consideration to economic, psychological, and social needs; gratification of one set of needs is not emphasized at the expense of minimizing others.

Management creates conditions which will keep the objectives of the company and employees as harmonious as possible by dealing with employees to their greatest advantage and by developing motivations which spontaneously generate employee efforts.

Having a basic faith in the employee's capacity and willingness to direct his behavior toward organization goals or sub-goals, as well as his capacity to assume responsibility, management strives to arrange work conditions and methods of operation so each employee can achieve his personal goals by the direction of his efforts toward organization objectives or sub-goals.

Relying upon the employee's self-control and self-direction, management seeks to provide guidance and opportunities for growth and development.

C.   Social Responsibility. The employee's standard of living, security, and welfare are intimately linked with the company's welfare.

1.   Work environment.
   a.   To provide good working conditions that appeal to the self-respect and dignity of employees.
   b.   To provide adequate protection for the health and safety of all employees.

2.   Economic security.
      To maintain personnel policies that provide adequate compensation, hospital and medical services, sickness and accident insurance, life insurance, and other feasible employment benefits.

3. Job security.
    To provide steady employment for employees in-
    sofar as possible by careful planning and good
    management.

D. Labor Concepts.

1. Consumer—Public.
    Satisfactory employee-management relations are the
    basis for public relations, and long-term profitable op-
    erations must be based on public, customer, and em-
    ployee goodwill and loyalty since these groups are es-
    sentially the same.
2. Partnership (Optional).
    Make each employee a full partner in the enterprise
    through profit sharing or stock ownership so that the
    employee shares in the profits and growth of the enter-
    prise.

II. Supervisor and the Work Group.

A. Social Concept of Labor.

Since social needs find expression through formal and informal
associations, both top management and supervisors are involved in
effectuating an adequate social work environment. Those measures
requiring the support of top management, since staff and engineering
assistance are required, and therefore only indirectly under supervisory influence, are as follows:

1. Supervisory training directed toward the promotion of
    leadership that is able to understand and cope with the
    social phenomenon of work.
2. The structuring of small work groups, built around
    common experiences and interests, and the concomi-
    tant physical arrangement of production.
3. Establishment of congenial groups of employees by
    sociometric grouping.

B. Immediate Supervisor

Activities that are necessarily implemented by the work group's
immediate supervisor are as follows:

1. Encourage employees to function as a social unit, both
    formally and informally by strengthening team work
    and group solidarity.
2. Promote group activities on the job and recognize
    group members for work performed collectively.
3. Apply group incentives when appropriate.
4. Assist the development of a common positive purpose

while working under a minimum of supervisory pressure.
5. Encourage the group to develop its own means for internal self-control.
6. When practical, respect the standards, norms of behavior, and values that the work group believes are proper.
7. Identify and cooperate with informal group leaders to minimize conflict and to assure that the informal leadership is promoting company objectives.
8. Use consultation and participation in the making of decisions to minimize conflict of managerial objectives and group values before technological innovations are made and to solve problems that involve the group as a whole.

III. Supervisor and the Employee.

   A. Humanistic Labor Concept.

     1. The practice of employee centered leadership.
       a. To provide a gratifying personal relationship through considerate and understanding treatment.
       b. To provide direction based upon persuasion and suggestion.
       c. To provide a gratifying work relationship through general directions and the evaluation of performance.
     2. Respect for the right of each employee.
       a. To be treated as an individual and respected as a person.
       b. To fairness and justice in all his relations with fellow employees and superiors.
       c. To prompt, fair adjustment of complaints of every kind.
     3. Communication.
       a. To provide each employee with the knowledge of where he stands in terms of job performance and promotion potential.
       b. To inform the employee on matters that may affect his economic, psychological, and social well-being.

   B. Citizenship Labor Concept.

     1. Free expression.
       To assure each employee the right of free expression on matters that concern his own and company welfare.

2. Consultation.
   To give each employee an opportunity to contribute to the best of his ability in the solution of common problems.
3. Participation.
   To encourage each individual as a group member to participate in discussing and solving problems that involve the group as a whole.

IV. Individual and Job.

    A. Uniqueness Labor Concept.

        1. To select differentially and fill all jobs with the best applicants available so as to provide the individual with purpose and satisfaction in his daily activity.

        2. To encourage and foster individual development and advancement by training each employee to his maximum capacity.

        3. To base promotions on merit and seniority; all other things being equal, the employee with longest service should be given preference.

    B. Humanistic Labor Concept.

        Provide a psychologically gratifying job function insofar as possible and give adequate attention to job enlargement and job rotation when necessary.

V. Company and the Union—Labor Relations.

Management works with the union on a fair and businesslike basis when employees choose to bargain collectively. Labor relations are conducted willingly and frankly with the employees' authorized representatives and with regard for the rights and responsibilities of the union.

Since positive advantages are seen as accruing from bargaining with a strong and well-disciplined union, management encourages workers to support their union.

Labor-management relations are based upon consultation and cooperation, rather than unilateral imposition or working around the union. Management separates areas of conflict and mutual interest as a means of increasing cooperation.

Management accepts the viewpoint that it is possible for employees to be loyal to both the company and their union—dual loyalty.

Management recognizes the compatibility between sound personnel relations and collective bargaining with the elected representatives of their employees. Labor relations do not preclude the need for personnel relations, and consequently, management strives to maintain a balance between its relations with employees as a group and as individuals.

VI. Personnel Management for the Total Personality Personnel Philosophy.

To implement the philosophy previously outlined requires that the personnel management function be characterized by the following conditions.

Top management accepts the ultimate responsibility for personnel relations, and personnel management is accepted as a basic function of management.

Personnel executives or managers have assimilated the ethical and philosophical foundation of personnel administration as a scientific discipline. Consequently, both behavioral principles and techniques provided by the social sciences are employed to promote harmonious personnel relations.

The personnel manager is an active participant in top management planning when policies are formulated that have an impact upon human relations and advises management of the personnel implications of proposed policies or courses of action. Consequently, human values, motivation, and attitudes are considered prior to the adoption of managerial plans and programs.

Personnel management is a major function of every person having supervisory responsibilities. Consequently, each person in a managerial capacity is in effect a "personnel manager" who fully understands the personnel philosophy, policies, and procedures formulated by top management.

Labor relations are integrated with personnel relations in order to achieve a consistent and balanced program of employee relations.

The personnel program contains the essential elements of personnel management, supplemented by relevant, appropriate techniques; such techniques and tools, however, are only a means to the promotion of personal satisfaction and job adjustment.

EVALUATION OF THE TOTAL PERSONALITY PERSONNEL PHILOSOPHY

The foregoing model does not promise to solve all the problems pertaining to the human side of an enterprise; it does, however, offer some hope for alleviating some of the numerous personnel difficulties that beset a management. Most significantly, the model outlines the requisite leadership by top management if an environment conducive to such a philosophy is to prevail. Equally important, the personnel function is accorded the status and position needed to implement such an enlightened personnel philosophy.

The total personality personnel philosophy holds promise of solving the problem of integrating individual needs and group relations as well as management's need to achieve the firm's objectives. Management would have less misgivings about potential conflicts between its own goals and work group norms, because consultation and participation would tend to reconcile their divergent purposes. In turn, the individual would not find himself caught between the different reward and penalty systems of management and his own work group or associates.

A cooperative approach to labor relations also would reduce conflict by cultivating areas of mutual agreement and abandoning the struggle for employees' loyalty and allegiance. Labor and personnel relations would be appropriately integrated to insure a more logical and consistent program of employee development and maintenance.

Finally, it is apparent that the fulfillment of all psychological needs will be greater for the employee, since emphasis is placed on the total personality. The safety needs find more expression because of the more supportive type of leadership; the worker is in a much less dependent relationship to his supervisor as compared with other personnel rationales. Furthermore, the human relations personnel philosophy is forceful in those need areas that are least effectively provided for by other rationales—social, self-esteem, and status-prestige. Social needs are provided more opportunity for expression by formal managerial objectives designed to foster the formation, functioning, and continued existence of social work group activity. This ranges from the planned structuring of small work groups around common experiences and task completion to supervisory practices oriented toward full cultivation and utilization of group forces and aspirations.

Such participation provides additional opportunities among employees for interaction and also for contributing their ideas and know-how to operating problems occurring at their level of employment. Additionally, this joint endeavor is conducive to mutual influence between foremen and subordinates. As a result, a promising environment is created which tends not only to facilitate the attainment of social or membership needs, but the self-esteem and status-prestige needs as well. The self-actualization needs are provided some opportunity for expression by participation in the discussion and solving of problems that involve the work group as a whole; consequently, there is a better correspondence of managerial objectives and group goals.

SUMMARY

Since, as we have observed throughout the present study, personnel philosophy is dynamic, a "total personality" philosophy may be the next direction or level of development for some chief executives and personnel officials. Such a rationale would provide opportunities for the satisfaction of employee needs—social, self-esteem, status, and prestige—that are ignored or inadequately considered by other personnel philosophies. Some of the concepts in the model just presented are projections of the thinking and ideals barely on the horizon in the field of personnel administration; others have been implemented and widely accepted. Consequently the total personality philosophy model represents a blend of both old and new concepts.

No executive, line or personnel, may be able to accept the total personality philosophy in its entirety; and even if a number do so, it would be unrealistic to expect the model's content to be accepted with the same degree of conviction or implemented with comparable effectiveness. Such expected variance will be contingent upon the individual executive's fund of knowledge in the personnel area, the historical antecedents of his company and associated industry, and other unique factors. However compatible the model's concepts may be with an executive's personal viewpoints, he has a framework which may be used as a guide or point of departure for structuring a personnel philosophy to meet his own peculiar situation.

IX

A BRIEF LOOK BACKWARD

SIGNIFICANT GENERAL TRENDS

We have observed how a generalized rigid insistence upon maintaining the status quo gave way to a partial alignment with the social values of the public and employees. The narrow individualistic attitudes toward business and social problems prevailing at the outset of the twentieth century have slowly been modified. This new orientation was eventually manifested by the acknowledgment that business existed to render a service to society and to a lesser extent, by an acceptance of moral and social responsibility for employees' wellbeing. The economic system had become so interdependent that individuals were subject to conditions beyond their control; protection by employers against unanticipated emergencies reflected an effort to bring the objectives and values of executive personnel philosophy more in alignment with those of the public. Employers, to some extent, have endeavored to harmonize their economic and social obligations. Worker welfare was perceived as interwoven with the welfare of business and industrial enterprise.

The employee has been approached with increasing consideration, as employers are more inclined to see the laborer not only as a worker entitled to treatment as a human being with specific rights, but also as a consumer and a member of the public to whom industry acknowledges responsibilities. Sound consumer and labor relations increasingly have been made complementary goals to the objective of profit maximization. Executives are now inclined to consider themselves as trustees who must properly balance the rights and interests of the public, stockholders, and employees. Whereas management had previously been associated with ownership, it has tended to become synonymous with trusteeship, identified with the long-run continuity and public welfare objectives of industry. Neither the employees nor the public should be exploited for the sole purpose of financial interests.

Numerous firms, especially during the 1930's, made explicit and public for the first time their policies and practices governing employee-employer relations. The sequel to this for some industrial executives consisted of an exploration and formulation of the firm's basic philosophy underlying such personnel policies. Statements of management philosophy generally were organized around the parties with whom an enterprise was directly or indirectly associated— stockholders, public, consumers, and employees. Therefore, the personnel rationale often was expressed as an integral part of management philosophy.

Although a majority of industrial enterprises do not have a written personnel philosophy as such, their rationale is reflected to some extent in policies primarily concerned with wages, hours, work conditions, etc.—management's intention or commitment to justice and fair practices in these areas. The basic personnel philosophy, whether written or unwritten, explicit or implicit, and the manner in which company policies are administered provide the real impact in determining the tone of employer-employee relationships. Personnel relations are fundamentally the results of the way a company lives, and therefore, a firm's philosophy may not be clearly or completely conveyed by its personnel rationale.

While formal statements of personnel philosophy are found only in a small minority of industrial enterprises, there is an increasing interest and tendency to formulate such rationales as many industrial firms look for or endeavor to make explicit the philosophy underlying policies and their practice of human relations. In implementing this task, personnel executives have made significant contributions to such philosophical formulations by virtue of training and experience. Many, however, have been unable to do so since they are unaware of the ethical and philosophical bases of their profession and discipline.

It would seem industry would logically progress from philosophy to policy, and then to techniques or implementation, but the American industrial experience has tended to be just the opposite. Generally speaking, the years from 1910–1930 were most notable for the development of techniques, 1930–1940 for formulation of policy, and 1940–1960 for the limited attention being directed to personnel philosophy. Overall, however, there has been a basic trend in personnel philosophy and practice toward a more humanistic approach which gives recognition to a broader range of human needs.

The above generalized trends have not been smooth nor the results of long-range planning or study by top executives. Rather, periods of greatest change in personnel philosophy have occurred during turbulent years—war, depression, rapid technological growth, and governmental intervention. Therefore, alterations in philosophy have been due to pressures, not to a serious, rational evaluation of the interrelation of technical and human factors. The very necessity for such compulsion is indicative of the extent to which a do-nothing rationale of personnel has permeated industrial practices, especially prior to 1930. Industrialists have not always been sensitive to community and employee values, but political, economic and social upheavals have precipitated reevaluations.

One of the most significant instrumental forces in the formulation of personnel philosophy is that of executive leadership. The mediating effect of top level executive leadership between external and internal forces shaping personnel philosophy and its content have been noted throughout this study. Since top management achieves enterprise objectives through others within the organization, leadership determines how others are induced to strive for personal and organizational goals. Industrial leadership has varied from a rigid insistence on the status quo to flexibility, from complete immunity to receptivity of public and employee values, and from disclaimers to sincere acceptance of employees' welfare. Reaction to scientific disciplines, also greatly influenced by top executive leadership, was significant because of the labor concepts and behavioral insights provided administrators. The tenets of a personnel philosophy are significantly affected by the extent to which scientific techniques or behavioral concepts, or both, are utilized, or ignored, by management.

However, there has been a considerable lag between the fund of knowledge available to top executives responsible for personnel philosophy and that which has been assimilated and utilized. Many factors contribute to this state of affairs. In some instances the training of executives in the social sciences has been deficient, and the quality and training of supervisory personnel who would implement many of the behavioral concepts is even more limited. Also there is a basic conflict between some of the behavioral concepts and the strongly entrenched authoritarian principles and practices, for example, the participation of rank-and-file employees in the decision-making process. Somewhat disturbing have been the language barriers between industrial officials and the social scientists. Finally the scientific investigators have not been without fault themselves. Much of the work has been fragmented, inconclusive, and conducted out of the context of significant, crucial industrial variables. Consequently, much of the knowledge prohibits generalizations useful to understanding employee behavior, much less any which might be included in a personnel philosophy.

A majority of top executives have accepted personnel management as a general managerial function, and accordingly the personnel official has been given an enhanced status and voice in policy determination. Although having acknowledged managerial responsibility for the personnel function, the perception of this function differs so widely that it gives rise to radically different personnel philosophies. This has ranged from an emphasis upon economic incentives and a rigid, authoritarian, structured work setting to an emphasis upon multiple psychological needs and a planned work environment to gratify such human drives. Consequently, regardless of manifested concern for social responsibility and the integrity and dignity of employees by top management, daily job satisfaction will vary greatly. Additionally, the language of human relations and behavior has often been adopted and utilized extensively, but frequently one finds no concrete expression in personnel philosophy or day-to-day work relationships.

CONCEPTS OF LABOR RECONSIDERED

Having traced developments in personnel philosophy, it is appropriate to note those labor concepts having only historical significance and those remaining an integral component of current personnel rationales. The *master-servant* concept is no longer a managerial attitude toward employees. Having been brought from England, this viewpoint strongly influenced the pattern of work relations as America became industrialized, but was displaced in the wake of economic, social, and technological changes.

The view of labor as merely a *commodity* no longer exerts a significant influence on the thinking of a majority of managers. For those employees who still entertain the commodity viewpoint, some of the harshness of the economic law of supply and demand and the attendant irresponsibility toward employees has been mitigated by state and federal law pertaining to wages, hours, and working conditions. Additionally, the union, in many instances, has functioned as a buffer between managements inclined to apply the commodity concept of labor and their employees. Such protection, however, fails to protect the employee against a work environment deficient in human values that enhance personal satisfactions.

The *machine concept* of labor, like the commodity concept, is too barren a viewpoint of the employee to be accepted by many employers. While management considers labor capable of a certain amount of productivity and installs incentive systems, when appropriate, to encourage a specific output, rarely will one find that this concept embodies or dominates employers' personnel relations as it did in the past.

Both the commodity and machine concepts of labor were notable for their failure to consider factory operatives as individuals possessing rights and human aspirations which should receive the serious consideration of management in its daily employee relations. However, for some few executives today, the basic managerial attitudes forming the foundation for personnel philosophy are identical with the attitudes prevalent when the designations of commodity and machine were more appropriate to trading and commercial activities. Since such attitudes reflect a lack of concern for the human element, the modern counterpart of this viewpoint may be labled as an impersonal concept of labor.

Chronologically, the commodity and machine concepts of employees were tempered by the *goodwill or paternalistic* concept; instead of complete indifference toward employees, however, the paternalistic view of workers went to the opposite extreme of over-solicitude. Such benevolent autocracy, both at work and at home, lacked a basic understanding of human motivation, especially the drives for independence, integrity, and self-esteem. This attitude toward labor denoted an emphasis upon economic motivation and provision of better work conditions. The paternalistic approach still finds expression when employers seek to obtain loyalty and goodwill primarily by means of wages and benefits without an honest appeal to other mainsprings of behavior. As a result, it falls short in developing the individual's total personality, and it generally fails to stimulate cooperation or convey a community of purpose.

The *natural resource concept* of labor was also of passing significance during the period 1900–1920, and reflected an upsurge of interest in protecting employees against harsh industrial personnel practices. Arising from an analogy to the nation's exploited, depleted natural wealth and accompanied by a surge of humanitarianism, the natural resource concept of labor found expression in efforts to improve the health, safety, hours of work, and wages of employees, all of which gradually became the subject of state and federal laws. The modern worker is protected to an even great extent by laws covering such matters, but he is seldom viewed as an impersonal natural resource.

Chronologically, the natural resource concept of labor was supplemented and finally replaced by the *uniqueness* concept of labor, cognizant of individual differences and seeking to utilize them more judiciously. While many employers may not appreciate the range of such individual differences, few are ignorant of their existence whether revealed through academic training or first-hand observation. This concept of labor is a part of most current philosophies of personnel and finds expression in the selection, placement, and training of employees.

The *humanistic concept* of labor likewise is a popular one in the personnel rationale of many employers. Extensive programs have been made to insure that work is a rewarding experience, not only financially but psychologically as well. This has been implemented by job enlargement, job rotation, and human relations training programs for supervisors. Technological efficiency is seen as limited or contingent upon sound personnel relations.

Perception of the employee as a *consumer* and member of the public became a concept of labor that assumed considerable importance in the 1930's and now appears to be generally recognized by a majority of employers. When the identity of plant employees with the public and consumers was first perceived, it attracted considerable attention; now, however, this relationship is generally realized and accepted. Employee relations and public relations are seen as delicately interwoven with one another.

The *partnership concept* of labor is predicated upon a mutuality and coincidence of interests and needs between management and employees. Manifested in stock-ownership and profit-sharing plans, numerous firms currently seek to secure cooperation and an identification of employee-company objectives.

Granting a voice in the decision-making function to rank-and-file employees, the *citizenship viewpoint* remains basically an academic matter, not an industrial practice. Regardless of the advantages of democratic management and leadership indicated in studies conducted by the social sciences, industry has not included participation as expressed in decision-making into either practice or philosophy to any appreciable extent.

Finally, and only slightly less controversial than citizenship implications, is the viewpoint founded upon the *social function of work.* While recognizing, to some extent, that the employee is affected by values, norms, and attitudes of his work associates, most managements have not structured any programs or courses of action to utilize constructively the social system of work relationships.

PERSONNEL PHILOSOPHY

In the course of examining the emergence and development of personnel philosophies, some of the major factors contributing to their evolution and the resulting content were examined. The survey just completed revealed five clearly discernible rationales; two of these—laissez-faire and paternalism—are primarily of historical interest only. While the paternalistic philosophy is infrequently observed today, vestiges of this rationale are still reflected by employers who seek to purchase loyalty and goodwill through generous wage scales, liberal employee benefits, and attractive working conditions. It is still believed that employees will show their appreciation of management's generosity by being happy and productive. Furthermore, it represents an attempt to find an easy solution to employee relations and reflects a refusal or inability to utilize some of the contributions by the social sciences to formulate a personnel philosophy and program more consistent with employees' desires, needs, and aspirations.

Many of the same forces that contributed to the evolution and development of a technique personnel philosophy also were instrumental in shaping the humanistic rationale. This is most evident in the utilization of contributions from scientifically oriented disciplines. As for the humanistic philosophy, while the personnel tools were employed, the philosophy of the scientific contributions has been more generally accepted.

Frederick W. Taylor's philosophy of cooperation, harmony, maximum production, mutuality of interests, and development of each employee to his greatest efficiency and prosperity is compatible with both philosophies, but the means of implementing these goals have varied considerably. The humanistic rationale has prompted the structuring of an organizational environment that better facilitated the attainment of Taylor's objectives and assigned a high priority to the gratification of basic psychological needs. In contrast, the technique philosophy has relied primarily upon economic incentives and adjustment of the individual to job and organizational demands. In facilitating this alignment of worker to the job, personnel selection and related procedures have been employed extensively.

Both the technique and humanistic philosophies became more dynamic with the deterioration of narrow, individualistic attitudes toward business and social problems, which in turn have facilitated the subsequent acceptance by employers of social responsibility for employees and the emergence of a sense of trusteeship. Economic depression and governmental labor policies in the 1930's also tended to increase management's sensitivity to employee sentiments and values. Good employee relations became the basis for sound public relations, and the identity of employees with the consuming public became a significant concept in executive thinking and action in personnel administration and philosophy.

Both the technique and humanistic personnel philosophies convey top management's intention to render a worthwhile service to consumers and to deal with all parties with whom it is associated, including its employees, in a fair way. In doing so, a company has structured the basis for good employee relations but much more is required before an employer can claim to practice such. Therefore, in attempting to discern a given company's personnel rationale, it is significant to note that a sense of trusteeship or social responsibility does not guarantee a humanistic philosophy of personnel administration. Likewise, both philosophies proclaim an acceptance of responsibility for the personnel function but the manner in which such obligations are discharged becomes the significant differentiating factor.

The technique personnel philosophy with its strong emphasis upon authoritarian principles has many favorable aspects that should not be dismissed because of possible negative connotations pertaining to techniques and their utilization within an authoritarian structure. Recognition of individual differences among employees and the utilization of psychological techniques produces a much better alignment of job demands and individual capacities in the personnel areas of selection, placement, transfers, promotions, and wage administration. This is no small achievement. Both the technique and humanistic philosophies reflect an awareness that the human resource has potential which may be better developed to the mutual advantage of employer and employee.

Given this basic similarity, however, the technique and humanistic rationales begin to diverge sharply. While making a commendable start through a better utilization of the unique characteristics of employees, further individual growth and development is thwarted by an emphasis upon economic motives rather than upon the broad spectrum of needs by the technique personnel philosophy. This myopia is further augmented by an intensive utilization of direction and control in daily work activities and procedures and also by the centralization of authority and responsibilities when operating conditions make it feasible to do otherwise. In essence the individual is required to occupy a dependent and passive role within the organization after being relatively well matched with the job duties he is to perform.

The humanistic philosophy of personnel makes the uniqueness concept of labor a point of departure for a fuller implementation of the humanistic concept of labor. Placing a premium on the human side of production, management is dedicated to promoting a work environment more compatible with the individual's broad range of psychological needs. Such activities consist of a rearrangement of job duties, more reliance upon self-direction and self-control, and the utilization of limited forms of participation. A broad range of motives is tapped; the economic incentive is merely a foundation upon which to structure a better balanced motivational framework. Significantly, the employee is encouraged to become a more independent and active member of the organization.

The above comparison of technique and humanistic philosophy

provides a partial clue as to why the technique philosophy only solicits limited cooperation—the employee does not conceive such cooperation as fulfilling his own needs to any significant extent. With only a very restricted emphasis upon the human side of production, self-respect and self-fulfillment needs are frustrated and employees are not challenged to optimum effort. Consequently, management fails to develop an identity of purpose between its collective goals and those of its employees. Part of the responsibility for the failure to create a satisfactory synthesis of the goals of employees and management rests with the personnel function, which should apprise management of the human side of its enterprise. Instead one finds that the personnel function often fails to aid top management in developing a sound framework of human relationships or in bringing the human factor to the attention of management, since it is based primarily upon tools and techniques that are perceived as the essence of its activity and purpose for being.

In looking back upon the developments in personnel philosophy, it appears that the technique rationale of top management has not advanced much beyond the basic philosophy of Frederick Taylor. It is an enlightened engineering approach to work problems, embodying a limited concept of motivation and the personnel function, yet conveying an awareness of social responsibilities. A high degree of task specialization in many industrial organizations, coupled with the technique philosophy, has precluded fruitful explorations of ways to make the work environment and task a more rewarding experience.

In measuring the humanistic personnel philosophy against the fund of information provided by our scientific disciplines, it appears that the philosophy enunciated by Taylor and the basic ideas provided by industrial psychology provide the main nucleus of concepts for this philosophy. Industrial leadership was provided some of the psychological insights requisite to the cultivation of sound personnel relations concerning concepts of individual differences with corollary emphasis upon selection, placement, and training. Psychology also made available to business leaders a human orientation toward the problem which recognized the multiple needs of employees and, equally important, the necessity of structuring a work environment consistent with these needs. As noted, the humanistic philosophy is characterized by a broader conception of human behavior and motivation as well as the personnel function. Rather than attempting to adjust the worker to the demand of industrial organization, as in the case of a technique rationale, the humanistic approach has sought to provide a work environment more consistent with the satisfaction of human needs. While this appears to have led to the adoption of a general type of supervision, the social concept of work, employee participation in decision-making, and democratic leadership have been ignored or at best been implicit in managerial thinking and practice. The present state of affairs represents some departure from traditional authoritarian practices and principles with the promise of further action being taken along such lines.

While America still needs an industrial philosophy that will suit its machine technology and the nature of man, one may derive some consolation from the fact that such a philosophy is being sought by many enterprises. Furthermore, we have seen that in seeking to achieve some semblance of balance between these two complex variables, the record has generally been a dynamic one. In the industrial milieu of our nation, this pursuit has been initiated, with few exceptions, by external and internal forces and pressures rather than by self-initiative or long-range planning. The response to such stimuli has generally been motivated by self-interest and the desire to avoid more public controls. Nonetheless, by adopting a flexible posture, industry as a whole, whatever its motivations, has made a contribution to the preservation of our democratic institutions and existing system of enterprise.

NAME INDEX

SUBJECT INDEX

American Code of Personnel Administration, 214–15
American Management Association, 124
Bureau of National Affairs, Inc., 173, 179, 181
Codes of ethics, 116–17
Concepts of labor: colonial labor systems, 24–31; current status, 238–40; do-nothing philosophy, 129; humanistic philosophy, 204; laissez-faire philosophy, 55–56; master-servant, 9; paternalistic philosophy, 94; pre-industrial, 16–17; technique philosophy, 164
Department of Commerce, 116
Economic security, employee, 137
Employee participation, growth of, 159
Employee relations policy, examples of, 119–21
Employee welfare: executive concern, 84–88; physical, 86–87; psychological aspects, 87
Employer associations: National Association of Manufacturers, 85, 88; National Founders Association, 54; Stone Founders' National Defense Association, 54
Employer philosophy, personnel administration, 91–92
Fair Labor Standards Act, 137
Group dynamics: acceptance of, 184–86; participation, 183–84; role of supervisor, 181
Hawthorne investigations, 155–57

Humanitarianism, tide of, 57
Human relations: assumptions, 157–58; communications, 180; executive reaction, 158–60, 186–87; management confusion, 183; origin, 157; programs, 182; social needs, 181–82
Incentives: do-nothing philosophy, 129–30; fear, 113; humanistic philosophy, 205; laissez-faire philosophy, 56; paternalistic philosophy, 94–95; social, 155; technique philosophy, 164–65; use of, 12–13
Industrial Commission on Industrial Relations, 82, 84, 85, 88
Labor concepts:
 citizenship, 11
  current status, 240
  emergence, 126
  employee representation plans, 124–25
  group participation, 184–85
  rejection of, 143
 commodity, 9
  current status, 238
  do-nothing philosophy, 20
  laissez-faire philosophy, 17, 48, 53–54
 consumer–public, 11–12
  current status, 240
  humanistic philosophy, 204
  origin, 150–51
  technique philosophy, 164
 humanistic, 11
  current status, 240
  humanistic philosophy, 21, 204

249